NIGHT RAIN

A MIKE CONNOLLY MYSTERY

A NOVEL

JOE HILLEY

Good News in Fiction

COOK COMMUNICATIONS MINISTRIES
Colorado Springs, Colorado • Paris, Ontario
KINGSWAY COMMUNICATIONS LTD
Eastbourne, England

RiverOak® is an imprint of
Cook Communications Ministries, Colorado Springs, CO 80918
Cook Communications, Paris, Ontario
Kingsway Communications, Eastbourne, England

NIGHT RAIN
© 2007 by Joseph H. Hilley

This story is a work of fiction. All characters and events are the
product of the author's imagination. Any resemblance to any
person, living or dead, is coincidental.

"Turn Back the Hands of Time" copyright © Unichappell Music Inc.
and Warner-Tamerlane Publishing Corp.

Cover photo: iStock Photo
Cover design: Ray Moore/Two Moore Designs

First Printing, 2007
Printed in the United States of America

2 3 4 5 6 7 8 9 10 11

ISBN 978-1-58919-099-3

LCCN 2006932509

060607

But if I had just one more try
I would be yours, yours alone until the day I die
and we would have a love so divine
If I could turn back the hands of time

"Turn Back the Hands of Time"
Tyrone Davis
Words and music by Jack Daniels and Bonnie Thompson

Prologue

*D*arkness stared back through the windowpane at Dibber Landry as a howling gale ripped through the night, driving sheets of rain against the house. Thick black darkness punctuated by momentary flashes of lightning so bright it made him jump. In the bursts of light he could see the house next door and the one beyond it. He wasn't supposed to. For as long as he could remember, they had been blocked from view by a stand of pine trees with trunks larger than the reach of two men. That he could see past the edge of the yard meant only one thing. The trees lay on the ground, splintered and ruined.

He smiled. The trees were down. That was a good sign.

Dibber moved away from the window and eased into a worn and tattered recliner. Around him the house shuddered, resisting with all its might the hurricane's attempts to smash it to splinters too. Dibber pushed back with his hands against the arms of the chair. A footrest popped out as the chair reclined. He propped up his feet, folded his hands across his lap, and closed his eyes. Better rest awhile. Before long, the eye of the storm would pass overhead. Then there would be work to do.

An hour or two later, the wind died away. The house, still cloaked in darkness, became quiet and still. Dibber's eyes popped open. He sat up, awake and alert.

"The eye," he whispered.

He hauled himself up from the chair, hurried across the room to the door, and stepped outside to the porch.

Around him the night air was thick and humid. Rainwater dripped from the eaves of the house in a steady, rhythmic cadence. Above him stars shone bright against the dark sky, but as he scanned the horizon, there was not a light to be seen in any direction.

A broad grin spread across his face.

"Power's out all over the island."

From the porch, Dibber moved down the steps to the yard and started across to the dock. Even without a light he knew how to find it. He'd been there thousands of times. On the mantle in the house there was a picture of him in his daddy's arms, standing near the end of the dock, looking across the pass to Heron Bay. But that was a long time ago. Before that day his aunt came and took him out of school. He remembered her bloodshot eyes and the way her red nose dripped. She took him by the hand and led him outside under the oak trees on the playground. They sat on the swings, the ones with the big thick chains that hung down with bottoms made of rubber cut from Mr. Vann's old truck tires. They sat there for a long time, her staring at the ground, him staring at her—and then she told him. A carload of kids skipping school. The car swerved across the road. Hit his daddy's pickup. Dibber was seven. In Mrs. Williams' second-grade class. It was as far back as he could remember.

But his feet remembered. They took him through the night to the dock without need of conscious thought. In less than a minute he felt the toe of his sneaker strike the first board. He reached into the darkness with his left hand for the first piling, a telephone pole driven into the ground where the yard ended and the dock began. His hand found it without searching. He moved forward with a confident stride.

Twelve paces out he knelt at the first cleat and found the line that was wound around it. He grasped the line and gave it a tug. By then his eyes had adjusted to the darkness, and he could see the faint outline of the boat. It was two-thirds full of water, but it had survived the first half of the storm without sinking. He steadied himself against the dock and stepped into the boat.

One side of the boat was tethered bow and stern to the dock. The other side was tied to large pilings that had been driven into the muddy bottom just far enough away from the dock to allow a boat to slip between them. Dibber opened a storage compartment in the bow of the boat, took out a five-gallon bucket, and started bailing water. In no time at all he scooped out most of it and untied the boat from the pilings. Freed from the mooring, he pushed the boat back with his hands, walking it hand over hand away from the dock. When it was clear, he moved behind the steering wheel. The boat rocked from side to side in the waves. Water sloshed around his ankles. He felt along the console for the switch, then pressed a button beside the steering wheel. The engine turned over. Once. Twice. Then came to life.

With a quick scan of the shoreline, Dibber turned the wheel and gunned the engine. The boat started across the water.

There on the leeward side of the island the waves were not too large, but still the boat struggled to climb over them and wallowed from crest to crest. He glanced over his shoulder toward the engine. The water that had been around his feet had moved to the back and splashed against the transom. He slowed the boat and flipped a switch for the bilge pump.

Minutes later, he reached the west end of the island and turned south toward the open water of the Gulf. As he rounded the island, the boat plunged headlong into six-foot waves. The first one crashed over the bow of the boat, sending spray into the air and drenching Dibber to the bone. He tossed back his head and laughed out loud.

When he was past the end of the island, he turned east and followed the shore along the southern side. To the left the hulking remains of mangled beach houses lurked in the shadows. What remained of their frames stood just above the water that flooded the western half of the island.

A satisfied grin stretched across Dibber's face. He slowed the engine and surveyed the damage.

A Category Three hurricane, the storm had pushed a wall of water ahead of it, sending the Gulf across the beach and running the surf all the way to Bienville Boulevard. Many of the beach houses were gone, swept away as the storm blew ashore. Most of the ones that remained were severely damaged.

Dibber scanned along the shoreline, then focused on a small frame house that stood on pilings a few feet above the water. It was damaged but seemed to be intact. He turned the boat toward it and slowed the engine to an idle. Waves coming from behind carried him forward. As the boat picked up speed, he nudged the throttle and used the engine to keep it pointed in the right direction.

Just before it would have slammed into the pilings, Dibber shoved the engine in reverse and pushed the throttle all the way forward. The engine screamed as it revved to full power. The prop churned the water and dug in against the waves. Pilings that supported the house loomed ahead. Closer and closer they came. Then, at the last moment, the engine overcame the momentum of the waves and backed the boat away.

Dibber pulled back the throttle and slowed the engine. He bumped the shifter with the heel of his hand and knocked it out of gear. The boat came to a stop, then drifted beneath the house. Dibber ducked to avoid banging his head on the floor joists that passed above him.

From a compartment beneath the steering wheel, he took out a spotlight and flipped it on, shining it at an angle toward the water to reduce the chances of being seen by anyone crazy enough to ride out the storm in the neighboring houses. With his free hand he grasped one of the floor joists to steady the boat.

"Water must be up seven ... eight feet."

In the glare of the light he could see pieces of boards and bits of debris sloshing in the chocolate brown water around the boat. A jet ski bobbed a few feet away. He worked the boat in that direction, grabbed the jet ski, and tied it to the stern with a heavy rope.

In the far corner was a storage closet. The door flopped back and forth with the waves. He pushed the boat over to it and held open the door. Inside, the tops of several fishing rods poked out above the water. He pulled the first one up and found a Shimano reel attached to the other end.

With a freshwater bath and a little oil it would be good as new. He laid the rod and reel in a rack along the gunnel of the boat. Three more rods were in the closet. He took them, along with a tackle box from a shelf above the water.

When he'd emptied the closet, he moved the boat from underneath the house to a stairway on the side facing the road. He tied the bow to the railing and took a large flashlight from beneath a seat along one side of the boat. Steadying himself against the railing, he put one foot on the bottom rung and tested it to make sure the steps would hold his weight. Satisfied it wouldn't give way, he shifted his weight and swung free of the boat.

The steps led up to a landing at a door to the house. When he reached the top, Dibber leaned his weight against the door and pushed. It didn't budge. He tried again, but it still didn't open. Then he stepped back and gave it a hard kick. The bolt of the lock tore through the facing as the door flew open and crashed against the wall. Dibber stepped inside and found himself standing in the kitchen.

To the right was a refrigerator and sink. Farther around was a stove. The top of it was greasy, and there was a strange odor in the air. A countertop separated the kitchen from the living room. Across the living room, a large sliding glass door offered a view of the beach. A sofa sat facing the view with chairs on either end. Between the sofa and the counter, a hallway opened to the right through the center of the house. Dibber moved around the end of the countertop and started up the hall. A few feet from the living room he came to a bedroom on the left. He leaned through the doorway and glanced inside.

In the center of the room was a bare bed frame. Across from it was a dresser. There was a closet in the corner. He moved around the bed frame and opened the closet door. The closet was empty. Not even a hanger. He stepped back to the dresser and opened the top drawer. There was nothing inside it, either. Frustrated, he turned to the door.

At the end of the hall was a second bedroom. Standing at the doorway, he caught a whiff of the same odor he'd smelled in the kitchen. It was stronger now, but he paid it no attention as he entered the room.

Along the wall by the door was a dresser. A bed sat to the right. Blankets and sheets on the bed were wadded and tossed in a mess. On the dresser top was a wooden box. Next to it was a blue vase. Scattered around them were bits of paper, loose change, and pieces of this and that deposited there from pockets and purses over time. He raked through it with his finger, picking up loose change as he moved things around. With the flick of a wrist, he sent a can of spray deodorant tumbling to the floor. Behind it he found a class ring. He picked it up and held it between his fingers. In the glare of the light he could see the inscription. Class of 1985. It was heavy. Maybe gold. He bounced it in the palm of his hand, then put it in his pocket.

In the corner of the room, beyond the dresser, was a closet. The door was ajar, and inside he could see clothes still on hangers. Holding the light with one hand, he raked the clothes aside with the other. Behind them he found an automatic shotgun leaning against the wall. He picked it up and held it under the light. Convinced it was in good shape, he tossed it on the bed behind him, then turned back to check the shelf above.

Near the front was a shoe box. He took it down and knocked off the top with the flashlight. In it were pictures and a handful of seashells. He dropped the box on the floor and ran his hand back over the shelf. A pair of boots. A folded sweatshirt. Behind them was a cigar box. He took it down and raised the lid. Inside was a one-inch-thick stack of twenty-dollar bills bound with a rubber band.

"Bingo."

Dibber took a seat on the bed and set the box in his lap. He took out the money, fanned through it with his thumb, then shoved it in his pants pocket.

Beneath the money, the box was stuffed with thin, rectangular pieces of paper. In the glow of the flashlight he could see they were money order receipts. The ones on top were made payable to Southern Nursery Supply, but near the bottom he found one that caught his eye. He took it from the box for a closer look.

The money order had been purchased at the Snack In A Bag, a convenience store on Halls Mill Road. Whoever filled it out had included, in the lower left corner, the name of the person who bought it. As his lips whispered the name, his heart sank. He knew the—

Bam!

Below him the boat banged against the steps. He glanced out the window. The stars were gone. The wind was picking up again. The eye of the storm was moving past. In a few minutes the back half of the hurricane would hit, and it would be the worst part. He closed the box, slipped it inside his shirt, and turned for the shotgun. As he reached for it, the beam of the flashlight swept across the bed. Two eyes peered at him from the tangled folds of the sheets.

Dibber gasped.

The eyes were open wide, the face around them fixed in a look of terror. Dibber stared, unable to move, unable to breathe.

Bam!

The boat banged against the steps once more. Dibber caught his breath and darted toward the door.

One

Mike Connolly stood to the side, waiting. When he'd reached the age of fifty-five, he thought he'd seen all there was to see in life. Drug dealers. Prostitutes. Thieves. He'd defended all kinds and heard stories no one would ever believe. But over the past four years he'd seen things he could never have imagined before. Now he was witnessing one more.

In front of the judge's bench, Hollis Toombs locked arms with Victoria Verchinko, a petite, dark-haired woman with large brown eyes and beautiful olive skin. Hollis gazed at her with a look that seemed both intense and soft at the same time. They looked happy, she in a blue silk dress, he in a gray suit.

Connolly smiled. He never had seen Hollis cleaned up before.

Mrs. Gordon stood behind them. Seventy-five now, she still beat Connolly to the office each morning and somehow managed to keep him organized and out of trouble. Beside her was Barbara. Connolly glanced at her. It had been six years since they divorced. Six years. It really didn't seem that long. It didn't even seem like they were divorced at all. Not now, anyway. Just a bad fight and a long, slow makeup.

On the far side of them was Raisa. All the way from Croatia ... or Bosnia ... sometimes he couldn't remember which. But he remembered the first time he saw her, living with the others in a makeshift apartment in the top of that warehouse. Penned like animals. Taken out each morning. Forced to sell themselves every day.

Well, at least that won't happen anymore.

Now, all but Victoria and Raisa had been resettled with new identities and new lives.

Raisa glanced over at him, a sad look in her eyes. She turned away. He knew what she was thinking.

A moment later, the door opened behind the bench. Judge Bolin appeared. Barbara caught Connolly's eye and waved him over with a snap of her fingers. He moved closer and stood beside her.

"Act interested," she whispered.

Connolly stared ahead.

"I am interested." He mumbled under his breath. "But I know a bookie on Dauphin Street who's taking bets on how long this will last."

She punched his thigh with her fist and clenched her teeth, trying not to laugh.

"Hush."

Judge Bolin took a seat at the bench.

"Okay," he began. "I see we have a wedding today."

Victoria grinned and looked away. Hollis smiled.

"Yes, Your Honor."

Bolin glanced at the marriage license, then looked up at Connolly.

"Mike, good to see you. Haven't seen you in my courtroom in quite a while."

"No, Your Honor. Don't get to probate court much anymore."

Bolin nodded.

"You still living in Lois Crump's guesthouse?"

"Yes, Your Honor."

"Y'all have much damage from the hurricane?"

"A few trees down. A little roof damage. That's about it."

"You got off easy."

Bolin glanced at the license again, then looked at Hollis.

"You're Hollis Toombs?"

"Yes, Your Honor."

Bolin looked at Victoria.

"And you are Victoria Ver ..."

She helped him with the name.

"Verchinko."

"Yes. Verchinko." He glanced at the license once more. "And the two of you want to get married."

Hollis and Victoria nodded in reply. Bolin cleared his throat.

"Very well. Victoria, will you have Hollis to be your husband?"

"Yes."

"And, Hollis, will you have Victoria to be your wife?"

"Yes."

Bolin smiled.

"Very good. Then by the power granted to me by the State of Alabama, I pronounce that you are husband and wife." He nodded to Hollis. "You may kiss your bride."

Hollis turned to Victoria and gave her a brief kiss. Mrs. Gordon and Barbara gave Victoria a hug. Connolly shook Hollis's hand.

"Congratulations."

Hollis nodded.

"Thanks. You need to sign the license."

"Oh. Yeah. Sure."

Connolly moved between the women to the judge's bench. The license lay in front of Judge Bolin. Connolly took a pen from the pocket of his jacket and scrawled his signature across the document as a witness. Barbara slipped in beside him. He handed her the pen. She signed her name below his.

Judge Bolin reached across from the bench and shook Hollis's hand.

"I wish you much success in your marriage."

"Thank you, Your Honor."

Victoria flashed a smile. Bolin stepped away and disappeared through the door behind the bench.

Connolly turned to Raisa.

"We better get you to the airport. You have a plane to catch."

"Yes. I suppose I do."

Connolly tried to sound hopeful.

"In a few hours you'll be back home in Bosnia."

She rolled her eyes.

"Ah, yes. Lovely Bosnia. Land of opportunity at the pickle factory."

"But it's home."

"This should be my home."

Barbara touched Connolly on the elbow. She smiled at Raisa.

"We better get going."

Connolly slipped his hand into the pocket of his jacket and turned to Hollis.

"Okay, Hollis. You're on your own now."

Hollis grinned.

"We'll be back in a few days. See if you can stay out of trouble till then."

Connolly lay one hand on Hollis's shoulder. As he did, he drew the other hand from his jacket and pressed it against Hollis's palm. In the exchange Connolly slipped Hollis a handful of cash. Hollis leaned closer.

"Thanks," he whispered.

Connolly patted him on the shoulder.

"Have a good time."

Behind him Barbara and Raisa said good-bye to Victoria. Connolly moved beside her and kissed her on the cheek. Tears filled Victoria's eyes.

"I don't know what to say."

Connolly gave her a hug.

"After two weeks alone with Hollis, you'll have plenty to say."

She grinned. Everyone chuckled. Connolly stepped aside. Barbara and Raisa started down the aisle. Near the door he glanced back at Hollis and gave him a wave, then stepped outside to the lobby.

Two

Connolly escorted Barbara and Raisa across the lobby and down the courthouse steps. Heat and humidity engulfed them as they walked up the sidewalk to Connolly's car. A dark-blue 1959 Chrysler Imperial, it was parked at the curb on the next block. He opened the front passenger door for Barbara, then held the rear door for Raisa.

From the courthouse downtown they drove west through the urban clutter on Airline Highway and made their way toward the airport. Raisa gazed out the window as they passed the purple building that had once housed the tanning salon where she and the others had been forced to ... work.

"What will they do with the building now?"

Connolly glanced at her in the mirror.

"The bank sold it to a group from Jackson. I think they're going to turn it into a restaurant."

Raisa shook her head.

"They should burn it to the ground." She stared a moment longer, then turned away from the window. "What about the warehouse?"

"I don't know. They'll probably find a tenant for it, eventually."

Raisa sighed and rested her head against the back of the seat.

Twenty minutes later they reached the airport. Connolly took Raisa's suitcase from the trunk of the car and carried it to the ticket counter. He stood with her while the ticket agent checked her in, then he and Barbara walked with her as far as the security checkpoint at the entrance to the gates. There, Raisa turned to face him.

"Well, I guess this is good-bye for good."

Connolly gave her a somber look.

"Have a safe trip."

Tears streamed down Raisa's face.

"Thank you," she whispered.

Connolly put his arm around her and pulled her close. She rested her head on his shoulder. He spoke to her in a quiet voice.

"Everything will be all right. Someone from the State Department will meet your plane and take you to the hotel. An FBI agent will go with you when you speak to the Bosnian authorities. They will do everything possible to keep you safe."

She pulled away and wiped her eyes.

"I think it will not be good ..."

Connolly offered her his handkerchief. She took it and wiped her nose.

"... but someone has to speak up." She looked him squarely in the eye. "At least Victoria will have a good life."

Connolly nodded.

"Yes, she will. And the others too." He squeezed her shoulder. "You have the calling card?"

She nodded.

"You remember how to use it?"

She nodded again.

"Yes. I remember."

"If something happens, you call me."

She looked at him and forced a smile.

"I will."

He guided her toward the security officer.

"You better get going. Your plane is already boarding."

Suddenly, Raisa turned to him. Before he could react, she kissed him full on the lips. Then, just as suddenly, she pulled away and stepped through the checkpoint. Connolly could only watch. As he did, Barbara came to his side.

"What was that all about?"

Connolly stared after Raisa and wiped her lipstick from his lips.

"She's scared."

Past the checkpoint Raisa turned to look at them one last time. She gave them a forlorn look and waved. They waved in return and watched as she disappeared around the corner.

When she was gone, Connolly turned aside and offered Barbara his arm. She took his elbow. They started toward the door. As they stepped outside, Connolly's cell phone rang. He took it from his pocket and checked to see who called.

"Mrs. Gordon," he grumbled. He pressed a button and answered the call. "Yeah."

"Carl Landry is here."

"Did he have an appointment? I don't remember having anyone this afternoon."

"Said it's an emergency."

"Emergency?"

"Says he knows you. His nephew was arrested yesterday."

"Check my calendar and give him an appointment sometime tomorrow. I can't come down there now."

Connolly switched off the phone and shoved it in his pocket. He and Barbara walked to the Chrysler. As he opened the door for her, the cell phone rang again. Barbara took a seat in the car. Connolly pulled the cell phone from his pocket. He pressed a button on the phone to take the call.

"What is it now?"

"He says he doesn't want to see you tomorrow. He needs to see you now."

Connolly sighed.

"All right. I'll be down there in a little while."

He switched off the phone and glanced at Barbara.

"Sorry about that."

He closed the door and moved around the car to the driver's side. He shoved the phone in his pocket and took a seat behind the steering wheel.

Barbara glanced over at him.

"Trouble at the office?"

"Carl Landry."

"Isn't he the guy who came to you that time about his nephew? The one they caught stealing a highway sign from the interstate?"

"That's him." Connolly grinned. "Caught him cutting down the stop sign at the end of the Broad Street exit ramp."

Barbara frowned.

"I've always wondered about that. What was he going to do with a stop sign?"

The grin on Connolly's face grew wider.

"Wasn't the stop sign. It was the pole."

"The pole?"

Connolly started the car and backed it out from the parking space.

"Wanted it for an exhaust pipe on his pickup truck."

Barbara laughed.

"Think it would work?"

"He said they worked great. Had one on the left side already. Needed one for the right. That's when they caught him."

Barbara shook her head.

"Whatever happened to that boy?"

Connolly put the car in gear and started toward the exit.

"He was arrested yesterday."

"What's the charge?"

"I don't know, but I think I'm about to find out."

Three

Connolly took Barbara home to her house on Ann Street, then drove downtown. His office was located in the Warren Building, a 1920s-style high-rise on Dauphin Street across from Bienville Square. It was after three when he arrived. He parked the Chrysler up the street near the Port City Diner and walked to the lobby entrance.

Inside he crossed to the elevator and pressed the button for the third floor. As the doors closed, he leaned against the back wall and thought of Raisa. Her body pressed against him as he held her for one last good-bye. The smooth skin of her cheek against his. The look in those brown eyes. Sadness swept over him, and he wondered if he'd done the right thing. She would have been glad to stay. Glad to—

A bell sounded. The doors opened on the third floor. Connolly stepped out to the right and made his way down the corridor to the office. Mrs. Gordon was seated at her desk when he entered. She rolled her eyes and pointed down the hall.

"He's waiting."

Connolly glanced at his watch.

"I hope this doesn't take long."

Mrs. Gordon brightened.

"Plans?"

He leaned over the desk and whispered to her.

"I planned on not being here right now."

She whispered back.

"Well, get moving and you can still get to Barbara's in time for dinner."

Connolly gave her a look to say she was meddling. Mrs. Gordon ignored him.

"Go on."

She waved him past. He started toward his office. A little way down the hall he could see Carl Landry sitting in a chair in front of the desk.

Carl was a short man, about five and a half feet tall, and though he had a slight build his body formed a perfect V with broad shoulders and a narrow waist. Lean and hard, he looked like a construction worker, or a boxer, or one of those guys on a crew who moved heavy machinery by hand. He looked like anything but what he was, the owner of a dozen low-end discount grocery stores.

He stood as Connolly entered the office.

"Mike."

"Keep your seat."

They shook hands. Carl gave him a nervous smile.

"Glad you could see me."

He slipped back to the chair.

Connolly moved behind the desk and took a seat.

"What's this all about?"

Carl leaned to one side in the chair, his arm propped on the armrest.

"Dibber's been arrested."

"What for?"

Carl raised his eyebrows.

"Capital murder."

Connolly frowned.

"Murder?"

"Yeah."

"What happened?"

Carl shrugged.

"I don't know for sure. He's been living down at our place on Dauphin Island for the last few months. Had a good job on a construction crew up in Virginia, but he got in a fight. Hit the foreman a couple of times." He sighed. "That was the end of that."

"So, he's working for you now?"

"No." Carl shook his head. "Tried that once before. Ran off half the customers." A wisp of a smile crossed his face. "And that's pretty tough to do in my stores. I got a lot of customers who don't have anywhere else to go."

Connolly nodded.

"So, how'd he get charged with murder?"

"They say he broke into a house on the island during the hurricane. Looting, I guess. Only someone was inside. They say Dibber shot him. Something about murder during a robbery."

Connolly nodded again, but his face quickly clouded with a question.

"They think he was in someone's house during a hurricane?"

"Yeah."

"Sounds a little strange."

"Wouldn't be the first time that's happened."

"He's done this before?"

"No, no, no. Not Dibber." Carl paused a moment as if giving his answer a second thought. "At least I don't think so. I meant looters. Wouldn't be the first time somebody tried to steal something in a hurricane. Those people who ride out storms on Dauphin Island ... or Coden, or Grand Bay ... they aren't crazy like the news reports make it seem. They got people down there who come around, most of them wait until right after the storm, but they come around and pick through the houses. They don't care. They just go right in and take whatever they want before anyone can get down there to see about their stuff. Sometimes they don't even wait for the storm to end. I caught some guy trying to get into my house down there one time."

Connolly shook his head.

"So, that's what they think Dibber was doing?"

Carl shrugged.

"I guess."

"Who do they say he killed?"

"They don't know yet. They haven't been able to identify him."

Carl slipped his hand inside his jacket and took out an envelope.

"Look, I know you don't come cheap. But maybe this will get you started. Dibber ... he doesn't have any money, and he's one big aggravation." He paused long enough to give a heavy sigh. "But he's Shorty's boy. I have an obligation to look after him." He laid the envelope on the desk. "You'll take his case?"

Connolly glanced at the envelope. Through the fold of the flap he could see it was stuffed with hundred-dollar bills.

"Sure. I'll take his case."

"Good."

Carl stood.

"You're a busy man. I won't take any more of your time. Dibber's down at the jail. He can give you all the details. He tried to tell me about it, but I told him he should wait and speak to an attorney and not talk about it to anybody."

Connolly stood.

"That's pretty good advice."

"Yeah, well ... I've seen how they work down there. You never know who's listening."

He thrust his hand toward Connolly. They shook. Carl gave him a sober look.

"Call me after you talk to him. Let me know what the fee is. I'll find a way to take care of it."

He turned toward the door. Connolly came from behind the desk. He scooped up the envelope as he followed Carl out. They walked up the hall in silence. When they reached Mrs. Gordon's desk, Connolly moved ahead and opened the door to the corridor. Carl paused and looked Connolly in the eye.

"Dibber's done a lot of things in his life. But he isn't a murderer."

Connolly nodded.

"We'll get to the bottom of it."

Carl stepped outside to the corridor and walked toward the elevators. Connolly closed the door and turned to Mrs. Gordon. He handed her the envelope.

"Take care of this."

She took it from him, pulled the flap open, and glanced inside. Her eyebrows lifted.

"Carl Landry ..." Her fingers flipped through the bills. "... is a nice guy."

Connolly moved down the hall toward his office.

"Yes, he is. But I'm not so sure about Dibber."

Mrs. Gordon laid the envelope aside and took out the receipt book.

"Dibber," she chortled. "How'd he get a name like that?"

She opened the book, picked up a pen, and began writing a receipt. Connolly straightened his jacket.

"I'll ask him."

Mrs. Gordon glanced up.

"You're not going over there now, are you?"

"Yeah. Why?"

"I thought you and Barbara were going to dinner."

Connolly cocked his head to one side.

"Stop worrying about that."

"I'm not worrying. I just think the two of you—"

"Myrtice," Connolly interrupted.

Her eyes narrowed in a scowl.

"That's the second time you've called me that."

Connolly smiled playfully.

"Your mother gave you that name." He opened the door. "You should wear it like a badge of honor."

With a flick of her wrist, Mrs. Gordon sent the pen in her hand sailing toward him. He ducked out the door. The pen flew past his ear and struck the wall across the corridor. He laughed as the door closed behind him.

Four

From the office Connolly drove across town to the county jail. Ten stories high, it stood near Water Street across from the banana wharfs that lined Mobile River. Built of dark-brown brick, it had a hulking, formidable appearance. Steel bars, rusted from the salt air that drifted in from the bay, covered the windows and added to the building's imposing character. Built in the 1950s and never remodeled, it was dirty, worn, and cramped. Filing cabinets lined every inch of the walls around the entrance lobby and down the hallways. Wedged between the cabinets was a metal detector used for scanning visitors, the building's lone public acknowledgment of modern technology. Beyond the metal detector was a large steel door that led to the booking area.

A guard sat at a desk near the door. She looked up as Connolly approached.

"What you need?"

"I'm here to see a prisoner."

"Name?"

"Landry. Dibber Landry."

The guard checked a list of prisoners.

"Don't have any Dibber." She glanced at the list once more. "Got a Dilbert." She looked up. "That him?"

"Yes," Connolly replied. "I'm sure it is."

She pointed to a basket on the desk.

"Empty your pockets and step through the metal detector."

Connolly laid his car keys and cell phone in the basket and walked through the detector. The guard handed him his things and banged on the steel door with her fist. She shouted in a shrill voice loud enough to be heard two blocks away.

"Visitor!"

The door swung open. Connolly stepped inside past the booking area to the elevator near the rear of the building. Dibber was waiting for him in the interview room on the eighth floor.

Like his uncle, Dibber was short with broad shoulders. But he was much heavier, with a thick neck, a muscular chest, and a stomach that spilled over the waistband of his pants. His hair was long and stringy. His face scruffy and unshaven. Wrinkles at the corners of his eyes and the leathery texture of his skin made him look old, but Connolly knew he wasn't much past thirty.

Dibber was standing in the center of the room as Connolly entered. They shook hands, then moved to a table on the far side of the room. Dibber moved around the table and took a seat.

"Uncle Carl talked to you?"

"Yes."

The table was made of stainless steel with benches that were bolted to the floor. Connolly laid a yellow legal pad on the table and took a pen from the pocket of his jacket.

"They have you charged with capital murder."

Dibber snorted.

"They're crazy. I ain't never killed nobody in my life."

"Why don't you begin at the beginning and tell me what happened."

"Everything?"

"Yes. Everything. The advice I give you is based on what you tell me. So make sure you tell me everything. It will come out one way or the other, and it's better if I find out now rather than on the witness stand in court."

Dibber nodded.

"Okay. Well, I guess it begins with the storm."

"The storm?"

"Yeah. The hurricane." Dibber leaned away from the table and rested his back against the wall. "I was down on the island, Dauphin Island. I live in a house down there. Belongs to Uncle Carl. Used to be my grandparents' house. They died. He got it."

Dibber paused. Connolly jotted down a note on the pad and nodded for him to continue.

"I was down there when the storm hit. Eye passed right over the house. When it went over, I got in my boat and rode around to see what I could find. Uncle Carl's house is on the north side, faces toward Heron Bay. I rode around to the south side, the Gulf side. Lot of beach houses around there. Storm was pretty bad. Worse than they expected. I figured there'd be a lot of stuff floating around out there. So, I went to see what I could find."

"You were looting."

Dibber's face twisted in a scowl. He took a deep breath and folded his arms across his chest.

"I ain't no looter." The breath escaped him in a long, heavy sigh. "Storm like that comes in, stuff's just floatin' around all over the place. All you got to do is ride along and pick it up. Ain't no way of telling whose it is. People that owned it don't even know. Half the time, nobody even comes for it. I got a friend lives in Bayou La Batre, found a boat after the last storm. Nobody ever claimed it. He peeled the numbers off the side, got new ones, been using it ever since."

Connolly nodded.

"You went around to the south side of the island to see what you could find."

Dibber glared at him.

"I ain't no murderer, and I ain't no looter neither."

Connolly nodded. Dibber took another deep breath.

"I come around the west end. Came up the beach a little way. First couple of houses were gone. Nothing but pilings sticking out of the water. Water was way up past the road. About three or four houses up, I come to one that was still there. It was in bad shape, but it was still pretty much in one piece. Water was up underneath it. I floated the boat under the house. Found a little bit." Dibber gave a concerned look and shook his head. "But the house was in bad shape. Deck blowed off. Stairs kind of rickety."

"You went inside?"

"Yeah. I found a little stuff underneath it. A jet ski drifted by. I got it. Then, I went inside to look around."

"What did you find?"

"Not much really. Shotgun in the closet. A few trinkets. Then I seen that fellow on the bed."

"Someone was in the bed?"

Dibber shook his head.

"Not in it. On it. Sort of rolled up in the sheets. Eyes staring out at me." He chuckled. "Spooky. Especially after I seen the blood."

"Blood?"

"Yeah. Looked to me like the mattress was soaked."

"What did you do then?"

"I started to leave, then I seen he had on a nice watch."

"You took his watch?"

Dibber gave a nervous smile.

"Yeah." The smile became a grin. "But he was already dead. Looked to me like he'd been dead awhile." He moved his hands to his side and rested them on the bench. "I mean, if I didn't get it, somebody else would."

"You're sure he wasn't alive?"

"That man was stone cold dead. Maybe even a little stiff. Most of the blood was dried."

"Then what?"

"I took the watch and the other stuff and hightailed it out of there. Back half of the storm was coming in. Waves was starting to kick up. I got back to the boat and run around to the house."

"Which way did you go?"

"Same way I come. Back around the west end. Too rough to go on around the other way. By then there was white caps three foot high in the road."

"In the road?"

"Yeah. Water was five foot deep as far in as the road."

Connolly nodded.

"What did you do with the things you took?"

Dibber shot a look across the table.

"Found."

Connolly glanced up from his notepad.

"Excuse me?"

"The things I found. I didn't take nothin'. I found it."

"All right."

"I ain't no looter."

Connolly nodded again.

"What did you do with the things you found?"

"Took most of the jewelry to a guy in Chickasaw."

Connolly cocked his head to one side. His face wrinkled in a frown.

"Jewelry? You called it trinkets before."

"There was some in the bedroom. You know, the watch ... stuff like that."

"Who did you take it to?"

"A guy I know."

"What's his name?"

Dibber shifted positions on the bench.

"I'd rather not say."

Connolly folded the pages of his notepad and closed his pen.

"Then I'd rather not represent you."

He moved to stand. Dibber held out his hand.

"Wait. It ain't that big a deal. I'll tell you."

Halfway up from the bench, Connolly paused. Dibber waved toward it.

"Sit down."

Connolly stared at him.

"I'm waiting."

Dibber sighed.

"Lootie Shaw." Dibber sighed again. "His name is Lootie Shaw."

Connolly wasn't sure Dibber was being honest, but the irony of the name struck him as humorous.

"Lootie?" He dropped onto the bench, grinning. "You took this stolen loot to some guy named Lootie?"

Dibber scowled. His face turned red.

"I told you ... it wasn't stolen. I ain't no thief." He looked away, then turned back to Connolly. "I think he pronounces it Loo-Tay now."

Dibber chuckled. He drummed on the table with his fingers. Connolly glanced across at him.

"You took some of it to Chickasaw."

Dibber nodded.

"Yeah. But he didn't want the jet ski. I held on to it for a week or two and took it to a pawnshop in Saraland."

"They didn't have a problem taking it?"

"No. I'd cleaned it up by then."

"Cleaned it up?"

"Scrubbed off the license numbers. Waxed it. Made it look good as new. I could have got fifteen hundred for it on the street, but I didn't want to worry with it."

"Which pawnshop?"

"Golden Nugget."

"What did they give you for it?"

"Three fifty."

"All right. You pawned off the stuff. What happened after that?"

"Nothing, at first. Then the other morning I was asleep at the house ... day before yesterday. Cops came in, rolled me out of bed. Put me in cuffs and hauled me down here."

"Did they tell you what you were charged with?"

"Not when they arrested me ... I don't think. I can't remember. Might have. They took me downstairs late that night after they brought me in. Judge came in. Told me I was charged with capital murder. Said I killed some guy in a house on Dauphin Island."

"What did you say?"

"I said I ain't never killed nobody in my life."

"Did anyone try to question you? Since they arrested you?"

"Yeah. When they brought me in, they put me in a room downstairs where they fingerprint you. Came in with a tape recorder. But I told them I didn't have nothing to say about nothing. One of them started to ask me some questions about the jet ski, and I told him I was waiting on my lawyer. They left me alone after that."

Connolly glanced over his notes, then looked up at Dibber.

"That it?"

Dibber nodded.

"That's it."

Connolly folded the pages of the legal pad and put the pen in his jacket pocket. Dibber looked at him.

"Think I got a chance?"

"There's always hope." Connolly stood. "I'll have to see what the DA has. Find out some details about what you've told me. Check on a few things. I'll get back to you in a day or two."

Dibber stood and followed Connolly toward the door.

"How long am I gonna be in here?"

Connolly turned to one side and answered him over his shoulder.

"They have a bond set for you?"

Dibber shook his head.

"No. Told me I wasn't gonna get no bond."

Connolly nodded.

"It'll take about a year to get your case to trial."

"I'll be in here a year?"

"If your case goes to trial."

Dibber shook his head.

"That ain't right."

They were in front of the door by then. Connolly rapped on the window for the guard, then turned back to Dibber.

"Look, don't talk to anyone about this except me. You understand?"

Dibber nodded.

"And don't get discouraged. I'll see what the DA has and then we'll know a little more about what you're facing."

Dibber nodded again.

The guard opened the door. Connolly stepped outside to the hall and started toward the elevator. He glanced over his shoulder in time to see Dibber disappear inside the cell block.

Five

The streets downtown were deserted by the time Connolly left the jail. In the distance beyond the buildings, the sun was sinking below the horizon, setting the blue sky ablaze with streaks of purple and red. Twilight was approaching.

With a glance in the mirror he made a U-turn and drove through midtown to Ann Street. A moment later he brought the car to a stop at the curb in front of Barbara's house.

A two-story white frame, it had dormer windows across the front above the porch. A walkway ran from the street to steps that led up to the porch. He liked that house. The first time he saw it, he knew it was home. But that was then. Now, the house seemed like a trap. Like the vortex of a whirlpool sucking him down to the depths of a black hole he knew all too well.

He wanted none of it.

Connolly reached for the key and switched off the engine, then opened the door and climbed from the car. He slipped on his jacket and started up the sidewalk toward the front steps. On the porch, he rang the doorbell and waited. In a moment the door opened. Barbara appeared.

She smiled at him.

"Wasn't sure you'd make it, after that call."

He smiled back at her.

"It wasn't that important."

She held the door open and stepped away.

"Come on in and have a seat. I'm not quite ready."

Connolly glanced in from the doorway, unable to move. Barbara looked puzzled.

"What's the matter?"

He turned aside.

"I ... ahhh."

"Are you all right? Has something happened?"

He shook his head.

"I can't."

She frowned.

"You can't? You can't go?"

"No. Not that. I mean ... I can't come inside."

She gave him a quizzical look.

"What do you mean? You've been in here thousands of times."

"That was different." He sighed. "I can't." He backed away. "I'll wait for you out here."

He took a seat at the edge of the porch and rested his feet on the step below. Behind him he heard the door close. From inside he heard Barbara's footsteps as she moved upstairs. He propped an elbow on his knee and rested his chin in his hand.

As he waited, his mind drifted away to a time when the world was right and everything seemed normal. Memories that were precious stones to him, jewels he took from the box of his mind and rubbed between his fingers in the quiet of the day.

The sun was well below the horizon by then. Evening was fading into night and with it the sidewalk at the bottom of the steps disappeared. In its place he saw Rachel rolling a ball across the yard. The ball was almost as big as she, her head just high enough to bump her chin on it with every step. She learned to walk by pushing that ball around the yard. Pushing. Running. Giggling.

"Daddy. You see me, Daddy?"

A smile crept across his face. Behind it tears forced their way toward the rims of his eyes.

Then he felt something brush against his cheek. A fragrance filled the air. The ball faded from the front yard. Steps appeared beneath his feet once again.

Barbara was beside him on the porch. Smiling.

"I'm ready now."

He stood and took her hand.

"You look nice."

She gave him a playful grin.

"Thank you."

At the sidewalk, she wrapped her arm in his and glanced over at him.

"Are you all right?"

"Yes. I'm fine."

They started toward the car.

"Where are we going?"

He shrugged.

"How about The Silver King?"

She gave his arm a squeeze.

"Great."

The Silver King was a restaurant located on the causeway at the northern end of Mobile Bay. The building sat on the north side of the highway near the edge of the marsh. Upstairs, large windows afforded a stunning view of the bay to the south, the Mobile skyline in the west, and the bluffs along the eastern shore.

Connolly turned the Chrysler off the highway into the parking lot and brought the car to a stop near the valet's stand. An attendant opened the door for Barbara. Connolly stepped out and took a ticket from the parking valet. He caught the young man's eye.

"Take it easy with my car."

The valet slipped in behind the steering wheel.

"Yes, sir. Treat her just like she was my own."

Connolly rolled his eyes.

"That's what I was afraid of."

The car moved away.

Inside, the restaurant was packed. Connolly scanned the dining room, wishing now he'd made a reservation. The maitre d' approached. He had a look on his face as if he recognized Connolly.

"How many?"

Connolly knew him from somewhere.

"Two."

The maitre d' smiled at Connolly again and gave him an odd look. Connolly glanced around, trying to remember how he knew him.

"Looks like you're full."

"Busy night. Convention in town. Summertime."

Connolly pointed across the room.

"Any way you could get us by the window?"

The maitre d' turned to look, then glanced back at them.

"Just a minute."

He stepped away and disappeared through a door at the back of the dining room. A few minutes later he appeared with men from the kitchen carrying a table and two chairs. They scooted a table of vacationers aside and squeezed the new table in place by the window. The maitre d' caught Connolly's eye and gestured for them. When they were seated, he moved away.

Barbara gave Connolly a questioning look.

"How'd we get seated so fast?"

Connolly had a mischievous grin.

"I think he thinks he knows me."

Barbara smiled at him and shook her head. A waiter appeared.

"Could I get you something to drink?"

Connolly looked at Barbara.

"Just water."

He turned to the waiter.

"She'll have water. I'll have a cup of hot tea."

The waiter nodded.

"Very good, sir."

Barbara glanced across the table at Connolly.

"That sounds good."

Connolly caught the waiter's eye.

"Make that two cups of tea."

The waiter nodded and moved away from the table. Barbara gave Connolly an amused look.

"When did you start drinking hot tea?"

He shrugged.

"I don't know.... Tonight?"

Barbara laughed. Her eyes sparkled. Connolly glanced out the window.

"Nice view."

She turned to look. The lights of the city glowed against the night sky and reflected off the dark water of the bay.

"Nice to be inside where it's cool." She turned back to him. "Tell me what's on your mind."

He gave her a puzzled frown.

"What do you mean?"

"That thing at the house. What was that all about?"

Connolly looked away.

"I can't ..." He stared out the window for a moment, then turned to face her. "That place is like a trap for me."

"A trap?"

"Like every time I get around Rick."

"Rick? What's your brother got to do with the house?"

"Nothing. But every time I get around him, he still sees me as some little boy on a bicycle, and he keeps bringing up all the stupid things we did when we were kids. Something I said or something I wore. And the next thing I know, I'm talking and acting like that kid he remembers."

"That's the way people are."

"And that's the way that house is. I love that house. I liked it the minute that realtor showed it to us. But every time I come over there, I feel myself being pulled back to what I used to be. I see what I used to be. I hear what I used to be." He ran his fingers through his hair. "All these—"

"Memories, Mike. They're just memories."

He shook his head.

"No. They're more than that." He tossed up his hands in a gesture of frustration. "I don't even think they're memories. I can't remember much of it. It's just this feeling I get. Like there's some kind of ... momentum there. Pushing me back to where I don't want to go."

Barbara looked hurt.

"I didn't realize—"

He cut her off.

"It's not you." He reached across the table and took her hand. His voice became a whisper. "It's not you. It's that place."

The waiter appeared with their tea.

"Are you ready to order?"

Connolly let go of Barbara's hand.

"Give us a minute, if you don't mind."

"Certainly."

The waiter set the tea on the table and moved away. Barbara picked up a menu. Connolly took a sip of tea.

"What looks good?"

"I think I'll have the crab jubilee."

Connolly set the tea cup on its saucer. He glanced across the room and gave the waiter a nod. The waiter came to the table.

"Yes, sir."

"She'll have crab jubilee. I'll have grilled amberjack."

"Yes, sir."

The waiter took the menus and moved away. Connolly took another sip of tea. Barbara shifted positions in her chair.

"So … did you find out why Dibber is named Dibber?"

Connolly nodded, smiling.

"Dilbert."

Barbara lifted an eyebrow.

"That makes sense." She took a sip of tea. "In a twisted sort of way."

Connolly glanced at his watch, a playful look on his face.

"What do you suppose Hollis and Victoria are doing now?"

Barbara arched her eyebrows.

"I'd rather not think about that. Where were they going?"

Connolly chuckled.

"She wanted to see Disney World."

Barbara grinned.

"Disney World?"

"Said she'd always heard about it. Dreamed of going there as a little girl. That was all Hollis needed to hear."

"How would Hollis Toombs have enough money to take her to Disney World?"

Connolly took another sip of tea. The waiter appeared at their table with bread and plates. He glanced at Connolly. Connolly nodded. The waiter moved away.

Barbara smiled across the table at him.

"Mike? How did Hollis get the money to go to Disney World?"

Connolly gestured toward the bread.

"They still bake this stuff in their own kitchen. How does it taste?"

Six

A fter dinner Connolly drove Barbara home and walked her to the door. She paused there and turned to him with a playful look.

"You want to come in?"

Connolly felt nervous. He backed away.

"I don't think so."

"Just for a minute?"

Connolly shook his head. Barbara's countenance changed. Her shoulders slumped.

"All right."

Connolly leaned forward and kissed her.

"I better go."

He moved across the porch to the steps and waited while she opened the door. She glanced at him over her shoulder.

"Mike?"

Their eyes met.

"I enjoyed dinner."

His face softened.

"I did too."

He made his way down the steps to the sidewalk and out to the Chrysler. As he moved around the rear bumper, he looked across the car toward the house. A light came on in the kitchen. He moved to the driver's door and got inside.

Connolly left Barbara's house and drove to Tuttle Street. Within minutes he turned into the driveway at The Pleiades. The main house was a four-story mansion built in 1901 by Elijah Huntley, a broker who made a fortune importing bananas from Costa Rica. In its day the house had been an architectural marvel. Now owned by

Huntley's great-great-granddaughter Lois Crump, the house and grounds still evoked wonder and awe, but it was not a practical residence. By the time it passed to Lois, she was living in Birmingham and had little time or money for maintenance. To make the place more affordable, she rented out the guesthouse. Connolly was the latest in a succession of tenants. He brought the car to a stop at the end of the driveway and got out.

Standing there, he glanced up at the night sky. Haze and the glow of city lights obscured most of the stars, but behind the trees on the far side of the garden the moon was rising, full and round with an orange hue. It seemed so close he could touch it. He stared at it a moment, taking in its beauty and grandeur.

Built as an afterthought at the insistence of Huntley's third wife, the guesthouse was larger than many suburban homes. It had its own kitchen, three bedrooms, and two marble bathrooms.

The door from the driveway opened at the end of the house, between the living room on the left and the kitchen on the right. Beyond the kitchen was a dining room. Past the dining room a hall led through the center of the house.

A lamp was on in the living room. It sat on a small table at the end of the sofa next to the wall and bathed the room in a warm incandescent glow. At the base of the lamp was the telephone, and next to the phone was an answering machine. A red light on the machine blinked.

Connolly shoved the keys in his pocket and crossed the room. He pressed a button on the answering machine and wandered to the kitchen while he listened to the messages.

The first was from Mrs. Gordon, reminding him he needed to be in Judge Pearson's court the following morning. The machine beeped at the end of that message and began another.

In the kitchen Connolly flipped on a light and opened the refrigerator door. He took out a bottle of Boylan ginger ale and twisted off the top.

The second message described a free vacation he had won, three nights at any Royal Hotel in the country. His for only a ninety-nine-dollar processing fee.

He turned up the bottle and took a drink. The message came to an end. The machine beeped. Connolly swallowed. The next message began.

"Hello, Mike."

The sound of her voice struck deep in his soul. A tingle ran across his shoulder and down his arm. He froze with the bottle of ginger ale still at his lips.

"This is Raisa. I'm in Atlanta. The plane is delayed so they sent us to the restaurant for dinner. They say I will still make the one in New York. I miss you. I'll call you later."

The machine beeped and turned itself off.

Connolly took another drink from the bottle then crossed the room to the answering machine and pressed the button. Raisa's voice filled the room once again.

Sadness crept over him. Then, worry.

He didn't like the idea of her being in the Atlanta airport. Mrs. Gordon had tried to get her on a direct fight to New York. When that didn't work, they tried to route her another way, but there was no other choice. The best they could do was a layover of about an hour. Now, even that had fallen apart.

A frown wrinkled his brow.

"No telling who will see her there."

He pressed the button on the machine and listened to her voice again. Images of the first night he'd seen her filled his mind. Her petite frame. Those brown eyes. Standing there in the darkness of that warehouse she and the others called home. Forced to—

The message ended for the third time. He reached to press the button again, then hesitated. There was nothing more he could do about it now. He sat on the sofa, kicked off his shoes, and propped his feet on the coffee table. He sat there sipping the ginger ale and thinking of Raisa. He knew he shouldn't, but he was tired of struggling to resist the thoughts.

Seven

All through the night, Connolly dreamed of Barbara and Raisa. Crazy dreams that made no sense. Dreams that kept him on the verge of being awake. Never quite sound asleep. He rolled out of bed the following morning more tired than the night before. It was after eight when he left the guesthouse. Judge Pearson was halfway through the docket call when Connolly arrived in court. By the time he reached the office, he was feeling grouchy and tense.

Mrs. Gordon glanced up as he came past her desk.

"You look rough."

Connolly groaned in response. Mrs. Gordon looked concerned.

"Something wrong?"

She handed him a stack of phone messages. He paused long enough to take them from her.

"No." He started down the hallway. "Any of these important?"

Mrs. Gordon scooted her chair across the floor.

"Only to the people who called. How was Barbara?"

He continued down the hall.

"Fine."

She called to him once more.

"You sure you're all right?"

He turned to her as he reached the office door.

"Everything's fine. Had a wonderful time last night. Just had a tough time getting to sleep."

Mrs. Gordon smiled and turned away. Connolly hung his jacket on the coatrack beside the door. He moved to the chair behind the desk and took a seat. In a moment the clicking sound of Mrs. Gordon's fingers moving across the computer keyboard drifted down the hall.

Connolly spent the morning returning phone calls and working through the files that had gathered on his desk. Business was better than it had been in a long time, or so Mrs. Gordon seemed to think. He couldn't remember much about how things used to be, except the way the floor felt when he awakened from sleeping on it. And the clanking sound the gin bottles used to make when he opened the bottom drawer of the desk.

At noon he took a notepad from the desk and stepped to the coatrack by the door. He slipped on his jacket and started up the hall. Mrs. Gordon glanced at him as he passed her desk.

"You've been mighty quiet back there."

"Working." He stopped to straighten the sleeves of his jacket. "Pushin' paper."

Mrs. Gordon frowned.

"Sleeping."

He smiled at her.

"I'm finished with the files on the desk. I left you some notes."

She scowled at him.

"Thanks. Take me all day to decipher your scribble."

He chuckled as he started out the door.

From the lobby on the first floor, Connolly slipped out the back of the building through the service door to Ferguson Alley. At the end of the alley he crossed Government Street to the courthouse in the middle of the block and rode the elevator to the fourth floor. There, the doors opened to a reception area outside the district attorney's office.

A row of chairs lined the wall to the left. Windows to the right gave a view of the atrium and the lobby below. Along the far wall was a counter that stood chest high. Hidden behind it was a desk and Juanita, the receptionist.

No one at the courthouse was really certain about Juanita's age. She'd come to the DA's office the year Connolly entered law school. He'd thought she was near forty the first time he saw her. Still, there was an ageless quality about her appearance, and she had piercing eyes that rolled up when she looked over the top of the reading glasses she kept perched at the end of her nose.

She raised her head just high enough to glare at him over the countertop as he approached.

"May I help you?"

Connolly stepped to the counter.

"I need to see Henry McNamara."

"What about?"

The tone in her voice put him on the defensive.

"A case."

"Which court?"

Connolly frowned.

"Which court? How many courts is he handling these days?"

"Mr. McNamara supervises all three district courts."

"Supervises?" Connolly chuckled. "Henry got a promotion?"

Juanita tilted her head even lower. Her eyes grew dark.

"Which court?"

Connolly grinned at her.

"Judge Cahill, I guess. I haven't checked the file. It's a—"

Juanita turned away and punched some numbers on the telephone.

"That would be Ms. Underwood. I'll see if she has time to meet with you."

Connolly moved away. There was a water fountain on the wall near the elevator. He started toward it. Behind him he heard Juanita drop the telephone onto the receiver.

"Ms. Underwood will be out in a minute." Her voice was loud and flat. "Have a seat."

Connolly took a drink from the fountain, then found a seat in a chair as far away as possible.

In a few minutes a door opened near Juanita's desk. An attractive woman about five feet tall appeared. She was dressed in a gray suit with a white blouse and was older than most of the prosecutors Connolly had dealt with in the past. Older, but not old. Her brunette hair was pulled back from her face and held in place by a barrette. The expression on her face was all business, but not her eyes. They sparkled with irrepressible laughter. She was ... different. Connolly liked her before she even said a word.

She caught his eye.

"Mr. Connolly?"

"Yes."

Connolly rose from his seat and crossed the lobby. She offered him her hand.

"I'm Gayle Underwood."

He shook her hand.

"Glad to meet you."

She held the door for him as he stepped past, then led him down the hall.

"I'm handling the cases in Judge Cahill's court. What case do you have?"

"Dibber Landry."

She glanced at him over her shoulder with a questioning look.

"Landry? I'm not sure I have that one. I don't remember it." Her face brightened. "But that's not unusual. I have a lot of cases."

Connolly liked her sense of humor.

"It's a capital murder."

"Oh." She seemed startled. "I haven't handled a murder docket yet."

At the end of the hall they turned left past a row of cubicles to a small conference room on the other side of the building. Sparsely furnished, the room held only a plain folding table and four chairs. The walls were bare and windowless. A florescent light in the ceiling above the table made the room seem even more stark. She paused at the door and gestured for him to enter.

"Have a seat. Let me check with Henry and see what we're doing with this case."

She stepped away. Connolly took a seat at the table and waited.

In a few minutes she returned. Behind her was McNamara with the file. Gayle took a seat across the table from Connolly. McNamara closed the door.

"Mr. Connolly." McNamara tossed the file on the table. He and Connolly shook hands. "Good to see you again. I understand you have this Landry case."

"Yes."

McNamara took a seat at the end of the table to Connolly's right.

"Ms. Underwood is handling the cases in Judge Cahill's court now, but I'll still take the murder cases for a while. What do you want to know?"

Connolly shrugged.

"What happened?"

McNamara opened the file and leafed through the papers inside.

"Well, let's see." He paused a moment. "Looks like the sheriff's office got a call from somebody down on Dauphin Island. They found a body inside a house down there."

"Who made the call?"

"Uhh ... I'll give you the name and address if you won't tell your client. Some of these people are a little worried about getting harassed by criminals. Especially murderers."

Connolly twisted the corner of his mouth in a sarcastic smile. He glanced at Gayle.

"Don't let him infect you with that attitude."

She smiled.

"They're teaching me a lot."

Connolly nodded to McNamara.

"Nobody's going to harass your witnesses. What's the name?"

McNamara glanced at the file.

"The call came from Amy Wilburn. Address we have for her in Mobile is 4155 Yorkhaven Road. She and her husband own a house on Dauphin Island. The body was found at 8925 Bienville Boulevard. That's way out on the west end of the island. They were down there cleaning up after the hurricane. Smelled something. Went over to have a look. Found the body. Called 911."

Connolly scribbled the address on his legal pad.

"Who's the detective?"

"Brian Hodges. He's with the sheriff's office."

"What's the victim's name?"

McNamara shook his head.

"Don't have a name. Body hasn't been identified yet." He read from the file. "White male. Midthirties, early forties. Took him to Mobile General." He glanced up at Connolly. "Looks like he died from a single gunshot to the head. I don't think we have an autopsy report yet."

McNamara glanced at the file. Connolly continued.

"So, how'd you get to Dibber?"

"Dilbert Landry." McNamara grinned. "Good ol' Dilbert pawned a jet ski at the Golden Nugget Pawn Shop in Saraland." His voice had a sarcastic tone. "The owner of that fine establishment filed the proper paperwork like all good pawnshop owners do. Stolen property unit checked it against the stolen property database. They called us. Guy at the pawnshop is ..." He checked the file for the name. "... Tommy Porter. You want the address?"

"I know where it is."

"The jet ski was registered to Inez Marchand. She owns the house where the body was found. You want her address?"

"Sure."

"She lives at 125 Upham Street."

Connolly wrote down the address.

"She doesn't know who the dead man is?"

"No. Hodges took a statement from her. Said she'd never seen him before. Didn't know who he was. Didn't know why he was in the house and didn't know anything about what happened to him."

Connolly shrugged.

"And your theory is ...?"

"Squatter."

Connolly's forehead wrinkled in a puzzled frown.

"Squatter?"

"Yeah. Lot of those houses aren't used that often. Drifter comes along. Needs a place to stay. Finds an empty one. Breaks in. Stays till he gets thrown out."

"So, what makes this capital murder?"

"The dead man was living in the house. Landry was out there looting after the storm. Got in the house. Surprised the man. They got in a fight. Landry shot him." McNamara flipped through the file to the warrant. He scanned through it and handed it to Connolly. "Murder during the course of committing a burglary."

Connolly glanced at the warrant.

"Squatter, huh?"

McNamara leaned away.

"Doesn't matter if the dead guy had permission to be there or not. He could have been Landry's accomplice. Wouldn't make any difference. Landry was committing a burglary. Dead man was killed during the burglary. That's all it takes."

Connolly laid the warrant on the table.

"You have the gun?"

"Not yet."

"What kind was it?"

"Thirty-eight caliber."

Connolly thought for a moment.

"How do you know Dibber was in the house?"

"Prints. His fingerprints were all over the place."

"And how do you put him there at the time this man died?"

McNamara cut his eyes toward Connolly.

"I don't have to prove it to a mathematical certainty."

Connolly glanced at Gayle. A wisp of a smile appeared on her face. Connolly ran his fingers through his hair.

"Got any physical evidence?"

McNamara leaned forward and flipped through several pages in the file.

"I'm sure we do." He scanned across a page. His eyebrows rose. "Looks like they found a small bottle in the kitchen. Point one-two-five grams of meth in it."

"Dust."

McNamara shook his head.

"Not angel dust. Methamphetamine."

"I know what meth is. What you found was dust. In the bottle. Point one-two-five is residue. Residue in a Pseudaphed bottle. Could have been residue from the Pseudaphed."

McNamara chuckled.

"I don't think so."

"You think Dibber was doing meth?"

"I don't know, yet."

Connolly leaned away from the table.

"You don't know much about this case, do you?"

"I've read the file."

Connolly sighed.

"This is thin, Henry. Mighty thin."

McNamara closed the file.

"Looks like a good case to me."

"Anybody see Dibber at the house?"

"Not that we know of, yet."

"You want to plead him out to first-degree theft?"

McNamara shook his head.

"I'll let him plead to straight murder. Take his chances on a sentence with the judge."

Connolly smirked.

"He'll never go for that."

"Beats the death penalty."

Connolly felt the muscles in his neck tighten.

"I can't ..." He stopped himself and gestured toward McNamara's file. "Give me a copy of the reports, and I'll get out of your way."

McNamara handed the file to Gayle.

"Gayle will give you what you're entitled to." He stood. "Tell Landry to think about my offer."

He stepped out the door and disappeared up the hallway. Gayle stood.

"Come on. I'll get your copies for you."

Eight

Connolly left the courthouse and retraced the route up Ferguson Alley to the office building. He cut through the lobby to Dauphin Street and made his way to Port City Diner in the next block. It was after one when he arrived. Most of the lunch crowd was gone. He took a seat in the back at the end of the counter.

A waiter appeared.

"Mr. Connolly. Having your usual?"

"Yeah."

The waiter scribbled on an order pad.

"Turkey on whole wheat. Swiss cheese. Mayo. Mustard. No onions. Sweet tea."

He turned to leave. Connolly called after him.

"Hey."

The waiter turned back.

"Change that. Give me a muffuletta instead."

"No problem."

The waiter tore the page from his order pad and stuffed it in the pocket of his apron. He scribbled down the order, then turned aside and disappeared through the door to the kitchen.

Connolly stared at the napkin dispenser on the counter and thought of Hollis. A smile spread across his face. Hollis. With Victoria. On their honeymoon. In Disney World. Hollis on a honeymoon was a reach, but seeing him in Disney World was more than Connolly could imagine.

Then he thought of Raisa. He took the cell phone from his pocket and dialed the office. Mrs. Gordon answered.

"Has Raisa called?"

"No. Was she supposed to?"

"She called from Atlanta. Left a message at the house last night. Said her flight was delayed."

"And you don't like it."

"No."

"Not much you can do about it."

"Leave me a note to call somebody and find out where she is."

"They won't tell you."

"Maybe not. But leave me a note anyway."

He switched off the phone.

The waiter appeared with the sandwich and a glass of tea. He set the plate on the counter in front of Connolly and put the tea beside it.

"Best muffuletta in town." He took a knife and fork from under the counter and arranged them on either side of the plate. "Enjoy."

The waiter stepped away. Connolly took a bite of the sandwich.

After lunch Connolly walked from the diner toward the office. Up the street ahead of him a girl leaned against the corner of the building, smoking a cigarette. She was not more than five feet tall, and her skin was pale and chalky. Her short blonde hair was dull and lifeless and lay flat against her head. She was dressed in blue jeans and a pink tank top that exposed her shoulders. For shoes, she wore a pair of black Converse high-tops.

As Connolly drew closer, he could see she had a diamond stud in her nose and a silver ring in her eyebrow at the corner of her left eye. When he was a few feet away, she turned her head to one side and twisted her shoulders as she exhaled cigarette smoke from the corner of her mouth. Her left shoulder rolled forward. Under the strap of her shirt he could see the edge of a tattoo just below the neckline.

She stepped toward him as he passed.

"Mr. Connolly?"

He was surprised she knew his name. He stopped and turned to face her.

"Yes."

"We need to talk."

A frown wrinkled Connolly's brow.

"How do you know who I am?"

"I seen you on TV. At The Pig."

"The Pig?"

"Whistlin' Pig."

The Whistlin' Pig was a barbeque restaurant on Holcombe Avenue. It had been around since Connolly was a little boy, but he hadn't been there in ... he couldn't remember ever being there.

She continued.

"Buster makes sure the local news is on every night. I seen you on there when you got that guy off on killin' that lawyer."

Connolly nodded. She took another puff on the cigarette.

"Everybody says you're the man to see if you're in trouble."

"Are you in trouble?"

She shook her head.

"We need to talk."

"About what?"

Her eyes darted around, as if checking the street.

"Dibber."

"What about him?"

She glanced around again.

"Not here."

Connolly gestured toward the building.

"Come up to my office."

She nodded.

"All right."

Connolly watched as she took one more drag on the cigarette, then dropped it on the sidewalk and rubbed it out with her foot. When she turned to walk away, he saw more of the tattoo. What he'd seen before on her left shoulder was the tip of a wing that stretched across her back from shoulder to shoulder. A dark outline was visible through the thin cloth of her shirt. From the look of it, the tattoo extended all the way down her back. He watched her as she walked ahead of him to the front entrance of the building, trying to decide how old she was. One minute she looked fifteen. The next he was sure she was thirty. He'd seen girls like that before. And he'd taken one home with him a time or two.

The thought of those days made him shudder.

They rode the elevator to the third floor and walked down the corridor to Connolly's office. Mrs. Gordon was in the break room when they entered. Connolly ushered the girl down the hall. At the office door he pointed her toward a chair in front of the desk.

"Have a seat."

Connolly reached to close the office door, then thought better of it. He moved away and took a seat in the chair behind the desk.

"So, you know Dibber?"

"Me and him's been datin' for the last year or two. I didn't know—"

Connolly held up his hand to stop her.

"Wait. How about if we begin at the beginning. What's your name?"

"Tiffany."

"Tiffany?"

"Tiffany Previto."

He jotted the name on a legal pad.

"You and Dibber have been dating?"

"Yes."

"How did you meet Dibber?"

"He come in The Pig one day. Me and him got to talking. First one thing then another."

Connolly nodded.

"What did you want to tell me?"

"I didn't know what they was doing, really."

"Who?"

"Them people in that house."

"What people?"

"Nick and that bunch he has working for him."

"What are you talking about?"

"Tinker asked me to help him. I helped him. Now they think I put Dibber up to breakin' in."

Connolly leaned forward and propped his elbows on the desk.

"Wait a minute. Start over. Who's Nick?"

"Nick Marchand."

"Marchand. Related to Inez Marchand?"

"I don't know. He runs a nursery in Wilmer."

"Okay. And you know Nick."

"Sort of. I know Tinker. Tinker knows Nick."

"Who is Tinker?"

"Tinker Johnson. One of them guys that works for Nick."

"At the nursery."

"Yeah."

"How do you know Tinker?"

"We ... we been friends a long time."

"And why do you think Nick thinks you put Dibber up to breaking in the beach house?"

Tiffany sighed.

"Look, I was helpin' them out."

"Helping who?"

"Nick and them."

"Helping them do what?"

"Tinker come to me one day and asked me if I wanted to make some extra money. I got a kid. I can use all the help I can get. So, I said, 'Sure.' All I had to do was go to the store and get some money orders. They'd give me some money. I'd go buy money orders."

"So, you did it?"

"Yeah. Sure. I mean, it ain't nothing illegal about buying no money orders."

"How many did you buy?"

"At first it was maybe two or three a week."

"And later?"

"Last week I did it before the storm I bought twelve."

"For how much?"

"Thousand dollars."

"Each?"

"Yeah."

"And what did you make out of it?"

"Started out at twenty dollars a piece. That last week it was forty."

"Forty for each one?"

"Yeah."

"And you gave the money orders to Tinker?"

"No. I gave them to Nick. Tinker just got me the job."

"How do they know about you and Dibber?"

Her eyes darted away.

"Tinker come by the house one day. Dibber was there. They was with him. I guess Tink told them who he was."

"When's the last time you saw Nick?"

"Right before the storm."

"How do you know Nick thinks you put Dibber up to breaking in the beach house?"

"Tinker come by the house right after the law picked up Dibber." She glanced at the floor. "Nick kept a lot of stuff down there."

"You've been to the beach house?"

"I went with Tinker a couple of times." She looked up. "Before I knew Dibber." She grimaced. "Dibber's in a lot of trouble, ain't he?"

"Yes."

"Think you can get him off?"

"It would help if I knew what was going on. Where did they get this money? The money they gave you for the money orders?"

She gestured with both hands.

"I didn't ask."

"But you have an idea?"

"I could come up with one."

"Drugs?"

Her eyes darted away.

"Maybe."

"How were the money orders made out?"

"Southern Nursery. Most of them."

"Most of them?"

"At first I had them made out to Nick, but he got mad about it. Said he didn't want his name on none of them. So then we used Southern Nursery."

"That's the name of Nick's nursery?"

"I guess."

"What did Nick do with them?"

"I don't know. I gave them to him. He paid me. That was all I wanted to know."

"You did this every week?"

"Every Thursday. Tinker brought me the money in the morning. I made my run that afternoon. Then I'd meet Nick and give him the money orders."

"Where did you meet him?"

"Winn-Dixie parking lot. On Ziegler Boulevard. Most of the time. Met at the beach house a few times." She shifted in the seat. "Think any of this will help Dibber?"

"Maybe. Who was the dead man?"

She looked away.

"I don't know."

"Why was he down there?"

"I have no idea."

"Did Nick know him?"

"You need to talk to Tinker."

"I'd be glad to. When can I meet him?"

"I'll ask him about it." She scooted forward in the chair. "Look, I just wanted to let them know that I ain't got nothin' to do with Dibber breaking in that place."

She stood to leave. Connolly came from behind the desk.

"Ask Tinker to get in touch with me."

He handed her one of his business cards. She shoved it in her pocket and started up the hall. Connolly followed her to the door by Mrs. Gordon's desk and held it open as she stepped into the corridor.

Mrs. Gordon came from the break room.

"Who was that?"

"Tiffany."

"Tiffany?"

"Dibber's girlfriend."

"Oh."

Connolly took a seat in one of the chairs near the door. Mrs. Gordon scowled at him.

"Don't you have something to do?"

"I'm waiting."

"Waiting?"

Connolly nodded.

"Waiting for her to get out of the building. Then I'm going up to Saraland."

"What's in Saraland?"

"The pawnshop where Dibber pawned the jet ski."

"Jet ski?"

"Yeah. That's how they found him. He took the jet ski from the beach house. Sold it to a pawnshop. Pawnshop reported the numbers to the police department. Police department computer matched the numbers to a stolen property report. Somebody matched the address on that report to the one on the dead man. Bada-bing! Dibber gets arrested."

"Sounds a little tenuous."

Connolly pointed to her in a playful gesture.

"Thin."

Mrs. Gordon rolled her eyes. Connolly laughed and started toward the door.

Nine

When Connolly reached the lobby, he could see Tiffany standing out front. He moved to one side and watched as a yellow 1980 Chevrolet Caprice came to a stop on the street across from her. Tiffany crossed the sidewalk toward it. The windows in the car were tinted, but when she opened the front door, he could see a man sitting behind the steering wheel. She got inside. The engine made a sputtering sound as the car moved away. Blue smoke rolled from beneath it and trailed down the street. Connolly waited until the car was gone, then walked outside to the Chrysler.

The Golden Nugget Pawn Shop was located on Telegraph Road in Saraland, a bedroom community on the north side of Mobile. The shop occupied a building that had once been the Jiffy Stop convenience store. Connolly had been there before while defending Jerome Lewis. The thought of that case made him chuckle.

Lewis was a polite guy. Never much trouble. But one night, for reasons that were never quite clear, he decided to rob the Jiffy Stop. He entered the store, walked to the cooler, took out two bottles of beer, and brought them to the counter as a ruse to get the clerk to open the cash register. Because he was buying beer, the clerk asked to see Lewis's driver's license. Lewis handed the man his license and a five-dollar bill. When the clerk opened the register to give him change, Lewis pulled a pistol from the waistband of his pants and demanded the money in the drawer. The clerk backed away from the register. Lewis grabbed the cash and the beer and ran out the door. But in the rush, he left his license on the counter.

Connolly turned the Chrysler off the highway and parked in front of the building. He stepped from the car, still grinning from the memory of Jerome Lewis. A man in a pickup truck beside him gave him a puzzled look. Connolly acknowledged the man with a nod and went inside. A woman greeted him as he entered.

"Good afternoon."

Connolly gave her a pleasant look.

"Is Tommy Porter here?"

"He's in the back. Just a minute. I'll get him."

She disappeared through a door behind the counter. In a few minutes a man appeared.

"You wanted to see me?"

"I'm Mike Connolly. I represent a man named Dibber Landry. He—"

A grin broke across Porter's face. He didn't wait for Connolly to finish.

"Dibber Landry. Now there's a character for you."

Connolly nodded.

"He's that, all right."

"Don't make them like Dibber anymore."

"You know him?"

"Yeah. I know him." Porter leaned against a gun rack and folded his arms across his chest. "Been coming in here since the day I opened."

"The police say he pawned a jet ski here a few weeks ago."

Porter's face turned serious.

"Yeah. Surprised me. First time I've ever taken anything hot from Dibber."

"You have any paperwork on it?"

"Oh, yeah. I have paperwork." Porter moved to a computer terminal at the end of the counter. "Got lots of paperwork."

He punched a few keys. A printer under the counter began spitting out pages. Porter collected them and handed them to Connolly.

The first page was a bill of sale. The second was a sheet that contained information about Dibber. The third was a photograph of him standing in the store.

Connolly looked at Porter.

"You took his photograph?"

Porter leaned around a display case and pointed to a small, round digital camera on top of the computer screen.

"Right here." He lifted the camera for Connolly to see. A cord ran from it to the computer. "Takes a picture. Captures it on a disk."

"How many times has Dibber sold you stuff?"

Porter turned to the computer again. He pressed some keys and stared at the monitor.

"Let's see." He pressed a few more keys. "Looks like about a dozen ... no. Fifteen."

"Fifteen?"

"Yes, sir. Sold me stuff fifteen times. That jet ski was number fifteen."

"How did you find out it was stolen?"

"We run the numbers through the police file every time we take something in. We're wired to their system. Send them the model numbers off everything we buy. Their system compares our numbers to the numbers off their police reports. I bought that jet ski on August the fourteenth. They came out here and got it August the nineteenth."

"The police took it?"

"Loaded it on a pickup truck. I guess they took it to the impound yard. I don't know. They could tell you."

"And you were out whatever you paid him?"

"Yeah." Porter glanced at the monitor and pressed a button on the keyboard. "Three hundred dollars." He shrugged. "I don't need it." He gave a tight-lipped smile. "Tax write-off."

"You paid him three hundred, not three fifty?"

Porter glanced at the monitor.

"Yeah. It should be on those papers I gave you."

Connolly glanced at the papers in his hand once more.

"Did Dibber pawn anything else with it?"

"I don't think so." Porter checked the computer. "No. Before that the next time would have been in June. Sold me an outboard motor." He looked at Connolly. "I guess Dibber has a thing for water sports."

"I guess." Connolly thought for a moment. "He didn't pawn a pistol?"

Porter glanced back at the screen, then shook his head.

"No. No pistol." He pressed a key on the keyboard. "Sold me a shotgun last year. Double barrel. Stevens 311. Twelve gauge. That's the only firearm I see."

Connolly nodded.

"Did you ever hear of a guy named Lootie Shaw?"

Porter dropped his head forward and gave Connolly a knowing look. Connolly grinned.

"Bad guy?"

"Loo-tay cost me a lot of money."

"How so?"

"Lives in Prichard. Used to work for the city. Started bringing me stuff. Never had any problems. Then about two years ago he brought me some jewelry. Watches. Expensive stuff. I asked him about it. He said it belonged to his aunt. She had died recently. He was selling it for the family."

"It was hot?"

"Sizzling. I heard that's all he does now."

"Know where I could find him?"

"He had something to do with Dibber?"

"Not sure."

"Dibber needs to stay away from him."

"Sounds like it. Where does Mr. Shaw live?"

"You know where Main Street is in Prichard?"

"Yeah."

"Go out Main Street towards the interstate. There's a street out there. Dobbs or Hobbs or something like that. He lives out in there. Around the old railroad tracks. Back in there somewhere."

"Okay."

Connolly turned to leave. Porter called to him.

"Tell Dibber I hope it works out for him."

"I'll tell him."

"And tell him to stay away from Loo-tay."

Connolly nodded.

"I don't think that's going to be a problem for quite a while."

Porter grinned. Connolly gestured with the papers in his hand.

"Okay if I keep these?"

"Yeah. Let me know if you need anything else."

Connolly stepped to the door and walked outside.

Ten

From the pawnshop in Saraland, Connolly drove downtown to Mobile General, the county hospital on Broad Street. The main building had been constructed during the Spanish-American War on a lush campus in what was then the suburbs. As time passed, the neighborhood changed. One by one the outlying parcels were sold, leaving the hospital surrounded by office buildings. The once beautiful landscape was reduced to nothing but a single, large parking lot. The grand stairs that swept down from the main entrance to a green lawn now spilled onto the sidewalk at the street. The roof of the portico that towered five floors above the front entrance seemed to dangle over passing traffic.

Connolly turned the Chrysler into the parking lot and drove to the back of the building. He brought the car to a stop near the emergency entrance. Notepad in hand, he crossed the lot and went inside. He walked through the waiting area and moved past the receptionist's desk to a corridor that led to the interior of the building. A little way down the corridor, he turned right and came to double doors that separated the morgue from the rest of the hospital. He pushed open one of the doors and entered.

Directly across from the doorway was the county's single autopsy suite. From the hall Connolly could see the stainless steel table in the middle of the room. A light above it shone down on a cadaver that lay on the table. The chest of the body gaped opened. The scalp had been peeled from the head. The tile floor around it was splattered with blood.

Ted Morgan stood on the far side of the table. Next to him was an assistant, a young woman whose name Connolly could never remember. Morgan was talking to her when Connolly came through the doors. Neither of them seemed to notice his arrival.

"I'm finished here." Morgan stripped off the rubber gloves from his hands. "Clean this up and get those slides ready."

The assistant moved away. Morgan came around the table. Connolly caught his eye.

"Got a minute?"

"Yeah. Sure."

Morgan stripped off his surgical gown as he started toward him. When he reached the door, he tossed the gloves and gown in a waste bin. He paused just inside the room.

"What could I do for you?"

"Henry McNamara said you did an autopsy on a guy they found down on Dauphin Island."

"Yeah. " He pointed over his shoulder with his thumb. "Got him in the cooler."

"What can you tell me about him?"

"Let me wash my hands and I'll see what we have."

Morgan moved out of sight to the left of the door. Connolly heard the water running as he washed his hands. Morgan spoke to him from around the corner.

"Come on in. Have a look. That guy on the table's the one they fished out of the lake at Municipal Park."

"What happened to him?"

"Not sure yet." Morgan turned off the water. He appeared in the doorway, drying his hands on a towel. "Looks like he fell in and drowned." He tossed the towel in a hamper and started through the doorway. "Come on."

Connolly stepped aside to let him pass, then followed him to an office across the hall. Morgan moved behind the desk and took a seat.

"Unidentified male from Dauphin Island." He leaned back in the chair. "Nobody's come to claim the body yet. I need to get it out of here. Think you can find out who it is?"

"I thought that was your job."

Morgan shook his head.

"Not my job. Sheriff's office is supposed to take care of that. But they don't seem to be in any big hurry."

"What happened to him?"

Morgan slid his chair around to a filing cabinet behind the desk and opened the top drawer. Connolly stood in the doorway. Morgan glanced at him.

"Have a seat."

Connolly shook his head.

"Better stand. If I sit, I'll go to sleep."

Morgan chuckled.

"I know the feeling."

Morgan flipped through several files and pulled out one. He slid the chair back to the desk, laid the file in his lap, and pulled open one of the desk drawers. He propped his feet on the open drawer and glanced through the file.

"Gunshot to the back of the head." Morgan pointed with his finger behind his head. "Bullet entered at the base of the skull right above the neck. Traveled through the center of the brain, exited the forehead."

"That's the cause of death?"

Morgan glanced up.

"I'd say that did the job."

"Anything else?"

Morgan flipped through some more pages.

"Blood gases looked okay. No alcohol or drugs."

"No drugs?"

Morgan held the page as if Connolly could read the results of the tests.

"That's what it says."

Connolly nodded.

"What else?"

"Fingernails were clean. Nothing remarkable about the body other than the entry wound and the hole in his forehead." He glanced through the last few pages of the file. "Fully clothed. Underwear. Jeans. Socks. Shoes. T-shirt with a pocket."

"No bruises?"

"I didn't find any. Were there supposed to be some?"

"I don't know. You're the expert."

Morgan grinned.

"You're admitting that? Even before we get to court?"

Connolly smiled.

"Anything in his pants pockets?"

Morgan shook his head.

"Nope." He tossed the file on the desk. He took a deep breath as he ran the palms of his hands over his face and through his hair. "Had a tattoo on his chest. A rose. Not very large. Almost missed it." He leaned forward and picked up the file again. "Wait a minute." He leafed through the pages. "Yeah. There was one thing in the little pocket on the jeans."

"The little pocket?"

"Yeah. You know. Used to call it a watch pocket. I don't know what they call it now. Nobody carries a pocket watch anymore."

"What was in it?"

"A key. A door key." He tossed the file back on the desk. "Wasn't on a key ring. Just tucked in there flat."

"A door key?"

"Yeah. I mean, I'm no locksmith, but it looked like the kind of key you see that fits in the doorknob of an exterior door."

"Is that what it went to? An exterior door?"

Morgan shrugged.

"I don't know."

"What did you do with it?"

"Turned it over to the sheriff's office. I can't remember the detective's name."

"Hodges."

Morgan nodded and pointed at Connolly.

"Yeah. Hodges. He came by the other day. I gave it to him. That and the clothes."

Connolly folded his arms across his chest.

"What do you think happened?"

"To the dead guy?"

"Yeah."

"Somebody shot him in the head. He died."

"Not a suicide."

"Nah. Just about impossible." Morgan folded his hands in his lap. "Well, not impossible. But not very likely."

"Any way to tell where he was? You know, sitting, standing, that kind of thing?"

Morgan rolled his bottom lip over as he thought.

"I'd say ... the dead man was standing and the shooter was sitting. But that's just my opinion."

"Why do you say that?"

"Because I like to have opinions."

"No. About him sitting. Why do you think the shooter was sitting?"

"The location of the entry wound was low on his skull." Morgan gestured with his hand behind his head again, to the spot at the back of his neck. "Bullet entered down here. Traveled up and out near the hairline in front." He pointed to his forehead with the other hand. "Either the shooter was seated and the dead guy was standing, or the dead guy was seated and the shooter was lying on his back on the floor."

"You think—"

"Either that or the shooter was very, very short."

"So, you think the dead guy was standing."

"Yeah. I think he was standing with his back to someone he knew."

"Not an execution."

Morgan shook his head.

"No. In an execution the shooter is almost always shooting down at the victim. This wasn't an execution."

Connolly thought for a moment, then leaned away from the door frame.

"All right. Can I get a copy of your report?"

"You ask me that every time." Morgan moved his feet from the desk and stood. "Henry goes ballistic when I do that." He stepped toward the door. "Which is a good reason to give you one." He brushed past Connolly to the hall. "Come on. I'll get you a copy."

Connolly followed him past the autopsy suite to a photocopier that sat in the hall. Morgan opened the file and took out the report.

"This is fresh stuff, you know. I haven't even sent this to Henry yet."

Connolly grinned.

"They made Henry a supervisor."

Morgan arranged the pages of the report in the automatic feeder for the copier.

"I heard." He pressed the button on the machine. "Hard to think of Henry being in charge of anything."

Connolly grinned again.

"He's not too bad really."

Morgan collected the copies from the tray of the machine and handed them to Connolly.

"Nah. He's not too bad. I've seen worse."

Connolly took the report and slid it between the pages of the legal pad.

"Thanks."

Morgan nodded.

"Sure thing. Hope it helps."

Connolly started down the corridor. Morgan turned toward his office. At the double doors Connolly remembered one more question.

"Ted?"

Morgan appeared from his office. He waited for Connolly to continue.

"What about a time of death?"

Morgan stepped inside his office. Connolly walked back to the doorway. Morgan had the file open.

"By the time he got to me, he'd been dead about ten days. Maybe two weeks."

"When did they find him?"

Morgan flipped through several pages in the file.

"They found him on July third."

"So, he died sometime around June twenty-third."

"Maybe."

Connolly frowned. Morgan glanced at him.

"That a problem?"

"Hurricane hit June twenty-ninth."

Morgan nodded. Connolly brightened.

"He was dead before the hurricane?"

Morgan shrugged.

"Can't really say. Time of death isn't an exact science."

Connolly thought a moment. Morgan closed the file.

"Anything else you need to know?"

"You got anything else?"

"Not really."

"I didn't think so."

Morgan smiled. Connolly turned to leave.

Eleven

onnolly walked out of the hospital and across the parking lot toward the Chrysler. An afternoon rain shower had fallen while he was inside. Heat from the pavement rose around him like a sauna. Sweat trickled down his back. He loosened his tie as he got in behind the steering wheel. As he drove away, he thought about that key.

A door key. In the dead man's pocket.

According to McNamara, Mrs. Marchand told Hodges she didn't know the dead man. Had never seen him. Didn't know why he was in her beach house. Connolly found that hard to believe.

"But why would anyone lie about a thing like that? It's too easy to discredit."

Then he thought of Jerome Lewis and how he left his driver's license on the counter after robbing the Jiffy Stop. Wouldn't be the first time someone did something stupid either.

The traffic light at Government Street was red. Connolly brought the Chrysler to a stop. He glanced at his watch while he waited. It was four o'clock. Still time to get to the office and return a few phone calls.

Phone calls. Maybe there was a call from someone about Raisa. Maybe she called the guesthouse and left another message on the answering machine. His heart jumped at the thought.

The traffic light changed. Cars began to move through the intersection. Connolly glanced to the right to check for traffic, then changed lanes. At the corner he made the turn onto Government Street and drove toward Tuttle. Five minutes later he parked the car at the guesthouse and went inside.

From the doorway he could see the answering machine on the table at the far end of the sofa. The red light was blinking. There was a message waiting. He shoved the door closed behind him and crossed the room toward the table. His pulse quickened. He pressed the button. The machine beeped. A male voice began to speak. Connolly felt his heart sink.

A marketing firm telling him about a deal on a new swimming pool. The message ended. The machine fell silent. He lifted the cover and checked the tape to make sure that was the only message. A sense of sadness swept over him. The cover snapped closed. An image of Raisa came to his mind. He took a step back, then collapsed on the sofa and stared at the window across the room.

Afternoon shadows crept around him but he didn't notice. His mind was lost in thought. Maybe he'd made a mistake. Maybe he should have told her to stay. She would have stayed if he'd asked. The guesthouse wouldn't be empty. He wouldn't be alone. She'd be waiting for him when he came through the door.

Barbara had been the love of his life, but there was a lot of baggage with her. When they were married and he was drinking, she had to run the house, look after Rachel. At first she tried to cover for him. Then she nagged. Then she just took over. It had changed her. Not that it was her fault, but she was different than she'd been before. More controlling. Demanding. And always lurking in the background was the unspoken question whether he would stay sober. Suspicion. He couldn't live under constant scrutiny.

Raisa, on the other hand, didn't know about any of that. She didn't know anything about his past. Didn't know about the gin bottles in the desk. Nights at the office in a drunken stupor. Or Marisa at the Imperial Palace. Or any of the other women he'd seen. She just knew he'd rescued her from a life of misery, and that was all she wanted to know. She liked him and she liked him for who he was, not who he'd become after being who he'd been. No conditions. No strings. No ...

Well ... there was a bit of a language problem. She spoke whatever they speak in Bosnia and two or three other languages, but she didn't know much about the American version of English. Or American life. And she had all the problems that might be expected after being drugged, sold into the sex trade, and forced to work as a prostitute. But the way she felt when he touched her. The way he felt. Like his entire body ...

He rubbed the palms of his hands over his face and slid his fingers through his hair, then tugged at his hair by the handful.

"I need a hobby."

The sun was still bright outside, but the shade of the trees around the house had grown more dense. The room was getting darker. Connolly leaned over the end of the sofa and switched on a lamp. He dangled on the armrest after the light came on, thinking about Raisa.

Sometime later he pushed himself up from the sofa and trudged down the hall to the bedroom. He hung his suit in the closet and put on a pair of jeans and a T-shirt. A pair of Topsiders sat on the floor by the bed. He glanced down at them. Bending over to put them on seemed like a monumental task. Instead, he fell face first across the bed.

"Women." He groaned. "Can't live with them. Can't live without them."

He folded his arms for a pillow and rested his head on them. Images of Raisa and Barbara danced through his mind.

After a few minutes he felt his stomach growl. It had been a long time since lunch. He rolled over and raised himself to a sitting position on the edge of the bed. He slipped his feet in the shoes and started toward the kitchen.

In the refrigerator he found a jar of mayonnaise and twisted off the lid to make sure it was all right. With a few slices of a tomato and some bread from the bread box, he had his favorite sandwich. Dinner in hand, he started toward the dining room. Then he had another thought.

Why not do something different? He could eat outside. He moved the plate to his left hand, took a bottle of Boylan's from the refrigerator, and started toward the door.

A round concrete table sat in the center of the garden between the guesthouse and the main residence. In the late afternoon shade it looked inviting. He crossed the lawn and walked through the garden to the table. As he rounded a large azalea bush, a mosquito buzzed his ear. He tilted his head to one side and rubbed his ear against his shoulder.

In the center of the garden he set the plate and bottle on the table, then stepped over the bench and took a seat. He twisted off the bottle cap and took a drink. A mosquito buzzed his ear again.

He set the bottle on the table and swatted at the mosquito to chase it away, then picked up the sandwich. As he took a bite, a fly buzzed around his head and landed on the edge of the plate. He flicked it away with the back of his hand. A moment later a mosquito bit him on the forearm. He smashed it against his skin, leaving a red blob of blood.

"Enough of this."

In one quick motion he swung his legs over the bench and picked up the plate from the table. As he stood, he grabbed the bottle by the neck and started toward the guesthouse.

Inside, he set the plate and bottle on the dining room table and took a seat in a chair. He rocked the chair back on two legs and tipped up the bottle for another drink.

And thought of Raisa.

In his mind he could see her standing beside him that night when they were waiting for Hollis and the pickup. Her fingers were locked in his. Her head rested against his shoulder. He imagined slipping his arm around her. Pulling her close. Her head tilted back. Her dark eyes focused on his. He could feel her lips against his—moist, soft, excited.

He rocked the chair forward and set the bottle on the table.

"I really need a hobby."

He took a bite of the sandwich and forced his mind to think of something else.

That key. In the dead man's pocket.

What if the owner ... he couldn't remember her name. He laid the sandwich on the plate and walked outside to the Chrysler. The legal pad was on the front seat. He picked it up and flipped through it as he walked back inside.

At the dining table he held the notepad in one hand and picked up the sandwich with the other. He ate while he read.

Marchand. Inez Marchand.

He took another bite of the sandwich and read some more.

Inez Marchand. Nick Marchand. A nursery. Southern Nursery Supply. Tinker Johnson. Tiffany Previto. A dead man in the beach house. With a door key in his pocket.

"A man in Inez Marchand's beach house. And no one knows who he is." He took another bite. "What if that key fit the front door of the beach house?"

The beach house. He needed to see it, to feel it, to smell it, but the thought of going there made him remember his friend Peyton Russo. The smell of the house when he went in there that day was more than he could stand. Even now the memory of it made his stomach churn. And what he saw. The way he'd seen in his mind how they stabbed Peyton with the—

A shudder ran up his spine. He closed his eyes and tried to think of something else, but with his eyes closed his mind turned again to Raisa. The look in her eye when he saw her the first time. They had caught her by surprise. She was startled, but she wasn't scared. Her eyes. The way her hands—

"Ahhhhhhhhh!" Connolly struck the table with his fist. "Why can't I think about ... football ... or flowers ... or ... anything but women?"

Twelve

Connolly awoke the next morning long before dawn. He lay in bed, staring up toward the ceiling in the darkness above his head. A few minutes later he rolled on his side and felt for his cell phone along the top of the nightstand. When he found it, he pressed a button to check the time and squinted to read the numbers in the glare of the light from the screen.

Four in the morning.

The phone slipped from his fingers and clattered onto the nightstand. He dropped his head on the pillow and closed his eyes. Twenty minutes later he was still awake. Another ten passed. Finally, he threw aside the covers and crawled from bed.

When he had showered and dressed, he went to the kitchen. He made a cup of instant coffee in the microwave and took a doughnut from a box of Krispy Kremes in the cabinet. He stood at the sink and ate between sips of coffee.

The sun was almost up when he left the guesthouse. But for the street sweeper he passed near the library, the city was deserted and quiet in the gray predawn light. He lowered the window and let the balmy damp air blow against his face. When he reached Royal Street, he turned right and made his way behind the courthouse to St. Pachomius Church.

One of the oldest structures in the city, St. Pachomius sat behind the courthouse beneath the thick foliage of oak trees almost as old as the building itself. Steps led up from the sidewalk at the street to a portico supported by large round columns that stood like sentries guarding access to the entrance. Connolly parked the car in front and walked up the steps.

Inside, the sanctuary was cool and dark. Walls to the left and right were lined with stained-glass windows depicting scenes from the life of Christ. Down front, a railing separated the nave from the marble steps that rose from the floor to the chancel. Early morning light illuminated the vivid colors in the windows, bringing the images to life and casting a rainbow of color across the dark wooden pews.

Lecterns stood near the front of the chancel, on either side facing the nave. Toward the back, pews were arranged for a split chancel choir. Beyond the choir was still another railing and behind it was the altar.

Connolly took a seat in a pew near the back and let his eyes move slowly around the room. It looked old and smelled old, but far from being cold and dead, the building was alive with mystery and wonder.

Before long, others began to arrive for morning prayers. They moved quietly down the aisle past him. In a few minutes Father Scott entered the nave and climbed the steps to the chancel. His voice echoed through the building.

When the service concluded, Father Scott disappeared into the sacristy. Connolly waited until the others were gone, then lingered near the chancel rail. In a few minutes Father Scott emerged in street clothes.

"Hear anything from Hollis and Victoria?"

Connolly grinned.

"Not a thing."

Father Scott smiled.

"I guess he has other things on his mind besides us."

"I guess. Wish he would come on back."

"Miss him?"

"No. But I could use his help on a couple of things."

"Sorry I missed the wedding. We could have done it here."

Connolly nodded.

"I told him that. But he didn't want to do it here."

"My wife and I got married at the courthouse." Father Scott's eyes danced. "She had this elaborate wedding planned. Then, at the last minute, she got fed up with the whole thing. Came and got me one night about two in the morning."

"She came and got you?"

Father Scott grinned.

"Yeah." He laughed. "It was kind of strange." His laughter trailed away. His eyes sparkled. "Actually, it was rather exciting. A woman banging on your door in the middle of the night." He grinned again. "I opened the door. She didn't say hello or kiss me or anything. Just standing there looking at me all alive. 'Let's get married.' I said, 'We are. Day after tomorrow.' She said, 'No. Now.' So, we rode over to New Orleans. Got married at the courthouse. Came back the day of the wedding in time for the reception."

"How'd that go over?"

"Her mother was a little upset. Everybody else thought it was a hoot."

"Well, I hope Hollis and Victoria have a 'hoot' at Disney World."

Father Scott looked amused.

"Disney World?"

Connolly grinned and nodded.

"That's where Victoria wanted to go."

Father Scott shrugged.

"Everyone has their dreams." He folded his arms across his chest. "Did Raisa get away okay?"

"Yeah."

"You know that woman had it bad for you."

"That's what I hear."

"She asked a lot of questions about you when we were over on Cape San Blas."

"That's the last thing I need to hear."

"Think she'll be all right?"

"I don't know." Connolly snapped his fingers. "But that reminds me. I need to call about her."

"Something wrong?"

"We had her flight worked out so she could get to New York without much of a delay, but her connection in Atlanta was late. She left a message on my answering machine. I need to check on her."

"She's a brave woman. Going back over there like that."

"Yeah. She is."

Connolly turned to leave. Father Scott followed him up the aisle.

"If you talk to her, tell her I said hello."

"I will."

They reached the door. Father Scott held it open. Connolly stepped outside.

When Connolly reached the office, Mrs. Gordon was busy at the copier in the break room. He stopped at the doorway.

"Any calls from yesterday?"

"They're on your desk."

Connolly stepped away and walked to his office. He hung his jacket on the coatrack and moved behind the desk. A stack of phone messages lay on the chair. He picked them up, glanced through them, then took a seat and opened the bottom drawer of the desk. The sound of the drawer sliding against the desk frame caught his attention. He looked to see why he didn't hear the gin bottles clank together, then remembered he didn't drink anymore.

Mrs. Gordon spoke to him from the hallway.

"Old habits die hard."

The sound of her voice startled him.

"Yeah."

He took the phone book from the drawer and laid it on the desk. She came closer and stood in the doorway.

"What are you doing with that?"

"Calling Dave Brenner."

"I don't think he'll tell you anything."

"Maybe not. But I'm calling just the same."

Mrs. Gordon watched while Connolly searched for the telephone number.

"Want me to get it for you?"

"No." He ran his finger down the page. "I can read a phone book."

Three pages later he found the number and punched it into the phone.

Brenner was the agent in charge of the FBI office in Mobile. Their paths had crossed on a couple of previous cases. His office was coordinating Raisa's trip. If anything had gone wrong, he would know.

After several delays Connolly reached Brenner's assistant. Brenner was out. He left a message and hung up the phone. Mrs. Gordon was still at the door. Connolly glanced up at her.

"Think he's dodging me?"

"What do you think?"

Connolly shrugged.

"Hard to tell."

"Hard to tell? Did you really think he would take the call?"

"I don't know. Maybe."

"Listen, that woman wanted to do this. You didn't make her."

"But did I?"

A frown wrinkled Mrs. Gordon's brow.

"What do you mean?"

"What if I knew how she felt about me and pointed her toward the FBI and this trip as a way of getting rid of her?"

Mrs. Gordon thought for a moment.

"You aren't that clever." She turned away. "Or that devious."

She started up the hall, then came back.

"You told her what the risks were, right?"

"Yes."

"And you told her she could stay."

"Yes. But if I had said I wanted her to stay, she would have."

"But did you really want a relationship with her?"

Connolly sighed.

"No."

Mrs. Gordon pressed his answer.

"What?"

"Huh?"

"Did you want a relationship with her?"

Connolly blushed. His face felt warm. An embarrassed smile tugged at the corners of his mouth.

"This is not something that's easy to talk about with you."

"What? She was attractive? Vulnerable? Available? That makes you uneasy?"

"It makes me uneasy that I was attracted to her in that way."

She dismissed him with the wave of a hand.

"That's just hormones."

Connolly laughed.

"Hormones?"

Mrs. Gordon looked serious.

"It's just physical. You know what kind of business she was in. You know all you have to do is touch her in the right places and she'll—"

"Mrs. Gordon!"

"Well, it's true."

"I know it's true, but you don't have to say it."

"Might as well talk about it. Everybody knows all about it anyway."

"They know about what?"

"You think Barbara doesn't know how you react to Raisa? How Raisa reacts to you?"

"I hope not."

"Why?"

"Because I—"

"Because you don't want her to know what kind of things you think about when you see Raisa?"

"Yes."

Mrs. Gordon rolled her eyes and shook her head.

"You men are all the same."

"What does that mean?"

"It bothers you that you look at a woman and size her up. So you assume it bothers us that you see a pretty woman and have this idiotic reaction."

"It doesn't?"

She sighed and turned away.

"Men understand almost nothing about women."

Thirteen

That afternoon Connolly stayed at the office, sorting through files, cleaning out drawers, prowling through filing cabinets. A little after three, Mrs. Gordon appeared at his door.

"What are you doing?"

Connolly glanced at her over his shoulder.

"Going through old files."

"What for?"

"Taking the notes off the legal pads."

She frowned.

"Taking the notes off the legal pads?"

"Yeah. These files need to be closed, but they have legal pads in them that only have notes on two or three pages. No sense in closing out the file and wasting the rest of the pad."

She strode across the room and snatched the file from his hand.

"Move."

She elbowed him aside. Connolly glared at her.

"What are you doing?"

She stuffed the file in the filing cabinet and slammed the drawer shut, then turned to face him.

"You've been holed up in here all day. What is going on with you?"

"You tell me I don't spend enough time in here. Now you tell me I'm spending too much time."

"Look, whatever it is you need to do, just go do it."

"I don't want to."

"What is it?"

"I need to go to the Marchands' beach house."

"Dibber Landry?"

"Yes."

"So, go."

"I don't want to."

"Why not?"

"Last time I went to a place like that, I saw things I didn't want to see."

She frowned.

"What are you talking about?"

"Peyton Russo."

The drawer on the filing cabinet came open on its own. She pulled it out further, pushed the files around, and shoved it closed.

"You have a job to do."

The filing cabinet came open again. Mrs. Gordon jerked it out farther, grabbed a handful of files, and pulled them from the drawer. She shoved the drawer closed with her knee and laid the files on top of the cabinet.

"I'll take care of the files. You go to the beach house."

Connolly sighed and crossed the room to the door. He took his coat from the coatrack and slipped it on.

Connolly walked down the corridor to the elevator and punched the button. He stood there in the hall feeling like a little boy who'd been scolded by his mother.

His mother.

An image of her face flashed across his mind. He could always remember her face. And sometimes when he wasn't expecting it, he could hear her voice. But when he wanted to hear her, when he needed to hear her, he never quite could make it happen.

He rode the elevator down to the lobby and walked outside to the street. The Chrysler was parked on the next block. He got in behind the steering wheel. Mrs. Gordon was right. He had to go to the beach house. Hollis or no Hollis. He smiled at himself. Maybe he felt like a scolded little boy because he'd acted like a little boy. Dauphin Island lay at the mouth of Mobile Bay, forty miles below the city. The drive would take about an hour, depending on traffic. Plenty of time to get over whatever it was that made him want to avoid the trip. He put the key in the ignition and started the engine.

South of town, Connolly crossed Dog River to Hollinger's Island and descended into the lowlands that lay along the coast. Live oaks lined the roadway creating a moss-draped canopy overhead. The road became a tunnel beneath the foliage. A tunnel through time, sending Connolly's mind back to days he remembered all too well. When he was ten years old, his father died. His mother turned to alcohol to escape the worries of raising two children alone. Often in a drunken stupor, she frequently was gone for days at a time. Then she met a man at a truck stop in Loxley and left altogether. Forced to fend for themselves, Connolly and his younger brother crammed what they could into a pillowcase and hitchhiked down the bay to Uncle Guy's house in Bayou La Batre.

Uncle Guy knew everyone from Bon Secour to the mouth of the Pearl River, and when he wasn't on a shrimp boat, he enjoyed visiting as many of his friends as possible. He let Connolly tag along. Together they went to places along the coast most people didn't even know existed. Places like Gasque and Delchamps and Bayou Cateau. Places that opened their arms wide for a lonely young boy, wrapped his soul in a hot, steaming poultice of encouragement, and squeezed the trouble from his broken heart.

At Bailey's he crossed East Fowl River to Mon Louis Island. Just beyond the bridge he passed a sign made of plywood and nailed to a tree. The plywood was painted yellow with red letters in a simple message. Sprinkle's Store. One Mile.

He'd been stopping at Sprinkle's since his first trip with Uncle Guy. It was a cool Saturday morning in October, a long time ago. They had been to see Latham Graham in Delchamps. Latham and Guy spent the morning talking about oyster beds and hurricanes. Connolly spent the morning listening. When they left, Latham gave them a gunnysack full of oysters still in the shell. Guy didn't want to spend all afternoon shucking them, so when they got to Sprinkle's Store, he traded the oysters for lunch and a few groceries. They sat on the tailgate of the pickup and ate Vienna sausage from a can and split a pack of saltine crackers. Uncle Guy had a Buffalo Rock ginger ale. Connolly had a Nehi grape. A whole bottle, all to himself. The thought of it made him smile.

A few minutes later he rounded a curve in the road. The store came into sight. Connolly lifted his foot from the gas pedal and let the Chrysler coast from the pavement onto the parking lot.

Built of cypress lumber, the store had weathered to a dark gray. It had a steep tin roof rusted to a ruddy brown the color of tobacco spit. Long eaves hung five or six feet past the walls on either side, the ends supported by a row of posts that were covered with mold and mildew. Near the back, kudzu vines encroached on the building, winding their way up the posts and dangling in the sun above the roof.

A porch ran across the front one step above a parking lot paved with crushed oyster shells that crunched beneath the tires as the car came to a stop in front of the store. A drink machine stood near the door. Next to it was an assortment of chairs and empty bread racks. Two men sat nearby playing cards on an empty Dairy Fresh milk crate. To the left a young man dozed in a straight-back chair that was propped against the wall. His feet rested on a plastic five-gallon bucket turned upside down. Connolly nodded to the men playing cards as he stepped onto the porch and opened the door.

Inside, the building was stuffy and warm. Ceiling fans stirred the air at a lazy pace but did little to relieve the heat. To the left of the door was a wooden counter, burnished and smoothed by the wear of countless customers. Behind it a woman sat on a stool cooling herself with a paper fan from a funeral home in Pascagoula. She wore a sleeveless cotton dress that hung from her shoulders in a way that left the straps of her bra exposed. Her hair was bleached white and curly. Strands around her face were wet with sweat and stuck to her skin.

On the counter was a manual cash register. Beside it produce scales towered above a jar of peppermint candy and a square container filled with packages of Tom's Toasted Peanuts. To the right of the register was a gallon jar of pickled eggs tucked behind a dusty cardboard display of Kick no-doze pills.

Connolly moved down an aisle to a cooler along the rear wall next to a display case that held packaged meats. He opened the cooler and took out a pint-sized bottle of Milo's iced tea. On the way to the front he picked up a bag of Golden Flake pretzels. He set them on the counter by the register and took his wallet from the inside pocket of his jacket. The woman slid from the stool, glanced at the items, and punched some buttons on the register.

"'At's a dollar eighty-five."

Her voice sounded flat and tired.

Connolly handed her two dollars and slipped his wallet back in his pocket. She took his money and pulled a lever. The register made a clicking noise. A bell rang. The drawer opened. She handed him the change.

"You want a bag?"

Connolly shook his head.

"No, thank you."

She shoved the drawer closed.

"Kind of hot today."

"Yes, it is."

She returned to her seat on the stool.

"Where's that Hollis Toombs?" The words seemed to take forever to slide past her lips. "Ain't seen him in nearly two weeks."

She picked up the paper fan and began fanning herself once more. Connolly twisted the top of the bottle of tea and took a drink.

"He's on his honeymoon."

Her mouth dropped open.

"Honeymoon?" She stopped fanning. "Hollis Toombs got married?"

"Yes."

"I wish I'da knowed that." Her voice cackled. "I'da danced at his wedding."

Connolly grinned.

"I don't think he wanted anyone to know."

"He didn't? Why not? Ain't right somebody get married and not tell nobody."

Connolly shrugged.

"I think he was worried too many people would show up."

"Huh. More likely he was worried about what we might say about him. Who'd he marry?"

"You wouldn't know her."

"You don't know who I know. What's her name?"

"Victoria Verchinko."

"Victoria Ver-what-o?"

"Verchinko." Connolly took another drink. He glanced at her over the bottle. "I told you, you wouldn't know her."

"Where'd he find a woman with a name like that?"

"Long story."

"I know she ain't from around here. Ain't no Verchinkos anywhere I ever been. They gonna be livin' down there in that shack?"

"I don't think so."

"I hope he's got better sense than to do that to a woman. Even if her name is Verchinko. Garon's Bayou ain't no place for nobody to live."

"Yeah."

Connolly stepped toward the door. The woman continued.

"Off on a honeymoon." She had a twinkle in her eye and a lilt in her voice that made Connolly grin. He wasn't sure he wanted to hear any more, but she kept going. "Where'd they go?"

He stopped at the door and took another drink. If he told her they went to Disney World, the conversation would last another hour.

"Down to ... Florida, somewhere. I think."

She shook her head.

"Married. If that don't beat all."

Connolly nodded.

"It wasn't really something any of us could predict."

"I reckon not."

He opened the door and stepped outside. The woman's laughter drifted across the porch as he walked to the Chrysler.

Fourteen

*F*rom Sprinkle's Store, Connolly continued south. Twenty minutes later he reached the Dauphin Island Bridge, a two-lane span from Cedar Point to the north side of the island. There wasn't a car in sight. He pressed the gas pedal. The Chrysler picked up speed. Expansion joints in the concrete roadway slapped against the tires. The car rocked gently in time with the sound.

At the end of the bridge he let the car coast down the grade to the road. To the left was Grant's Pass Marina. Farther down on the right was the Ship-N-Shore. Since Zirlott's closed, it was the island's only grocery store. It was the only hardware, bait, and video store, too. Unlike most coastal resorts, Dauphin Island had no fast-food franchises, no amusement parks, and no gaudy souvenir shops. Just beaches and sunshine.

Past the Ship-N-Shore, Connolly turned right on Bienville Boulevard, a broad thoroughfare lined with palm trees that ran from east to west the length of the island. He glanced around as he drove.

For a barrier island that had recently weathered a hurricane, things didn't look too bad. Most of the commercial buildings were open and operating. Downed trees were still piled by the road, but houses near the center of the island looked to be in good shape. As he continued west, things began to change.

Beyond the public beach the western end of the island was a flat, treeless, sandy spit. Even in good weather a constant southern breeze swept unimpeded across it, blowing sand from the Gulf side and depositing it on the bay side. As a result, the western third of the island was less than three feet above sea level. But that hadn't stopped anyone from building on it. Beach houses lined both sides of the road in rows three and four deep from the pavement to the water. All of them perched atop pilings ten to twelve feet above the sand.

Connolly surveyed the houses as he drove past. There were houses with roofs missing. Houses with decks blown away. And pilings with no houses at all. Sprinkled in with the destruction was the occasional house that seemed to have escaped with little or no damage at all.

Farther down he came to the end of the road. The island continued for another mile, but a large sand berm blocked the way. Connolly turned the car around and made his way back up the road, searching for house numbers. There were none, of course, but it wasn't hard to spot the Marchands' house. It was the one with the yellow crime-scene tape wrapped around the pilings. The tape fluttered in the breeze.

Connolly brought the car to a stop at the edge of the road and got out. His foot landed in a puddle that filled his shoe with water. The breeze tousled his hair. A seagull called overhead. In the distance he heard the sound of an electric saw, and behind him someone was using a hammer. He stared at the beach house. A shudder ran up his spine. After a moment he leaned against the car and poured the water from his shoe, then stepped from the pavement and started toward the house. Sand filled his shoes as he slogged his way to it.

When he reached the house, he found the storm had blown away the bottom rungs of the steps and washed the sand away from the pilings. What was left of the stairs dangled above his head. The lowest rung was just beyond the tips of his outstretched fingers. He could jump for it, but there was no way of knowing if it would hold his weight.

The breeze blew harder. A loose board dangled from the eave. It creaked as it swayed from side to side in the wind. Connolly looked around. There wasn't much choice. He slipped off his jacket, gripped the back of the collar with his teeth, and tossed the tail of it over his shoulder. He could make it. The bottom step wasn't far way. He took a deep breath, bent his knees, and jumped. As his fingers locked over the edge of the first step, his elbows banged against the runners on the sides. Pain shot through his arms. He dangled there in agony.

Struggling with all his might, he pulled his chest toward the step, then reached with one hand for the next rung. Kicking and squirming, he worked his way up until his knees rested on the first step. He paused a moment to catch his breath, then grasped the railing and stood. The stairs swayed to the right. His heart jumped. He hesitated, then started up.

At the top of the steps he took the jacket from his mouth and slipped it on, then cupped his hands against the windowpane in the door and looked inside. Through the window he could see a large timber had smashed through the sliding glass doors on the Gulf side. Water and wind had ruined everything.

As he reached for the doorknob, he saw it was missing. The door frame was splintered where the bolt had torn through it when someone kicked the door open. It wasn't hard to figure out who. He shook his head and sighed.

"Dibber."

Connolly pushed open the door and stepped inside to the kitchen on the front of the house, facing the road. A countertop with a sink separated it from the living room area. Glass from the shattered doors was strewn across the room. From the look of things the timber had crashed through the doors, shoved a love seat across the room into the coffee table, jammed them both against a sofa, and rammed all of that against the countertop at the kitchen.

Connolly glanced around.

The kitchen was a mess. Dirty pans and dishes filled the sink. The stove was covered with grease and spatters of something that left charred black spots all over it. The cabinets were filthy. The refrigerator door was ajar. Molded, rotten food sat on the shelves inside. Sandy grit covered everything. Black mold grew along the lower half of the walls where the water had washed through the house.

Connolly climbed over the sofa to a hallway that opened off the living room to the right. A short way down the hall was a bedroom that faced the beach. Across from it was a bathroom. A door at the end of the hall led to a second bedroom. Connolly stared in at the first bedroom.

A dresser sat along the wall to the left of the door. In the middle of the room was a bare bed frame. A pair of blue jeans lay on the floor. Beside them was a black garbage bag stuffed with clothes.

Connolly stepped into the room and opened the top drawer of the dresser. It was empty. He tried the others. They were empty too. At the end of the dresser was a closet. He opened the door and looked inside. A single wire coat hanger hung from the bar. He backed away and glanced around the room once more, then moved across the hall to the bathroom.

Just beyond the open door was a sink on the wall to the right. A washcloth lay on it between the faucet and the wall. Beside it was a toothbrush. Above the sink was a medicine cabinet. Connolly opened the cabinet. Inside was a wrinkled tube of toothpaste and three disposable razors. He closed the cabinet and glanced around, then turned away.

In the bedroom at the end of the hall, there was a dresser along the wall near the door. The top of it was cluttered with bits of paper and things that collect on dressers over time. A bed sat in the middle of the room, but it had been stripped bare. A dark-brown stain covered the center of the mattress. Connolly moved to a closet on the far side. The door was open. Inside was a galvanized bar with a shelf above it. A pair of pants hung from a plastic hanger on the bar.

From the closet Connolly moved back to the dresser. He raked through the items on top with his finger. A pocket knife. A jewelry box with a paperback novel on top. A cobalt blue vase about twelve inches high. It had a wide mouth at the top and curved to a stem with a clear bubble in the center. Connolly knew what it was only because his aunt Ruby Poiroux had collected cobalt glass.

Alone on the dresser the vase seemed out of place. He picked it up for a closer look, then set it near the jewelry box. He moved the paperback book aside and opened the box. Inside was a Casio watch and two small photos of a baby. The baby lay on a bed, wrapped in a blanket, sound asleep. Connolly closed the box and picked up the book.

Dog-eared and worn, the cover showed a sketch of a man lying on the grass beside a motorcycle with one arm tucked behind his head. In his free hand he held a cigarette, and on his forearm was a tattoo. His feet were tucked against his thighs with his knees up, stretching his black leather chaps tight against his legs. A tough guy. With a tough ride.

Connolly read the title aloud.

"*Hotel Green.* By Randy Morris."

The book fell open at a spot where a black-and-white photograph had been stuck inside. A man and woman stood next to a car. Tall and slender, the man had a solid build, but nothing about him looked athletic. The woman looked much younger than he but not immature. Short and petite, she had curly hair with dark eyes. In the photo she stood next to him with her arm in his, her head resting just below his shoulder. The car behind them was a 1962 Galaxie 500. Connolly knew a guy who used to own one. June 1966 was stamped in the margin across the bottom of the picture.

Connolly flipped through the pages of the book. In front he found an inscription. To Billy and Frieda. Best regards, Harold.

He read it again, then stuck the photo in the book and laid it on the dresser.

From the bedroom he retraced his steps to the living room, climbed over the love seat, and moved around the counter to the corner by the door. Near the stove was a Dr Pepper bottle with some sort of brown liquid in it. Connolly stepped across the kitchen and picked it up. He swirled the bottle around. Tiny black pieces of something stuck to the sides of the bottle. He grimaced.

"Skoal spit."

He set the bottle on the counter and brushed his hands together.

A plate on top of the dishes in the sink had bits of food smeared over it. Connolly found a wooden spoon that was clean enough to touch and used it to push the dishes around. A roach ran out. He jumped to one side and swatted at it with the spoon. The roach disappeared through a crack under the lip of the sink.

Beside the sink was a frying pan. Connolly nudged it with the spoon, but it didn't move. He grasped the handle and tried to lift it, but it was stuck to the countertop. The pan had been burned black. Plastic on the handle was melted at one end. A stainless steel fork lay in the pan. The handle was shiny and smooth and bore the letters US Navy. The tines were corroded green.

Connolly let go of the pan and brushed his hands together again. They felt greasy and dirty. He glanced around the room once more then turned to the door and started outside.

Fifteen

The following morning Connolly arrived at the office as Mrs. Gordon unlocked the door. She gave him a questioning look as they entered.

"What's wrong?"

"Nothing. Why?"

She glanced at her watch.

"You're here and it's not even eight thirty."

Connolly shrugged.

"Ah, you know."

"That's the second time this week."

Connolly didn't reply. Mrs. Gordon moved to her desk and switched on her computer.

"Messages from yesterday are on your chair."

"Okay."

He started toward the hallway, then turned back.

"You know anything about a book called *Hotel Green?*"

She took a seat at her desk.

"Never heard of it."

"Written around 1966."

She turned toward him, her face wrinkled in a scowl.

"Is this a literature quiz, or do you want me to find a copy for you?"

Connolly shook his head.

"Just asking."

Mrs. Gordon turned back to the computer. Connolly walked down the hall to his office. He hung his jacket on the coatrack and moved behind the desk. The phone messages were on the seat of his chair next to a stack of mail. He moved them to the desktop and took a seat.

In a few minutes Mrs. Gordon appeared at the door, notepad in hand. She leaned against the door frame and read from her notes.

"*Hotel Green.* Published in 1966 by Worthen Press. New York. Written by Randy Morris. Morris was a pen name. His real name was Harold Schnadelbach. Lived in Atlanta. Taught English at Emory University."

She paused to turn a page. Connolly slid the trash can next to the desk and propped his feet on it.

"Where'd you find all of this?"

"The Internet."

"The Internet?"

"Learn how to turn on a computer and you could find it for yourself. You want to hear the rest?"

"Yes."

He leaned back in his chair and closed his eyes. Mrs. Gordon continued.

"Schnadelbach wrote three or four books. Had some success but nothing great. Hit the big time with *Hotel Green.* Became a best seller. Made it into a movie." She paused a moment. "I saw it at the Bama Drive-In. It was pretty good. Tommy Russell played the guy. If you look closely in a couple of scenes, you can see a very young Jane Manley."

Connolly opened his eyes.

"You went to the Bama Drive-In?"

She gave him a sarcastic smile.

"Yes."

Connolly grinned.

"With who?"

"With whom."

"Yeah. With whom?"

"None of your business."

Connolly chuckled.

"What else?"

She raised her eyebrows. Connolly laughed.

"Not about that. Is this a story about some guys in high school? Spend all their time talking about leaving the little town where they live. Gonna hit the road as soon as they graduate. Then when school is over none of them does it except this one guy?"

"Yes."

"I think I might have read part of it once."

"I can't imagine why."

"Neither can I. Anything else?"

"Not much. *Hotel Green* was a big success, but Harold never got to enjoy it. He died in a plane crash that summer, not long after the book was released. Crashed in a peanut field near Sylvester, Georgia."

Connolly sat up in his chair.

"That it?"

"That's it."

"All right." He turned back to the desk and the stack of mail. "Thanks."

Mrs. Gordon lingered by the door.

"Why are you interested in this book?"

"Found it in the beach house."

"The beach house?"

"The one they say Dibber Landry looted."

Mrs. Gordon cocked her head to one side in a thoughtful look.

"Might make a good beach book."

"This one was inscribed to somebody. Bill and Frieda, I think."

"By Morris?"

Connolly shook his head.

"Harold."

Mrs. Gordon shifted positions.

"Harold Schnadelbach."

Connolly looked up from the mail.

"Yeah." His eyes were wide. "Harold Schnadelbach. I should have picked it up."

Mrs. Gordon moved away from the door. Connolly spent the next hour or so reading through the mail and working on pleadings in some of his pending cases. As he worked, he thought about that book and the inscription in it. The more he thought about it, the more certain he was that it had something to do with this case. The only question was, how did it get in the beach house? Did the dead man bring it with him, or was it the Marchands'?

Shortly before ten he finished with the files on his desk. He put on his jacket, picked up the files, and started up the hall. Mrs. Gordon glanced up as he reached the door.

"Where are you going?"

Connolly laid the files on her desk.

"To see Inez Marchand."

"Who's she?"

"Lady who owns that beach house."

"Are you going to give her a literary quiz too?"

"I'm going to ask her a few questions."

Mrs. Gordon chuckled.

"Did they ever identify the dead man?"

"Not yet."

Mrs. Gordon shook her head.

"This is a really strange case." She turned to face the computer. "You've had some strange ones before, but this one is really weird."

"Yeah."

She grumbled as she arranged the papers on the desk beside her keyboard.

"Dead man in a beach house. Just before a hurricane hits. No one knows who he is. And we spend the morning talking about a novel written in 1966 by a man who died before it paid off." Her fingers began to move across the keyboard. "You attract a strange crowd."

Connolly opened the door and walked up the corridor toward the elevator.

Sixteen

Inez Marchand lived on Upham Street in midtown off Old Shell Road. The drive from the office took less than ten minutes. Connolly made a right onto the street and began looking for the house. He found the number painted on the curb in front of an overgrown lot that covered most of the block. Large oaks and magnolias grew near the street. Farther back he could see a few pecans and pines. Underneath was a tangled mass of vines and bushes. A picket fence ran along the sidewalk in front. It once had been painted white, but most of the paint was gone. The boards were rotten and green with mildew. A gate drooped from rusted hinges across a narrow brick sidewalk that led into the center of the lot. The bricks in the sidewalk were covered with moss.

At the far side of the lot past the sidewalk, Connolly found a gravel driveway. Most of the gravel had been worn to the sides by traffic going in and out, leaving bare dirt tracks that ran from the street toward the house. Connolly slowed the Chrysler and made the turn. The car idled up the drive.

The house was a single-story cottage constructed of concrete blocks that had been painted white. It had square windows that cranked out on either side. The gabled roof was set at a steep angle and covered with slate shingles. Bushes had once ringed the house just beyond the drip line, but they had been trimmed to the ground. Their stumps, hacked and splintered, sprouted fresh green leaves. A little farther out from the house, the undergrowth had been chopped back far enough to allow someone to walk all the way around. Spatters of paint dotted the ground and made a trail across the sidewalk near the front door. A wooden ladder leaned against a tree near the walk, surrounded by empty paint cans.

At the end of the drive was a garage. Pine needles covered the roof. The windows were gray with dirt and grime. A 1971 Mustang sat next to it. The car was covered with needles and leaves. Through the rear window Connolly could see the back seat was crammed with boxes.

Closer to the house a green 1989 Buick was parked by the side door. Connolly brought the Chrysler to a stop next to it and climbed out. He slipped on his jacket and glanced around. Through a window he could see a light was on over a table in the kitchen near the back of the house. But the tabletop was clean, not even a coffee cup or the morning paper. Across the room a portable television sat on a counter near the sink, but the screen was dark. The place had an odd feel and a strange look. Like someone had been there moments ago, but just left. Connolly glanced around again, then made his way past the corner of the house to the front door. As he reached to knock, the door opened.

A woman peered out from inside. The room behind her was dark, and she squinted against the glare of the sunlight through the opening. Her voice was craggy and wheezy.

"May I help you?"

She was short and stocky with a full neck that made her jaw-line smooth and soft but weighed against her chest to form a wrinkle in an arc just above the neckline of her faded blue house-dress. Over the dress she wore a blue housecoat that was open in front. Her gray hair was short and curly and looked as if she'd just rolled out of bed, but her dark eyes were bright and alert. On her feet she wore dirty pink slippers. One arm held the door. With the other she braced herself against the door frame. Something about her was familiar to Connolly, but he couldn't remember why.

Cold air rushed through the open doorway. With it came the smell of cigarette smoke and fried bacon. From behind her Connolly heard the yap of a small dog.

"Inez Marchand?"

"Yes."

"My name is Mike Connolly. I'm an attorney. I represent—"

The woman jerked her head to one side.

"Pixie!" she shouted at the dog. "Shut up!"

The dog continued to yelp. Inez leaned away. The door opened wider. Connolly could see the living room inside. A small table sat by the door next to a sofa with green upholstery covered with a clear plastic slipcover. Inez picked up a magazine from the table and threw it across the room. Connolly heard the click of the dog's paws on the floor as it scurried away.

Inez turned back to face him and pulled the door closer to her side.

"Who are you?"

"Mike Connolly. I'm an attorney. I represent Dibber Landry."

She shook her head.

"Never heard of him."

"He's—"

Her eyes opened wider. Her voice grew louder.

"Is he that man that stole that stuff from my beach house?"

"Yes, ma'am. He's the one they've accused of it."

Her look turned cold.

"What do you want?"

"I was wondering if I could talk to you."

"About what?"

"About the dead man they found in the house."

She stood erect.

"I'm not sure I want to talk about him. I don't know nothing about him."

"Well, when was the last time you went down there?"

"I don't know."

"Have you been down since the hurricane hit?"

"I haven't been down there in years."

"It looks like someone's been living there. Has anyone else been down there?"

A frown wrinkled her brow.

"You've been down there?"

"Yes."

She looked angry.

"What were you doing in my beach house?"

"It's a crime scene. I—"

"How'd you get in?"

"I—"

She cut him off.

"You broke in."

"The door was open."

"You broke in my beach house."

"I didn't break in. The knob's missing from the front door. There's a hole in the back big enough to drive a truck through. I didn't break into anything. Besides, it's a crime scene."

She glared at him.

"What'd you find?"

"Like I said, someone's been living down there."

"I imagine it was that fella they found. The dead guy. Or that man they arrested."

"Anyone else have access to the house?"

"My son uses it some."

"Your son?"

"Yes."

"What's his name?"

"Nick. Why?"

"Think he knows anything about him?"

"About who?"

"The dead guy."

"I don't know."

"Anyone else have access to the house?"

"No."

She was a difficult woman. Connolly struggled to think of another question. Then he thought of the key.

"The coroner said he found a key in the dead man's pocket."

Her eyes narrowed.

"A what?"

"A key. A door key."

She shifted her weight to the opposite side.

"So what."

"Did you give him a key to the house?"

Her eyes narrowed.

"I told you, I don't know anything about him. Do I have to talk to you?"

Connolly sighed.

"No."

"Good."

She leaned away and closed the door.

Connolly raised his hand to knock on the door again, then thought better of it. Instead, he turned aside and started toward the

Chrysler. As he reached the car, a pickup truck turned from the street into the driveway. It came to a stop in front of the garage. A man got out, dressed in khaki work clothes and carrying a metal lunch box. He moved around the truck and walked toward the house. He stopped when he saw Connolly standing in front of the Chrysler.

"You an insurance salesman?"

"No, sir. A lawyer."

"Huh," the man chortled. "Not much difference. What do you want?"

"Are you Mr. Marchand?"

"Yeah. What's she done now?"

"I was trying to talk to your wife, but she closed the door on me."

"She can be ornery sometimes. What do you need?"

"I represent Dibber Landry. He's accused of killing the man they found in your beach house."

Marchand shook his head.

"How do you do that?"

Connolly gave him a puzzled look.

"Do what?"

"Defend those guys. How do you get up in court and say your man didn't do it, when you know he did?"

Connolly smiled.

"That isn't exactly how it works."

"No?"

"No. When's the last time you were at the beach house?"

"I ain't never been there."

"Excuse me?"

"That beach house ain't mine. That's my wife's house." Marchand moved past Connolly and started toward the house. "If she don't want to talk to you about it, I can't help you."

Connolly persisted.

"You've never been down there?"

Marchand stopped and turned to him.

"Mister, I ain't been in it. I ain't rode by it. I ain't never even seen that house. And I don't plan on going." He turned toward the house. "I'd love to help you with your case, but I don't know nothing about it."

Connolly called after him once more.

"The dead man had a key. Looks like it was a key to the beach house."

Marchand was at the door. He stopped with one hand on the doorknob and turned again to face Connolly.

"Do what?"

"The dead man. He had a key in his pocket. Looks like it could fit the door at the beach house. Any idea why he would have a key to the house?"

"Like I said, anything you want to know about that beach house you'll have to ask my wife. And if she won't help you, there ain't much I can do for you."

He opened the door and disappeared inside.

Connolly backed the Chrysler down the driveway. As the car rolled into the street, his cell phone rang. The call was from Mrs. Gordon.

"Someone named Gayle Underwood is looking for you. Said she works with the DA's office."

"What did she want?"

"Wants you to call her. They've identified the dead man in Dibber Landry's case."

Connolly pressed a button to end the call. He brought the car to a stop behind a service van parked down the block and telephoned Gayle.

"You identified the body?"

"Hodges got a match back on the prints yesterday. His name is Stephen Ellis. Last address was in Lawrenceville, Georgia. We're still trying to track down relatives."

"Anything else?"

"Born April 11, 1967. Looks like he was forty years old."

"How'd you find him?"

"Arrested for possession of marijuana in Valdosta, Georgia, in 1986."

Connolly switched off the phone and headed downtown.

Seventeen

At Royal Street, Connolly turned right and drove behind the courthouse. He parked in front of St. Pachomius Church, but instead of climbing the stairs to the sanctuary, he walked across the street to the sheriff's office. A receptionist greeted him as he entered.

"May I help you?"

"I need to see Brian Hodges."

"Down the hall. Turn right. Third door on the left."

Connolly moved past her desk. He found Hodges sitting at his desk in a cramped office across the hall from a row of vending machines. Hodges looked up when Connolly appeared at the door.

"Mike Connolly. Let me guess. You're here about Dilbert Landry." Hodges gestured toward a chair in front of his desk. "Come on in. Have a seat." He stood and took a file from a stack on the windowsill behind him. "We just got an ID on the dead man in that case."

Connolly took a seat.

"I heard."

Hodges sat in his chair and opened the file.

"He's from Georgia."

"What do you know about him?"

"Not much." Hodges turned through the pages in the file. "Looks like his parents live in Lawrenceville, Georgia. Billy and Frieda Ellis."

Connolly felt his heart jump.

"Billy and Frieda?"

"Yeah. You know them?"

"No. Gayle Underwood said you were still looking for them."

Hodges nodded.

"We are. Have an address for them, but we haven't been able to reach them yet."

"How'd you come up with an address for his parents?"

"Busted for pot when he was nineteen. Student at Valdosta State. Once we got a match on the prints, we called the police over there. They gave us the information from his file."

Connolly nodded.

"Anything else?"

"No. Other than that one charge, he was a model citizen. No warrants. No traffic citations. Nothing."

"What about the beach house?"

"What about it?"

"What did you find?"

Hodges tossed the file on the desk.

"Well, not much, really. Place was a mess. You been down there?"

"Yeah."

"All that damage from the hurricane. Hard to say what was there before the storm."

"You didn't find anything?"

"Found some prints."

"Whose?"

Hodges picked up the file and leafed through it. He took out a page and glanced over it while he talked.

"We found prints for Inez Marchand. Her son, Nicholas Marchand. Dilbert Landry. The dead man, Stephen Ellis. Three more sets we haven't been able to identify. And some prints from Edwin Marchand, Inez's husband."

Connolly frowned.

"Her husband?"

"Yes."

"In the house?"

"Yes."

"Where?"

Hodges turned to another page in the file.

"Front door frame. Countertop in the kitchen. Door frame in the back bedroom."

"Did you talk to him?"

"Yes."

"What did he say?"

"Said he hadn't been down there in years."

"Think he's lying?"

Hodges shrugged.

"Prints stay around a long time."

Connolly thought for a moment.

"What else you got?"

"That's about it."

"That's not much."

Hodges shifted positions in the chair.

"It was right after a hurricane. We had several dead bodies to deal with. Power was out. Had to get some guys with chain saws to cut our way to a couple of them. Everybody was working round the clock. We didn't have time to process every scrap of paper in the place. Had a tough time just getting to the house."

Connolly nodded.

"Take anything from the scene?"

"Not much." Hodges looked at the file. "To tell you the truth, we had a hard time figuring out what was important and what wasn't. The place was a mess." He lifted a page from the file. "We took the sheets from the bed. A slug from the wall. Thirty-eight caliber. Found some empty Pseudaphed boxes in the first bedroom. That's about it." He tossed the inventory list on the desk. "I mean, the sink was full of dirty dishes. Junk piled around everywhere. We could have loaded a trailer truck if we'd wanted to, but none of it seemed that important."

Connolly scanned the inventory document.

"Pseudaphed?"

Hodges nodded.

"From the looks of that kitchen, I'd say somebody was cooking up some meth."

"You think that's what the dead guy was doing?"

"Wouldn't surprise me."

"Find any prints on the boxes?"

"One of the unidentified sets."

"Anybody else's on the boxes?"

"Can't say."

"Can't say?"

"Still investigating it."

Connolly tossed the document on the desk. A frown wrinkled his forehead.

"You found somebody's prints on the Pseudaphed boxes. You think that person was cooking meth in the house where the dead man was found. And you won't tell me who it was?"

"We're still investigating."

"I'm entitled to know who that person is."

"We're still investigating."

Connolly sighed.

"We'll see about that. How'd you find out the dead guy was in there?"

"Lady next door reported it." Hodges looked in the file again. "Amy Wilburn. You want the address?"

"Yeah. What did she say?"

Connolly already had the address from McNamara, but he didn't want to tell Hodges what he knew about the case. Better to keep him wondering. Hodges scribbled the address on a legal pad and tore off the page.

"Wilburns owned the house next to the Marchands." He handed the address to Connolly. "They came down to see about it after the storm. Noticed an odor. Husband went over to check it out. Called us."

"He went in the house?"

"I don't think so. Said he didn't. Said he got as far as the front door. Odor was pretty strong. I think there were flies in there by then. He didn't want to go inside."

"Body was in bad shape?"

"Not terrible. I've seen worse. But it was smelling pretty rank by the time we got there."

Connolly nodded.

"What about the son?"

"The son?"

"You said you found prints in the house for the Marchands' son."

"Yeah." Hodges glanced at the file. "Nicholas Marchand. Born August 3, 1970. Works at Southern Nursery Supply in Wilmer. I think they own it."

"Who?"

"Marchands."

"You talked to him too?"

"Yeah."

"What did he have to say?"

"Said he didn't know the guy. Never seen him. Didn't know why he was in the house."

"Did you ask him about your meth theory?"

Hodges smiled.

"Can't say."

"Can't say?"

Hodges leaned back in his chair and folded his arms behind his head.

"Still investigating."

Connolly didn't like the answer, but he resisted the urge to press the issue.

"What about the key?"

"What key?"

"Morgan said he found a key in the guy's pocket."

Hodges shook his head.

"Haven't checked on it yet. Been trying to find out who he was."

"Don't you think that key might be important?"

Hodges shrugged.

"I don't know."

"Well, if it fits the front door of the beach house, wouldn't you think maybe somebody's lying about not knowing who he is?"

"Maybe. Could have found it inside."

"And it could have fallen from the sky."

"What are you saying?"

"Nobody's going to believe he found the key."

"That's Henry's problem."

Connolly chuckled.

"Henry said you found Dibber because he pawned something from the house."

Hodges nodded.

"A jet ski."

"How'd you know it belonged to the Marchands?"

"They filed a report on it."

Connolly was taken aback.

"They reported it stolen?"

"Yeah."

"Doesn't that strike you as odd?"

"What?"

"These people are cooking meth in the house and they file a report with the police saying someone stole their jet ski."

Hodges smiled.

"I didn't say they were smart." He took a copy of the report from the file and handed it to Connolly. "They filed a report with the Dauphin Island police when they met with FEMA."

"FEMA?"

"After the storm. Disaster relief. Look on the back."

Connolly read the report. Hodges leaned back in his chair.

"It lists a bunch of stuff. Filed a report on it to back up their claim for property loss on their FEMA application."

The report was signed by Inez Marchand and listed a number of items besides the jet ski. Connolly pointed to the list.

"Are you accusing Dibber of taking all of this?"

Hodges shook his head.

"Not right now. Just the jet ski."

Connolly glanced at the report again, then handed it to Hodges.

"Could I get a copy of that?"

Hodges stood.

"Sure."

Connolly pointed to the file.

"How about a copy of those other things. The inventory of what you took from the house. The incident report when you went out there. Fingerprints. Whatever you have."

Hodges collected the reports from the file.

"Anthony Hammond was talking about you the other day."

"Yeah? What'd he say about me?"

Hodges came from behind the desk.

"Said if I didn't watch out, you'd walk off with the whole file."

"Did he tell you I'm one of the good guys?"

Hodges had a wry smile as he moved toward the door.

"Come on. I'll get you some copies."

Eighteen

fter lunch Connolly drove across town to Airline Highway. The Wilburns lived on Yorkhaven Road at the western edge of the city. Edwin and Inez Marchand hadn't helped at all. Morgan and Hodges weren't much better. Four days into the case and he still didn't know what had happened at the beach house. And for all their talk, he was sure Hodges and McNamara didn't either. Perhaps Amy Wilburn could fill in some details. He hoped someone did, and soon. He was running out of people to talk to.

The Wilburns lived in a two-story stucco house on five acres. A concrete drive ran from the road to a garage alongside the house. A walkway curved around the house from the drive to the front door. The walkway was lined with monkey grass and small accent lights with black covers. Boxwood shrubs trimmed in the shape of a ball grew just beneath the windows. A wooden fence surrounded the backyard. Over the top Connolly could see a play set. A Honda minivan was parked at the end of the drive.

Connolly turned the Chrysler into the driveway and brought it to a stop behind the minivan. He stepped from the car and walked to the front door. From inside came the heavy beat of music. He rang the doorbell and waited.

The music continued, then stopped. Someone was talking inside, but he couldn't hear what they were saying. He pressed the doorbell once more. In a moment the door opened, and a woman appeared. About thirty years old, she was tall and slender and dressed in a blue jogging suit. She had short brown hair cropped just below her ears in a way that made it flip toward the front. Her cheeks were red. Sweat glistened on her neck.

She took a deep breath and smiled.

"Hello."

Connolly smiled back.

"I hope I didn't take you away from something important."

"No." She took another deep breath. "I needed a break."

Connolly nodded.

"My name is Mike Connolly. I'm an attorney. I'm looking for Amy Wilburn."

She wiped her face with her hands.

"Well, you found her. Who's mad at me now?"

"You called the sheriff's office about a problem at a house on Dauphin Island."

"Yes."

"I was wondering if I could talk to you about that."

"Sure." She moved away from the door. "Come on inside."

Connolly stepped past her through the doorway. She closed the door behind him and led him to the kitchen.

"Would you like something to drink? Iced tea? Water?"

"No. I'm fine."

She took a glass from the cabinet and filled it with ice.

"Sure you don't want something to drink? I'm having tea."

Connolly shrugged.

"Okay."

He moved around the kitchen table and took a seat. She filled another glass and set it on the table in front of him.

"My husband is the one who thought something was wrong over there."

She found a napkin and laid it next to Connolly's glass, then took a seat. Connolly took a sip of tea.

"What made him think something was wrong?"

"We were down there after the storm, checking on our house. He and the children were wandering around looking at the damage to the other houses. They came back and said there was a terrible smell coming from that house. We all went over and had a look. Would have gone inside but the stairs were torn up." She frowned. "The smell was really bad. So, finally I just called and reported it."

"You didn't go inside the house?"

"No." She shook her head. "Glad we didn't, too." She took a sip of tea. "Did they ever identify the body?"

"Yes. His name is Stephen Ellis. Does that name mean anything to you?"

She shook her head.

"No. I don't know anyone by that name."

"Sheriff's office says he's from Lawrenceville, Georgia." Connolly took another sip of tea. "Does that help?"

Amy shook her head.

"No. Sorry."

"Have you had any trouble with people breaking into your beach house? Anything like that?"

"No."

"Any of your neighbors?"

"Not that I know of. It's pretty quiet down there. Most people in our area know each other. Not much happens."

Connolly nodded.

"That afternoon, when you noticed the smell. Did your husband go inside the house?"

"No. At least he said he didn't. I think he climbed up to the door and looked in."

"What about your children?"

"No." She shook her head. "They're five and three."

Connolly nodded.

"Did you talk to your neighbors about the smell?"

"Yeah. I mean, we all talked about it. Several of them were down there that same weekend."

"Any of them go in the house?"

"No. This all happened in just a few hours. We talked. I made the call."

"But your neighbors noticed the smell?"

She nodded.

"Several people were talking about it. You know, the ones who have houses around there. We were all down there after the storm, trying to see what was left."

"Do you know the people who own that house? The one where the body was found."

"I don't know them. I think I might have met the woman once. Marsh ..."

"Marchand."

"Yes. Marchand. I think I met her once. Older woman."

"Was she down there a lot?"

"I don't think so. They've had people in and out of there most of the time when we've been down there. But most of the time it was a guy about my age. I think it's the son of the people who own it. That's what they say."

"They?"

"The other owners."

"Anyone with him?"

She nodded.

"Two or three guys." She grimaced. "Not really the kind of people we hang out with."

"A rowdy group?"

"Yeah."

"Ever have any trouble?"

"Once or twice it got a little loud."

"Did you or your husband ever go over there to talk to them about it?"

She shook her head.

"We didn't."

"The neighbors?"

"I think some of them might have called about it."

"The police?"

"Yeah. Didn't do much good."

"Have you ever been inside that house?"

She shook her head.

"No."

"Was anyone living in it? You know, permanently?"

She frowned.

"I don't think so. But we're only down there on weekends, and not every weekend at that. So, I don't know what happened during the week."

"When was the last time you were down there? Before the storm."

"A day or two before it hit. We went down to board up the windows."

"Was anyone in the house then?"

She nodded.

"Yes. They were down there. Looked like they were getting things ready. You know, preparing for the storm. Like everybody else."

"What were they doing?"

"When we drove up, they had a pickup parked at the steps and were loading things on it."

"Things?"

"Mattress. Clothes."

"Did you talk to them?"

"No. We got busy doing what we were doing, and I didn't pay any attention. When we left, they were already gone."

"What time did you leave?"

"Just about dark. We got down there about two in the afternoon. Left right at dark."

"Did you ever see anyone else at the house? Other than the son and his friends?"

"Not really. I mean, there could have been other people. I wasn't watching very closely, and, like I say, we weren't down there every weekend."

Connolly took another sip of tea and set the glass on the table. He wiped his hands on the napkin and stood.

"Mrs. Wilburn, I appreciate your time."

"Hope I helped."

"You did."

She stood and led him through the house to the front door.

"My husband might be able to tell you more. He'll be in this afternoon."

Connolly stepped outside.

"Thanks. I may give him a call."

Nineteen

Connolly checked his watch as he drove away from the Wilburns' home. It was almost two. Talking to Amy Wilburn had taken less time than he expected. With an afternoon available he decided to look for Lootie Shaw, the man to whom Dibber sold some of the items from the Marchands' beach house. He wasn't sure what Lootie could tell him, but he wasn't getting very far with anyone else.

From Airline Highway Connolly cut across the city to Wilson Avenue in Prichard on the north side of Mobile, not far from Tommy Porter's pawnshop. He knew one person in Prichard. Tyrone Jackson. If Lootie Shaw was as notorious as Tommy suggested, Tyrone would know about him. And he would know where to find him.

As a young man Tyrone had lived a rambunctious life. In grammar school he was in a fistfight almost every day. Midway through the eighth grade he was suspended for selling beer from his locker. In the eleventh grade he was arrested for stealing radios from automobiles in an apartment complex near the high school. Then in his senior year he and two friends stole a beer truck. They stashed the beer in the woods behind Tyrone's house and abandoned the truck in front of the Dairy Freeze in Chickasaw. Only problem was, the Chickasaw police chief lived across the road from the Dairy Freeze. He knew about the missing truck and was on the lookout. Tyrone and his friends were arrested the next morning. The friends pled guilty and went to Mt. Meigs, a detention center for juveniles. Tyrone's mother hired Connolly. With some hard work he managed to get the charges reduced, and Tyrone was placed on probation. It was a turning point in his life. He finished high school, attended college, and opened his own business. Mid City Tire. He married, had four children, and served as a deacon at Eighth Street Baptist Church. Not much happened in Prichard that he didn't know about.

Connolly turned the Chrysler off the pavement and parked to one side of the building. He got out and stepped into one of the service bays. A car sat on the lift. Tyrone came from beneath it with a smile.

"Mr. Connolly." He wiped his hands on a rag. "Haven't seen you in a long time."

Connolly shook his hand.

"Too long."

"Yes. It has been too long. How's that car of yours running?"

"Doing well."

"Ready to sell it to me?"

Connolly chuckled and shook his head.

"Can't part with my car."

"Don't see many like it these days."

"No, you don't."

"What brings you up this way?"

"I'm looking for someone."

"Oh? What kind of someone?"

Connolly gave him a sober look. His voice took a serious tone.

"Trouble."

The smile disappeared from Tyrone's face.

"Trouble got a name?"

"Lootie Shaw."

"Client of yours?"

"No. He's a witness."

Tyrone looked away.

"Anything he witnessed can't be good."

"Probably not. You know where he lives?"

"Yeah. I know where he lives." Tyrone looked Connolly in the eye. "You got a pistol with you?"

Connolly chuckled. Tyrone didn't blink.

"I'm not kidding. The fire department doesn't go in there without a police escort."

Connolly sighed.

"I'll be all right."

Tyrone looked away, shaking his head.

"Go out Main Street to Price Avenue." He turned back to Connolly. "It's a little ways out. There's a club on the corner. Vee-Jay's Lounge."

Connolly nodded. Tyrone continued.

"Turn right. Go up a couple of blocks to Lucky Street."

Connolly frowned.

"Lucky Street?"

"It ain't really lucky, but that's the name. Turn left on Lucky. Go down about two or three blocks. Some of the blocks may be a little long in there, but two or three blocks. You'll come to Hobbs Avenue. Turn left. Loo-tay lives in a green house on the left. Just before you get to the railroad tracks."

"Green house on the left."

"Yeah. Green. Like, bright green."

"Okay." Connolly offered his hand. "Thanks, Tyrone."

They shook hands. Tyrone smiled.

"Sure is good to see you. You ought to come by here more often. I'll give you a good deal on some tires."

Connolly nodded.

"Might take you up on that."

"I can get you some bias-ply tires, just like the ones that came on it."

Connolly tossed a wave over his shoulder as he walked to the car.

Finding Lootie Shaw's house wasn't any trouble. Painted lime green, it was visible from two blocks away. With purple trim and a pink door, it looked like a Day-Glo sign. A small patch of dirt in front of the house was dotted with weeds and trash.

Connolly parked the Chrysler across the street and started toward the house. Just before he reached the steps, the front door opened. A young man came out. He looked Connolly over, then tipped his chin.

"You lost?"

Connolly smiled.

"I'm looking for someone named Lootie Shaw."

"What you want with him?"

"I'm a lawyer."

Connolly slipped his hand in his pocket for a business card. The young man's eyes were alert. He stood up straight and reached his hand behind his waist. Connolly stopped.

"It's okay." He pulled open his jacket in both directions. "I'm just getting a business card."

The young man smiled. Connolly took the card from his pocket and handed it to him.

"I represent a man named Dibber Landry."

The young man glanced at the card, then back at Connolly.

"White guy?"

"Yes."

"What's this got to do with Loo-tay?"

"Supposedly, he bought some things from Dibber. I need to talk to him about—"

The young man shook his head and backed away.

"Uhn-uh. Ain't nobody talk to Loo-tay about no missin' property. Whatever we got here is ours."

Just then the door opened, and another man appeared. Almost as wide as the door frame, his large stomach bulged beneath an oversized black and white shirt that hung over the waistband of his black pants. The legs of the pants were big and floppy and so long that they piled up on top of the black canvas high-tops on his feet. The sleeves of his shirt reached past his first knuckles, but beneath the cuff Connolly could see each finger bore a gold ring with a diamond in the center. Around his neck he wore strand after strand of gold chain. He stood at the top step, his eyes fixed on Connolly.

"What about Dibber?"

"You know him?"

"Maybe. What you want?"

"I'm looking for Lootie Shaw."

"Loo-tay."

Connolly wasn't sure if the man's response was a question or an answer.

"Yes. Lootie."

The door opened again. Two men came from the house. They were older and heavier than the young boy Connolly had talked to before. They stood on either side of the doorway, watching. Connolly felt uncomfortable. The heavyset man stared at him.

"Say it right."

"Excuse me?"

"The name is Loo-tay. Say it right."

Connolly felt confused.

"You know him?"

"Who?"

"Lootie."

The man stepped forward to the edge of the porch.

"I am Loo-tay. I want you to pronounce my name the right way."

"Oh." Connolly hesitated, wondering if he could get to the Chrysler before the other two men on the porch got to him. Rather than risking it, he gestured with both hands. "Sorry. Didn't mean to cause a problem, Loo-tay."

The big man smiled.

"All right. Now we can do some business. Come on inside."

He stepped into the house, followed by the two men standing at the door. Connolly didn't move. The young man he'd first seen on the porch gestured toward the door. Reluctantly, Connolly moved up the steps.

The door opened from the porch to a large room. Beyond it was a dining area and kitchen. To the left was a hallway. A large-screen television occupied the center of the room. A rug covered the floor in front of it with oversized pillows scattered across it. In the corner to the right was a leather recliner. A woman wearing red vinyl hot pants and a yellow vinyl halter top was sprawled across the chair. Loo-tay crossed the room toward her.

"Woman, get out of my chair."

She smiled at him but didn't move. He slapped her on the thigh. She grimaced in pain and pouted.

"That hurt!"

"Get out of my chair."

She rolled off the chair and stood. Loo-tay put his arm around her and kissed her. His eyes followed her as she crossed the room and disappeared down the hall.

Loo-tay took a seat in the chair. A man Connolly hadn't seen before entered the room and stood behind Connolly. With a wave of his hand Loo-tay gestured to Connolly.

"Ask Loo-tay what you want to know."

Connolly cleared his throat.

"Dibber sold you some jewelry a few weeks ago."

"That's what he says?"

Connolly nodded.

"That's what he says."

Loo-tay shrugged.

"Maybe he did. And, maybe he didn't. Hard to say."

"The pieces came from a beach house on Dauphin Island."

"I wouldn't know about that. He's not one of my people."

"But you know him."

"I know him. I do business with him. But he's not one of my people. Dibber's what we call a freelancer."

"Freelancer?"

Loo-tay nodded.

"Doesn't take orders."

"Orders?"

"Yeah. Orders. Like, somebody wants a television or a DVD player, they come to one of my people. Give them the order. Bring it to me. I look it over. If I got it, I sell it to them. If not, one of my people goes and finds it. Sell it to them at a reasonable price."

The man behind Connolly snickered. Connolly ignored him.

"So, Dibber doesn't do that?"

"No. He's on his own. Finds something he thinks we might be interested in, brings it to us. My people work on a sure thing. Dibber's is strictly speculation."

Three men entered the room, laughing. Loo-tay cut them off with a look. Connolly shifted his weight from one foot to the other.

"Did Dibber sell you a pistol?"

Loo-tay gestured with both hands.

"No weapons."

"He didn't sell you a pistol?"

"I don't deal in weapons. None of my people deals in firearms. I catch them dealing guns, they're out." His eyes bore in on Connolly. "You know what I'm saying? Out."

"I take it this wasn't the first time Dibber sold you something."

"Dibber and me go way back."

"A freelancer."

"Freest of the free."

The men around Loot-tay snickered again. Connolly kept talking.

"He said he tried to sell you a jet ski, but you wouldn't take it."

Loo-tay nodded.

"Wrong item for my business. This is where a freelancer gets hung up. Not much call for jet skis with my people. Motorcycles, yes. Jet skis, no. Not really the beach crowd, if you know what I mean."

Connolly nodded.

"Well, thank you for your time."

He turned toward the door. Loo-tay stood and moved across the room with him.

"Dibber's in some big trouble?"

"Capital murder."

Loo-tay sighed and shook his head.

"I could have told him she wasn't right."

"Who?"

"That skinny little thing he been hanging out with. Tiffany, or whatever her name is. Some bad stuff. Girl like that get you killed."

"You know Tiffany?"

Loo-tay shook his head.

"I don't know her. I seen her a time or two. She was with him the last time I saw him. A manipulator."

"She was with him?"

Loo-tay nodded.

"You ask me, she was the reason he was down there."

"Why?"

"Way she acted. Straight-up manipulator. Dibber, he's the kind don't see that kind of thing coming. Girl like that slip right up behind him, whack him in the head, he'd never know it."

"Tough?"

Loo-tay shrugged.

"Talker. Most of my people come in here, they women don't come with them. When they do, they stand in the corner and keep quiet." He pointed toward the hall. "You see I don't put up with none of that. I pop 'em they get to acting big with me."

"She did the talking?"

Loo-tay nodded.

"Dibber and me couldn't barely do no business with her around. Me, I would have left her at home." He grinned. "Well, I wouldn't never had her in the first place. But if I did, I'd leave her skinny behind at the house."

They reached the door. Connolly offered his hand to Loo-tay. The men around him jumped. Loo-tay smiled at them.

"It's all right, fellas."

He shook Connolly's hand and opened the door.

"You need anything? TV? DVD player?"

The men in the room snickered and ducked down the hall. Connolly shook his head.

"Not today."

Twenty

As he drove back to midtown, Connolly thought about what Loo-tay had said. He was a crook, but he wasn't stupid. Men like Loo-tay survived by their wits. What he'd said about Tiffany was true. She was a manipulator. A gamer. Playing off other people's needs. He could figure out what Dibber needed from her, but he had no idea what Tiffany wanted from him.

At the Loop, Connolly stopped at Hong Kong Buffet and picked up dinner, then went to the guesthouse. Twilight faded to evening as he sat at the dining table reading the newspaper and eating moo shu pork.

Around seven, the telephone rang. The call was from Tiffany.

"Tinker wants to talk."

"Good. Put him on."

"Not now."

"When?"

"Later."

"How much later?"

"Tonight."

"Where?"

"Parking deck across from the Essex Hotel."

"How will I find him?"

"Park on the third level. He'll find you."

"Will you be there?"

"He'll find you."

"Does he know what I look like?"

"That car ain't hard to spot."

"What time?"

"Nine."

Connolly hung up the phone and glanced at his watch. He had two hours before they were to meet. He finished eating, then crossed the room to the far side of the sofa and slipped on his jacket. As he started toward the door, he took the cell phone from his pocket and scrolled through the directory for Hollis's number. He pressed the key to dial the number, then remembered.

"Disney World."

With two hours to spare, he drove to Barbara's house on Ann Street. He parked the Chrysler out front and started up the walkway. On the porch he rang the doorbell and waited. In a moment the door opened. Barbara appeared. She leaned against the door frame and smiled at him.

"Still can't remember to call first, can you?"

Connolly gave her a sheepish grin.

"I guess not."

She gestured over her shoulder.

"You want to come in?"

He shoved his hands in his pockets.

"Can we sit out here?"

He smiled at her. She stepped outside and closed the door behind her.

"Bugs might carry us away."

They moved to the edge of the porch and sat together on the top step. Barbara glanced at him.

"What's on your mind?"

"Not much."

"Just in the neighborhood?"

"I have to meet someone in a little while."

"What's her name?"

"It's a guy."

She arched her eyebrows in mock surprise.

"Friend of yours?"

Connolly grinned.

"Supposed to know something about Dibber."

"Where are you meeting?"

"Parking deck."

"Sounds like a good spy novel."

Connolly nodded.

"Watergate."

"*All the President's Men*."

"Something like that."

"Well, meeting a man at night makes you look very ... contemporary. I'm not sure about meeting one in a parking deck."

Connolly gave her an amused look and gestured toward himself. His voice took on a self-deprecating tone.

"Contemporary?"

"Yeah. You know." Her eyes laughed. "'With it.'"

"'With it.' You mean like, 'groovy'?"

They laughed. She leaned back against her elbows.

"Seems like a long time ago."

Connolly nodded again.

"It was a long time ago."

"I know. But it seems even longer."

"Times aren't what they used to be."

"And what they used to be wasn't all that good."

"I don't know." He sighed. "It wasn't so bad."

She gave him a sarcastic look. He shrugged.

"Well ... you have a point."

Connolly leaned forward and propped his elbows on his knees.

"You ever wonder if you really know what's going on in life?"

Barbara chuckled.

"Wow. You really know how to talk to a girl."

"Sorry."

"Who did you see today?"

He gave her a questioning look.

"What do you mean?"

She sat up.

"When you first started practicing law, you used to run into these strange people sometimes. I could always tell when it happened because you'd come home and we'd have this conversation."

Connolly chuckled. She looked at him.

"So? Who was it?"

Connolly leaned back and propped his elbows behind him.

"Lootie Shaw."

Barbara had a pained expression on her face.

"What does he do?"

"Lootie Shaw is ... royalty."

"Royalty?"

Connolly nodded.

"He rules a special kingdom."

She rolled her eyes.

"Here we go."

"No. Really. It's there. The kingdom is there. But it's one you can't see."

"Do I need to call somebody?"

"Lootie's kingdom exists just beneath the thin veneer of our everyday life."

"Seriously, are you okay?"

Connolly kept going.

"He lives in a house in Prichard. Lime green with purple trim. He has courtesans who attend him. He has mistresses who cater to him. He holds power over his kingdom by keeping his subjects supplied with the things they need. And he makes a nice profit from it for himself and the members of his royal family."

Barbara frowned.

"You've been smoking something."

"No. He actually exists."

"He's a king."

"Royalty."

"He's in jail?"

"Not yet."

"But he's a crook."

Connolly nodded.

"But his kingdom is real. And he really rules it." Connolly sighed. His voice took on a faraway sound, as if with each word he was fading into the world he saw in his mind. "There is a life out there that we know nothing about. It's hidden by what we were raised to think of as normal. But for most of the world, we are abnormal. They are normal."

"Normal?"

He glanced at her with a confident look.

"There's more of them than there are of us."

"Majority rules."

"Something like that."

Barbara gestured over her shoulder.

"Sure you don't want to come inside? I can fix some coffee. You can sit in the den until this passes."

Connolly shook his head.

"I can't."

"Wrong kingdom in there?"

"I don't want to go back to who I used to be."

The laughter was gone from her voice.

"But you're not who you used to be."

Connolly shook his head again.

"Can't risk it."

Barbara gave a heavy sigh.

"Well, you won't have to."

Connolly jerked his head around to look at her.

"What?"

"I've been talking to a realtor."

Connolly sat up, his eyes alert, fully focused.

"About what?"

"About selling this house."

"Why?"

"It's too big for me by myself. You won't come inside. I can live somewhere else."

"Where?"

"I don't know. But if it's that big of a thing for you, maybe it is for me, too. Maybe I'm someone I shouldn't be."

"You can't sell the house."

"I can do whatever I want. It's my house."

"Don't remind me."

"You signed the papers."

"I said, don't remind me."

"Look, the past is the past. There's nothing you can do about what happened."

"If the past is the past, why is it always so present?"

"You are what you've been."

"Not anymore."

"Good. Let's go inside."

She stood. Connolly didn't move. She glanced down at him.

"You coming?"

Connolly stood.

"I need to go."

She shrugged.

"Suit yourself."

She turned away. He took her arm. She turned to face him. They kissed, then kissed again. He looked her in the eye.

"I don't want you to sell the house."

Her voice took a resolute tone.

"I don't want to live here if you won't come inside."

She turned away and opened the door. Connolly lingered there a moment, then moved down the steps and started toward the Chrysler.

The Essex Hotel was a downtown landmark. The main entrance opened beneath a large canopy on Royal Street. Brass revolving doors led to a lobby with a ceiling that soared four stories high above a marble floor. Around the corner on St. Michael Street was a second, less opulent, entrance. Across from it was the parking garage. Connolly turned the Chrysler off the street and up the ramp to the first floor.

The car idled past rows and rows of cars. Every space was filled. In the far corner Connolly pressed his foot against the gas pedal and turned onto the ramp. The Chrysler's engine rumbled as the car moved up to the second floor. Like the first, it, too, was filled.

At the third level a few cars were scattered across the floor, but most of the spaces were empty. He found an open spot on the side overlooking Water Street and backed the car into the space. From there he could see anyone who entered the floor long before they could see him. He checked to make sure the car doors were locked, and waited.

Nine o'clock came and went. By nine thirty Tinker still hadn't showed. Connolly opened the door and stepped outside. The damp night air felt cool against his face. He moved behind the car and leaned against the railing. A breeze blew in from the bay as he stared across Water Street toward the river. He watched as a ship glided past the docks. Two tugboats kept it straight in the channel. In the stillness of the night, voices of the crew echoed across the water.

After a moment Connolly turned to face the garage. He stood there, arms folded over his chest, listening to the sounds of the night, and waiting.

By ten he'd had enough. He got in the Chrysler and started down the ramp toward the street. As he passed the toll booth on the first floor, his cell phone rang. He pressed a button to answer the call.

"Tinker couldn't make it."

The sound of Tiffany's voice startled him.

"How did you get this number?"

"Somebody was watching us."

Connolly made the turn from the garage onto the street.

"How did you get this number?"

"I'll call you later."

"You didn't answer me." He wasn't even sure she heard him. "How did you get this number?"

"He really wants to talk. It's just, some people were around and it didn't look good. Tinker had a bad feeling. I don't blame him."

Connolly's voice took an angry edge.

"How did you get this number?"

"For a few bucks you can get anything you want. I'll call you."

The line went dead. Connolly switched off the phone. The traffic light at Royal Street was red. He came to a stop, then turned left in front of the hotel. As he rounded the corner, he glanced in the mirror. A yellow Chevrolet Caprice was parked down the street behind him. Headlights came on as the car made a U-turn and sped away in the opposite direction.

Twenty-one

The following morning Connolly appeared in Judge Cahill's court for a preliminary hearing in a robbery case. He arrived early. Walter, the judge's bailiff, was busy at his desk near the bench. He glanced up as Connolly entered the courtroom.

"You're here early."

"Thought I'd get at the head of the line."

Connolly set his leather satchel on the counsel's table. Walter caught his eye.

"We got a big docket this morning. You won't be first."

Connolly shrugged.

"I know."

He took a seat in a chair near the rail. Walter picked up a stack of files.

"You want some coffee?"

"Sure."

Connolly followed Walter through the door behind the judge's bench to the judge's chambers. Windows lined the wall opposite the door with a view of the street below. A coffeepot sat on a ledge below the windows. Judge Cahill's office was to the left. He called to Connolly as he passed the office door.

"Mike, how much time do you need on that murder case? Landry."

Connolly reached the coffeepot.

"I don't know yet, Judge."

"We need to schedule a preliminary hearing. Walter, what are we looking at?"

Walter filled a cup and handed it to Connolly.

"This month is almost full, Judge."

"Give Mike a date."

Connolly stepped to the office door.

"Judge, they just identified the body in that case." He took a sip of coffee. "We haven't been able to find out much about him."

"That's all right. If you need more time, we can see about continuing it later. I don't want this case to sit around. Walter'll give you a date. We can work with you if you need it."

The door behind them opened. Gayle Underwood entered. She passed Connolly and moved toward the coffeepot.

"We found Billy Ellis. The dead man's father in that Landry case. He's coming in this afternoon. You interested in talking to him?"

"Yes."

She filled a cup and moved near the door to Cahill's office.

"We're meeting with him around three. You can see him after we get finished."

Judge Cahill came from his desk.

"I think it would be good if you both talked to him at the same time. Save us some time."

Gayle frowned.

"I don't think Henry will agree to that, Your Honor."

Cahill's eyes were intense.

"I'm not asking Henry to agree." The cadence of his voice was all business. "I can order him to do it. I'm just saying, we need to get this case moving. I think it would help if you both talked to him at the same time. The man isn't going to be a witness to anything, is he?"

Gayle shifted the coffee cup to her right hand.

"That's just it. We don't know what he's going to say."

Cahill's tone became less strident.

"Well, I don't think it would hurt if the two of you talked to him together. If he has something interesting to say, you can always talk to him separately later. This way, you can both hear his story and then he can arrange to get the body and get out of here."

"I don't—"

Cahill's face went cold. Whatever he'd been holding inside broke free and burst from his mouth in a torrent of emotion.

"The man just lost his son! You want him to hang around here two or three days while Henry tries to figure out what to ask him?"

Cahill stepped into his office and slammed the door shut. Gayle set her coffee cup on the table by the door and walked out to the courtroom. Connolly took one more sip and followed her.

When the morning docket was finished, Connolly stepped outside the courtroom and started toward the elevator. As he moved down the corridor, he felt someone tug on his elbow. He glanced to the right to see Dave Brenner.

"Keep walking."

Connolly continued past the elevators to a conference room near the courtroom on the opposite end of the floor. Brenner guided him to the door. A man in a gray suit came from behind him and opened the door. Brenner pushed Connolly inside. The door closed behind them. Brenner stood just inches away. His face was stern, his voice demanding.

"Don't call my office anymore about this. In fact, don't call my office at all."

Connolly was undeterred.

"Where is she?"

"She's in Croatia."

"Croatia?"

"Bosnia."

"Which one?"

"Whichever one she's supposed to be in. She's where she's supposed to be."

Connolly was not reassured.

"Is she all right?"

"Yes. She's fine. She's working for an American service company. She's being taken care of. We have her under constant surveillance."

"You're just blowing smoke, right?"

"Listen to me. She is fine. She's being debriefed by their people."

"Alone?"

"No. We have someone with her."

"At the meetings?"

"Yes."

Connolly was still skeptical.

"I don't know whether to believe you or not."

"I don't care. I'm telling you what I know. You can believe me or not. It doesn't matter to me. The girl is safe. We're looking after her. They tell me she's adjusting. Apparently she's telling them things they need to know."

"She'll have to testify?"

"Yes. But their first trial won't be for another six or eight months."

"Then what?"

"I don't know." Brenner gestured with both hands. "How could I possibly know? The investigation has broadened some since we talked before. They'll need her as long as they need her."

"But then she'll be able to come back."

"Yes. If she wants to."

"Wouldn't you?"

Brenner looked away.

"I wouldn't have gone in the first place."

Connolly sighed. Brenner turned toward the door, then paused.

"Don't call me anymore." He jabbed Connolly in the chest with his finger. "You keep messing with this, and you'll screw up the whole deal. Leave it alone. You understand me?"

Connolly braced himself but held his temper.

"Yeah. I hear you."

Brenner jerked the door open. Connolly followed him out. They walked together as far as the elevator. Without a word Brenner turned left and disappeared down a hall. Connolly glanced around. The man who had held the door to the conference room was nowhere in sight. Connolly stood there a moment, thinking, then stepped to the elevator.

Twenty-two

At three that afternoon Connolly entered the waiting area outside the district attorney's office. He paused long enough to take a drink from the water fountain, then crossed the room to the receptionist's desk. Juanita saw him coming.

"Go on back, Mr. Connolly." She pointed to the door at the end of the desk. "They're waiting for you. End of the hall. Last door on the right."

Connolly moved past Juanita's desk to the door and made his way down the hall. At the corner he found a long, narrow conference room. In the middle of the room was a table with a dark-brown top designed to look like oak. Chairs with the same brown finish were arranged around the table. A photograph of the building hung at the far end of the room. A picture of Mobile Bay hung on the wall opposite the door.

Gayle sat on the far side of the table facing the door. Sitting across from her with his back to the door was a man who looked to be in his midfifties, wearing a plaid shirt and blue jeans. He had a bony frame with shoulder blades that poked out against the fabric of his shirt. His thin, narrow neck seemed lost behind the collar. A crease through his hair went around his head just above his ears as if he'd been wearing a hat. His legs were crossed, and in the shadows under the table Connolly could see he had on a pair of black cowboy boots with brass tips on the toes.

Gayle looked up as Connolly appeared at the door. The man turned to see who was behind him. Gayle stood. He did too.

"Mr. Connolly." Gayle gestured for him to enter. "This is Billy Ellis."

Connolly entered the room. The two men shook hands. Gayle continued.

"Mr. Ellis, this is Mike Connolly. He's the defense lawyer."

Billy nodded.

"You defending the man they say killed Stephen?"

"Yes, sir."

"Well, if he's innocent I hope you can get him off. But if he's guilty, I hope they fry him."

"I'm sorry you lost your son."

"Thank you."

Billy turned away and took a seat. Connolly moved to the end of the table and pulled out a chair. As he and Gayle sat down, McNamara entered.

"Well, I guess we can get started." McNamara laid his file on the table and took a seat at the opposite end from Connolly. "Mike, I'll let you begin."

Connolly nodded.

"You want to record this?"

McNamara shrugged.

"I'm not. If you want to, be my guest." He glanced at Billy. "As long as Mr. Ellis doesn't mind."

Connolly stared at McNamara a moment. Something about him made Connolly laugh, and something about him made him want to slap his boyish cheeks. He took a deep breath.

"It was just a thought, Henry." He turned to Billy. "Mr. Ellis, have they told you what happened to your son?"

"They said somebody found Stephen in a house."

"His body was found in a house on Dauphin Island. That's an island south of here on the Gulf. Near the mouth of Mobile Bay. He was found in a beach house. Do you know anyone who lives on Dauphin Island?"

"No."

"Have you ever heard of Dauphin Island?"

"I don't think so. Not before this."

"Never heard anyone mention it?"

"Not that I can recall."

"Bayou La Batre? Coden? Any of those places?"

Billy shook his head.

"No."

"Have you been over to the morgue to see the body?"

"Not yet."

Connolly thought for a moment, then continued.

"I think I better back up and begin at the beginning. Do you have a son named Stephen Ellis?"

"N ... Yes ..." Billy had a tight, thin-lipped smile. "Well, he's not exactly my son."

Gayle glanced in McNamara's direction. McNamara stared at Billy. Connolly continued.

"What do you mean?"

"Stephen was ... well, you might say we adopted him."

"Did you go to court and do a formal adoption?"

"No."

"What happened?"

"Stephen was ... My wife ... ex-wife ... Frieda, we was married at the time. She had this friend named ... I can't remember her real name right now. We called her Tiny. She was from down here somewhere. But she was a student back then at Emory. Emory University. Anyway, she got pregnant by this fellow who was a professor. You might have heard of him. Name was Harold Schnadelbach."

Connolly felt his stomach drop. He did his best to hide his surprise. Billy glanced around the table, as if expecting them to acknowledge the name. No one responded. He continued.

"He was a writer. Wrote under a different name ... I can't remember it neither. They made a movie out of one of his books." Billy paused and took a breath. "Tiny and Harold was seeing each other, but Harold was married."

Billy's voice faded into the background. Connolly's mind was on the book. The one on the dresser at the beach house.

Hotel ... Hotel ... Hotel Green.

Stephen Ellis was down there looking for his mother.

Connolly forced himself to listen again. Billy's voice came back into focus.

"Things was all right though, until Tiny got pregnant." Billy sounded like a man unburdening himself with something he'd held inside for a long time. "Harold wanted her to have an abortion, but she wouldn't do it. They fought about it some, but then he got killed. After that—"

Connolly interrupted.

"Who got killed?"

"Harold. Harold Schnadelbach." Billy's eyes brightened. He gestured with the index finger of his right hand. "Mary. That's her name. Mary. Mary Givens."

"Tiny?"

Connolly caught Gayle's eye and pointed to the legal pad on the table in front of her. She tore out a page and passed it to him. Connolly took notes as Billy continued to talk.

"Yeah. We all called her Tiny, but that was her name." He had a satisfied smile. "Mary Givens." He paused a moment as if remembering her, then continued. "After Harold died, Tiny wasn't the same. Things kind of fell apart for her. She had the baby, but she didn't have no way of taking care of him. So, she decided to go home." His face twisted in a pained expression. "But for some reason, she didn't want to take the baby with her. We tried to talk her into it, but she said she couldn't." He shook his head. "I don't know why." Billy sighed. "So, we took him." He looked over at Connolly. "Nice kid."

"Her home was here? Tiny's?"

"Yeah. That's what she said. Said she was going home to Mobile."

"To her parents?"

"I guess. I mean, that's what I always assumed."

"Do you know their names?"

Billy shook his head.

"I don't think I ever heard her say."

"Does your wife know Stephen is dead?"

Billy's voice took a reverent tone.

"She's dead."

Connolly wasn't sure he heard the response.

"Excuse me?"

"She's dead." He cleared his throat. "Frieda's dead."

"I'm sorry."

Billy nodded.

"She died ... last year." A puzzled look came over him. "Year before last." He lifted his head and stared into space. "No. Last year. Right at the end of the year." He turned again to Connolly. "I guess it hasn't been a year yet. We weren't married when she died. We got a divorce about fifteen years ago."

"When's the last time you saw Stephen?"

The puzzled look returned to Billy's face.

"I ... I don't remember." He shrugged. "It's been awhile. I think the last time I saw him was when he was in college. He went to Valdosta State. Got in a little trouble." Billy glanced over at McNamara. "Whoever called me the other day said that's how you figured out who he was."

McNamara nodded.

"Sheriff's office matched his prints through the FBI."

Billy smiled.

"Funny." He cocked his head to one side. "Wasn't funny then. But to think him getting in trouble solved a riddle after all these years."

Connolly continued.

"Do you know when he left to come down here?"

"No."

"Any way to figure it out?"

"Well, my sister said she saw him at Frieda's funeral. She died end of last year. I think her funeral was the day before New Year's Eve."

"Where was the funeral?"

"Collier's Funeral Home."

"What town?"

"Lawrenceville. Lawrenceville, Georgia. Up there where we live."

"Was he already living down here by then?"

"I don't know."

"But he was in Lawrenceville at the end of last year?"

"Yes."

"Any other time between then and now when you knew where he was?"

Billy thought for a moment, then shook his head.

"Nah. Me and him, we didn't get along too good."

"Any idea where Mary Givens lives?"

"No. Somewhere around here, maybe. But I don't know where."

"When's the last time you talked to her?"

"I haven't seen her since the day she left. She handed Stephen to Frieda, got in her car, and drove away. That's the last time I saw her."

"Thirty ... forty years ago?"

"Yeah. Forty years ago. Stephen was born in ... August ... of 1967."

"Did this professor ..."

"Harold."

"Yes. Harold. Did he have any other children?"

"Oh, yeah. He had children. I think he had three or four."

"What happened to him?"

"He died."

"I understand. But how did he die?"

Billy shifted positions in the chair.

"Died in a plane crash. Down there near Albany. Right outside Sylvester."

"Was he still married at the time he died?"

"I don't know."

"Do you know why Stephen was down here?"

Billy shook his head.

"I have no idea."

"Think he was looking for his mother? Tiny?"

Billy shook his head once more.

"He didn't know about her."

Connolly's forehead wrinkled in a frown.

"He didn't know about her?"

"As far as I know. I didn't tell him, and Frieda didn't either. At least not while I was around."

"Does the name—"

Billy interrupted.

"And I doubt she ever did. Frieda didn't care too much for Tiny after that. The way she just up and left the child and all. She was glad to have him." His gaze dropped. "We couldn't have kids of our own." He lifted his head and glanced at Connolly. "But she didn't think it was right for her to go off and leave him like that. Told me she wasn't going to never tell him about her."

Connolly nodded.

"Does the name Inez Marchand mean anything to you?"

Billy thought for a moment then shook his head.

"No."

"Edwin Marchand?"

"No."

"Nick or Nicholas Marchand?"

"Nope. Never heard of them. They's some Marchands live down at McDonough, not too far from me. But I don't know them very well."

"All right."

Connolly nodded to McNamara down the table. McNamara leaned back in his chair.

"Mr. Ellis, what did your son do?"

"What did he do?"

"Where did he work?"

"He worked on a road crew for the highway department. They say he's some kind of foreman."

"Did he inherit anything from Schnadelbach's estate?"

"I don't know. Never thought about it. Like I said, he didn't know about Harold, and we never did nothing about that."

McNamara twirled a pen between his fingers as he continued to ask questions.

"But Harold could have provided for the boy on his own. Did anyone ever come around asking about him or trying to talk about Harold's estate?"

"Not that I know of. I don't think Harold's wife even knew about Stephen."

"This trouble he had at Valdosta. What was that about?"

"Got caught with some marijuana."

"Did he go to jail?"

"No."

"He got probation?"

Billy smiled.

"I had a friend in Lawrenceville who was a hunting buddy with the district attorney down there. They worked it out."

"Did your son have a problem with drugs?"

"Not really."

McNamara stopped twirling the pen and leaned forward in his chair.

"What does that mean?"

"He was a good kid."

"Did he get arrested again, after that first time?"

"Not that I know of."

"Did he ever deal in drugs? Ever sell them?"

"Not that I know."

"Was he married?"

"No."

"Have a girlfriend?"

"I wouldn't know."

McNamara opened the file and leafed through the pages.

"Did the police or anybody ever come around investigating anything about your son?"

"What do you mean?"

"Did the police ever show up at your house asking questions about your son?"

"No. I mean, not while he was around me."

"Did you ever hear of him being in trouble or someone coming around like that?"

"No."

McNamara thought for a moment, then closed his file.

"I don't think I have anything else." He stood. "Thanks for your time, Mr. Ellis. Your son's body is at the hospital. Ms. Underwood will take you over there. I think they're finished with it. They'll tell you when you can get it."

McNamara stepped across the room to the door and disappeared down the hall.

Twenty-three

*J*uanita was on the phone as Connolly came out to the reception area. She glanced at him then turned away. He crossed the room to the elevator, stepped inside, and pressed a button for the first floor. As he waited, he thought about what Billy had just told them.

Stephen Ellis was the son of the man who wrote that book. Hotel ... Whatever. And, he was the son of someone named Mary Givens. All he had to do was find Mary Givens, before McNamara did. He smiled to himself. Not much chance McNamara would even look for her. But this new lady, Gayle Underwood. She might.

Gayle was already at the coroner's office when Connolly arrived later that afternoon. She stood to one side of Morgan's desk. Seated on a folding chair next to her was Billy Ellis. Connolly stepped through the doorway and glanced around.

"Have you seen Ted?"

Gayle gestured over her shoulder.

"He went down the hall. Said he'd be back in a minute."

As she spoke, Morgan appeared in the doorway.

"I'm right here." He brushed past Connolly to the desk and picked up a file. "Everyone ready?"

Gayle glanced at Connolly.

"Brian Hodges was supposed to meet us here."

The double doors in the hall banged open. Gayle smiled.

"Sounds like him."

Hodges appeared at the office door.

"Sorry I'm late."

Morgan turned to Billy Ellis.

"Mr. Ellis, you feel all right?"

Billy nodded.

"I'm all right."

Morgan stepped toward the door.

"Then let's go."

File in hand, Morgan brushed past Connolly and started down the hall. Gayle and Billy came from the office and followed him. Connolly and Hodges tagged along behind.

Past the autopsy suite they turned right. The cooler where the bodies were kept was built into the wall at the end of the hall. Six doors were arranged in two rows, one above the other. Like most things in the hospital, the doors were old and worn. They looked as if they'd been salvaged from old iceboxes.

Morgan opened his file and glanced at the top page, then stepped to a door to the right on the bottom row. He pulled it open. Through the opening Connolly could see a pair of feet, heels together, toes pointed up and out at an angle. The end of a sheet was draped between them. The body rested on a stainless steel rack. Cold air tumbled from the cooler to the floor. It swirled around his ankles and rose up his legs. With it came a stale, morbid smell. Connolly took a step back.

Morgan grasped the end of the rack and pulled. It clattered as it slid out, bringing with it a body covered with a white sheet. Morgan checked the toe tag.

"This is the body." He glanced at Billy. "Ready?"

Billy nodded.

Morgan moved to the other end of the rack. He lifted the sheet from the head and glanced underneath, then pulled it back and folded it across the chest.

Billy's shoulders sagged as if the air went out of him. The corners of his mouth twitched. His lips moved in a whisper.

Gayle leaned closer.

"Did you say something?"

Billy cleared his throat.

"That's not him." He looked at Morgan. "That's not Stephen."

Morgan frowned. Hodges moved to Billy's side. Gayle glanced at the body, then back at Billy.

"Are you sure? The body's rather bloated."

"I'm sure." Billy shook his head. "That's not Stephen."

She tried to prompt him.

"You said you haven't seen him in fifteen years."

"I know. But that's not him." Billy pointed at the body on the rack. "That's Stephen's roommate from school. The guy he got in trouble with in Valdosta. He's ..." Billy stepped away, his hand over his mouth. "What's that guy's name?"

Gayle looked at Connolly and shrugged. Connolly nodded to Morgan. Morgan pulled the sheet over the body and slid it back inside the cooler. The door clicked shut.

Billy wheeled around.

"Bobby ... Bobby John ... Junkins. Bobby Junkins." Billy pointed to the cooler door. "That's who that is in there. Bobby Junkins."

Gayle's forehead was still creased in a frown.

"You're sure?"

"Sure I'm sure. Why would I lie? That's not Stephen. That's Bobby Junkins."

Hodges turned to Billy.

"Do you know where your son is?"

"No, sir." Billy shook his head. "I have no idea."

Hodges nodded toward the end of the hall.

"Do you know of any reason why this man would have been in the house on Dauphin Island?"

"No."

"Do you know where he lived?"

"I think his father was a politician. A legislator or county commissioner or something like that. There was something about that when they got arrested."

"Where do they live? His parents."

"I don't know. Back then I think they lived over around Savannah some place. Statesville, I think."

"Statesville, Georgia?"

"Yeah."

Morgan started up the hall. Hodges and Billy followed. Connolly and Gayle came behind them. Gayle spoke in a low voice.

"You better call Henry. I think things have changed."

"You think he'll be interested in making a deal?"

"I think so."

That's how most of the prosecutors thought. Better to plead him to something than to spend more time working a case that ended in nothing. That's how Connolly approached his cases too—most of the time. But that was because most of the time his clients were guilty. Representing them came down to getting them the least time in jail. Acquittal usually wasn't much of an option for the people he defended.

A week earlier he would have done the same for Dibber. He would have pushed for a plea. Fought for one. Begged for one. But this case wasn't like most. Mrs. Gordon was right. This case was strange, and the more he found out about it, the stranger it became. Dibber wasn't guilty. Connolly had been sure of that the first time they talked. But he wasn't sure they could win. Now he was beginning to think there was reason to hope.

Connolly and Gayle walked together to the end of the hall. There, she and Billy turned right. Hodges followed them. Connolly turned left and made his way outside. As he started across the parking lot toward the Chrysler, he slipped off his jacket and flipped it over his shoulder. Finding out the dead man wasn't really Stephen Ellis after all had been interesting. But Connolly's mind wasn't on Stephen or Billy or finding Mary Givens or wondering why Stephen Ellis' fingerprints were matched with Bobby Junkins' body. His mind was on one thing.

"I need that book."

That book didn't get in the beach house by accident. It was a gift from Harold Schnadelbach to Billy and Frieda Ellis. Frieda gave it to Stephen. Stephen brought it with him when he came looking for his mother.

Loneliness swept over Connolly. Looking for his mother. He knew something about that. He hadn't gone looking for her, but he knew what it was like to wonder where she was and what she was doing.

Connolly opened the door and ducked inside the car.

That book was important. But to get it he'd have to drive back to Dauphin Island. Climb in the house. In the dark. By himself.

Connolly stuck the key in the ignition and turned it. The Chrysler came to life.

"Hollis, I hope you're having fun."

Twenty-four

From the hospital Connolly drove downtown to the jail. He was cleared through the security checkpoint in the lobby and rode the elevator to the eighth floor. Dibber was seated at the table in the interview room when Connolly arrived.

"What's up? I thought you'd be back before now."

Connolly crossed the room toward him.

"Didn't have anything to tell you."

"And now?"

Connolly smiled.

"I've been over at the morgue this afternoon. Sheriff's office thought they had an ID on the dead man."

"Who'd they think it was?"

Connolly stepped over the bench on the near side of the table and took a seat facing Dibber.

"Somebody named Stephen Ellis."

Dibber shook his head.

"Never heard of him."

"He's from Lawrenceville, Georgia."

"So, what happened?"

"You ever been to Lawrenceville, Georgia?"

"No."

"Know anyone from there?"

"No. What happened?"

"They got a match on the dead guy's fingerprints through the FBI. He had a record. They found his father in Georgia. Brought him here. I met with him. He doesn't know anything about the beach house. But they took him to the hospital. Showed him the body."

Dibber grinned.

"It ain't who they thought it was?"

Connolly shook his head.

"Stephen Ellis' father says the dead guy is Bobby Junkins. Used to be his son's roommate in college."

"Where's the son?"

"Don't know."

"How'd they get the prints matched to him?"

"They were roommates in college. Got busted together. I guess things got confused. Either of those names mean anything to you?"

Dibber had a blank look.

"Stephen ..."

"Ellis. Stephen Ellis."

Dibber shook his head.

"Never heard of him. What was the other one?"

"Junkins. Bobby Junkins."

"Never heard of him either. What else?"

"I wouldn't be surprised if they made us an offer."

"An offer?"

"A plea."

Dibber frowned and shook his head.

"I ain't coppin' to no plea."

"You better think about it."

Dibber continued to shake his head.

"I'm not pleading guilty."

"But you are guilty."

Dibber had an angry look.

"I didn't kill nobody."

"You're not guilty of murder. But you are guilty of trespassing. Theft."

Dibber's voice grew loud.

"I didn't steal nothing. That stuff was—"

Connolly cut him off.

"You were in the house. You took things that belonged to someone else—"

Dibber interrupted.

"Not that jet ski. It was floating in the water. That's all they got me charged with."

Connolly had an amused smile.

"Believe me. If you went to trial on a theft charge, you'd be convicted."

Dibber sighed and turned away. Connolly changed the subject.

"I talked to Tommy Porter at the pawnshop. He has a picture of you. Copy of your driver's license. No way to deny you sold him the jet ski."

Dibber shrugged.

"I already said that. I sold him the jet ski." He shot a look at Connolly. "But I didn't steal it."

"I talked to the detective. Hodges. The beach house is owned by Inez Marchand. Husband's name is Edwin Marchand. They have a son named Nick. Those names mean anything to you?"

"No."

"Nick works at a nursery out in Wilmer. Southern Nursery Supply. Know anybody that works out there?"

Dibber's eyes darted away. He shook his head once more. Connolly continued.

"They found some prints in the house. Yours. The dead man's. Three sets they can't identify. And some from Edwin, Inez, and Nick." Connolly caught Dibber's eye. "Was anyone with you?"

"No."

"You're sure?"

"Yes. They sayin' I had help?"

"No."

"When'll they find out who those other prints are?"

"I don't know. If they don't have an arrest record, they might never identify them."

Dibber looked away again.

"Did you talk to those people? The Marchands?"

Connolly nodded.

"I tried. They weren't too interested in talking. Inez closed the door in my face."

"Why'd she do that?"

"I don't know. But I talked to her husband. He told me he'd never been in the beach house."

Dibber looked up.

"I thought you said his prints was in the house."

"They were."

Dibber smiled.

"He's lying?"

"He's lying."

"Wonder why?"

"Good question."

Dibber propped his elbow on the table and rested his chin in his hand.

"What about the other guy? The son? Nick?"

Connolly leaned away.

"I don't know. I haven't talked to him yet."

Dibber fell silent. He stared past Connolly, his eyes fixed on a point over Connolly's shoulder. After a moment a frown wrinkled his brow.

"Why would they lie? I mean, if they didn't know him, why lie about being in the house?"

"That's what I'm trying to find out."

Dibber chuckled.

"I bet he was relieved."

"Who?"

"The guy they brought down here. The father."

"Yeah."

The faraway look returned to Dibber's face. They sat there a moment. Dibber staring past Connolly. Neither one saying a word. Then Connolly spoke up.

"There's one more thing. Your girlfriend came to see me the other day."

"Tiffany?"

"Yes."

Dibber's countenance changed.

"What's she done now?"

"Nothing. I think she's a little worried."

Dibber frowned.

"About what?"

"She's been talking to some guy named Tinker Johnson."

Dibber looked angry.

"What'd he tell her?"

"Nick Marchand thinks Tiffany put you up to breaking in the house."

"Why would I do that?"

"I don't know."

Dibber looked away, angry again. His voice was clipped and sharp.

"I told her she shouldn't have nothin' to do with him. Nothin'."

"What's going on, Dibber?"

Dibber slapped the table with his hand. His face was red. Connolly insisted.

"Talk to me, Dibber."

Dibber sighed.

"She and Tinker had this thing. She told me it was over. Then one day I came to The Pig to see her. That idiot was there talking to her."

"Who?"

Dibber's eyes were ablaze.

"Tinker. Had his car parked around back. They was out there talkin'. I knew she hadn't stopped."

"Hadn't stopped what?"

Dibber hesitated, as if thinking. Then he slapped the table once more.

"Tinker works for that guy you mentioned. Nick. I don't know him. I ain't never talked to him. But Tinker works for him. They're into all kinds of stuff. Use that nursery for a cover. He set her up with Nick to buy money orders."

"Buy money orders?"

"Yeah. He'd give her money every week. She'd go to convenience stores and buy money orders."

"Laundering money."

Dibber nodded.

"Get them money orders, then he could put them in the bank. Nobody'd ask any questions."

"So, you knew whose beach house it was."

Dibber sighed.

"Yeah. But I didn't kill nobody."

"What were you looking for?"

"Whatever I could find." Dibber smiled. "Hit the jackpot too."

"What did you find?"

"Money." He looked at Connolly. "And receipts."

"Receipts?"

Dibber nodded.

"Cigar box full of 'em. In the closet. Had a bunch of cash in it.

Underneath it was receipts for all them money orders. One of them had her name on it."

Connolly smiled.

"What did you do with the box?"

Dibber grinned.

"It's at the house."

"The beach house?"

Dibber shook his head.

"My house."

"Where?"

"You want it?"

"Yeah."

"It's in the closet in the back bedroom. Think it'll help?"

"It might. How can I get it?"

"Go in the front door. There's a hall down both sides of the stairs. Take the one on the right. All the way to the back of the house. Bedroom's on the right, across from the bathroom. Box is up in the top of the closet. Under a bunch of old clothes."

"How do I get in? Does Carl have a key?"

Dibber scowled and shook his head.

"Don't ask him. Just go down there. There's a key hanging on a nail behind the water heater."

"Where's the water heater?"

"Back porch."

Dibber fell silent. Then he slapped the table again.

"I told her not to have nothin' to do with him. Nothin'."

Connolly leaned away.

"Tiffany said she would see if Tinker would talk to me."

Dibber snorted.

"I wouldn't believe nothin' he says. Nothin'."

"I need to talk to him."

Dibber sighed.

"Better watch your back."

Twenty-five

Connolly left the jail and drove across town to the guesthouse. Cool shade from the oaks that surrounded the mansion engulfed him as the car idled to a stop at the end of the driveway. He switched off the engine and stared out the windshield, lost in thought.

If what Dibber said was true, if he had those receipts, they might have a chance. At least they would have something besides the dead man to talk about at the preliminary hearing. Connolly thought about it a moment then shook his head.

"Doesn't prove a thing."

And Judge Cahill would see right through it. Might help with a jury if the case went to trial, but it wouldn't do much good in a preliminary hearing. They could have all the receipts they wanted, talk about Nick Marchand and drugs and money orders and Tinker, and it still wouldn't make any difference. Dibber was charged with murder. McNamara had a dead body and Dibber's fingerprints at the scene of the crime.

Connolly took the key from the ignition and opened the car door.

"Makes more sense that they killed the guy over a drug deal than Dibber killing him for a jet ski."

Connolly's legs felt like lead as he stepped from the car and started toward the door to the guesthouse. The thought of driving all the way to Dauphin Island left him feeling weary. For a moment he considered not going. But he had to. He needed Dibber's receipts.

And, he needed that book from the beach house.

He looked up through the branches of the trees toward the sky.

The thought of going in that beach house after dark sent a chill up his spine.

From the door by the kitchen Connolly glanced across the living room to the table at the end of the sofa. The light on the answering machine was out. He crossed the room and pressed the button to play the messages anyway, just to make sure. The machine was silent.

In the bedroom he put on a pair of jeans and a T-shirt. He set his black winged tips on a rack in the closet and slipped on a pair of worn leather Topsiders. The shoes felt soft and comfortable against the balls of his feet.

Dressed and ready, he went to the kitchen. He stood at the sink and ate a piece of cold pizza left over from the night before, washed down with a bottle of Boylan ginger ale. As he took the last drink from the bottle, he checked his watch. It was six o'clock. He had stalled as long as he could. He set the empty bottle on the counter and walked to the door.

When Connolly crossed the bridge at Cedar Point, the sun was an orange glow behind a towering bank of dark clouds on the western horizon. Billowing high above the water, the clouds formed ominous shapes outlined in red and gold as the fading sun sent streaks of purple and amber across the evening sky. Connolly caught the scene in quick glances out the window as the car rolled across the bridge.

Lights were on at the Ship-N-Shore at the center of the island. There, Connolly turned onto DeSoto Avenue. Three blocks later the paved street came to an end in front of a rambling old two-story house that faced the sound between the island and the mainland. A lush green lawn ran from the house down to the water. Connolly parked the car on the grass at the end of the pavement.

The house had a porch that ran all the way around. In front there was a swing and three or four rocking chairs. Around back the porch was cluttered with an assortment of buckets and pails and three ice chests. Near the corner was a door to the kitchen. A washing machine and dryer stood to one side. The hot water heater sat on the other. Connolly stepped onto the porch and slid his hand behind the heater. A door key was hanging on a nail beneath a water pipe. He slipped it off the nail and shoved it in the lock above the doorknob.

The door opened to a kitchen that seemed as large as Connolly's house. Cabinets and counters lined the walls all the way around to a door on the opposite side of the room. A white porcelain sink sat beneath a window on the wall to the right. A stove stood along the far wall. A table sat in the center of the room.

Connolly moved across the kitchen and through the house to the front door. There, he turned, faced the staircase, and repeated Dibber's directions.

"Take the hall to the right." He started down the hall to the right of the stairs. "All the way to the end. Last door on the right. Across from the bathroom." He found the room and reached through the doorway for the light switch.

To his surprise, the bedroom was neat and clean. In fact, the whole house was clean and straight. Then he noticed it for the first time. He sniffed the air. Pine cleaner.

Someone had cleaned the place. He smiled to himself. Dibber wasn't the kind to clean anything. Tiffany? He shook his head. No way. She wasn't the kind either. More likely Carl hired someone. Connolly crossed the room to the closet and opened the door.

Clothes hung on hangers arranged neatly across a galvanized bar. Faded blue jeans and four flannel shirts were folded and stacked on the shelf above. Connolly slid his hand under the stack. Nothing. He moved the clothes aside and stood on his toes, reaching as far back as possible. Near the corner his fingers struck something. He worked it forward with his fingertips until he could see it was a cigar box. He took it from the shelf and sat on the bed.

Inside the box he found a small velvet sack with a gold drawstring. Bon Ton's Jewelry was emblazoned on the front in gold letters. The money order receipts lay beneath the sack. Connolly set the sack aside and looked through the receipts. All of them were carbon copies from the back of the money order forms. The ones near the top were made out to Southern Nursery Supply, but near the bottom of the box he found several made out to Nick Marchand, one of which bore Tiffany's name on the memo line in the lower left corner. Each of the money orders was for one thousand dollars.

Connolly stared at them a moment, thinking. Only one business generated both large amounts of cash and an accounting problem.

After a moment he set the box on the bed and picked up the velvet sack. He opened it and emptied the contents into the palm of his hand. Two silver earrings. A cheap bracelet. And a man's ring with a blue stone. He picked up the ring and turned it to one side to read the words inscribed around the stone. His heart skipped a beat. Lawrenceville High School. Class of 1985.

Connolly dropped the ring into the bag and pulled the top closed.

"I really need that book now."

Twenty-six

*D*arkness had fallen by the time Connolly left Dibber's house. In the distance a large red moon rose over the Gulf. Connolly walked across the grass to the car.

From Dibber's he made his way to Bienville Boulevard and turned right. The Chrysler rolled past the last dunes and onto the flat sand spit at the western end of the island. Ten minutes later he came to the berm at the end of the road. The car coasted to a stop across from the Marchands' beach house.

Connolly reached under the seat and took out a flashlight. He pushed the switch to make sure it worked then opened the door and stepped from the car. In the distance he heard the waves crashing on the shore beyond the house. The churning surf shimmered in the moonlight. He glanced around as he closed the car door then started across the sand.

When he reached the house, he came to a stop beneath the broken stairs that led up to the front door. He stood there in the dark and stared up at the bottom rung of the steps. Somehow it seemed farther out of reach than before. He stretched his arm above his head as far as it would go and tried to judge the distance, then jumped with all his might. His fingertips scraped across the end of a runner that dangled below the step.

Connolly shoved the flashlight in his hip pocket and backed off a little way. He took three steps forward and leaped into the air like a basketball player. His fingers slapped against the ends of the runners as he sailed past. A splinter jammed under his fingernail. He clutched his hand in pain and clenched his teeth.

"This didn't used to be so hard."

In the shadows near the pilings on the far side of the house, he

saw a red and white ice chest sticking from the sand. He gave it a
tug. It didn't budge. He knelt beside it and dug around the edges
with his hands. In a few minutes he worked it free and dragged it
beneath the steps. He flipped on the flashlight and glanced up to
make sure the chest was aligned with the stairs. Then he saw why
he was having so much trouble.

In the glare of the light, fresh wood shone at the ends of the
runners. The steps had broken off. He turned the light across the
sand. Pieces of the steps lay in a clump of sea oats a few feet away.
He switched off the flashlight, shoved it back in his hip pocket, and
stood on top of the ice chest.

With his knees bent he sagged as low as possible and pushed off
with all his might. His body sailed upward. Seconds later his outstretched arms banged against the runners on either side. He dug
in with his fingers, then worked his hands around the bottom step
and pulled himself up.

When he reached the top step, he glanced back toward the
Chrysler. Across the bay on the north side of the island, a boat was
headed toward the marina. Running lights on the bow blinked in
the distance as the boat rose and fell on the waves. Connolly turned
away and opened the door.

In the beam of light he could see the timber that had been lying
in the living room now lay at an angle away from the kitchen counter.
The sofa and love seat that had been piled against the counter were
in the center of the room. He flicked the light around and shone it
over the kitchen. Dishes and pans still filled the sink. Grease still covered the stove.

As he rounded the end of the counter, he could see the door to
the bedroom at the end of the hall. Across the room the floor
creaked. He glanced in that direction. Fear rose inside him, the
same fear he'd felt as a child when his mother turned out his bedroom light and closed the door and all the ghouls came from the
closet in his mind. He stuffed down the rising emotions and moved
into the hallway.

With each step forward, he felt his heart rate quicken. Midway
down the hall he passed the doorway to the bedroom on the left.
Moonlight streaming through a window caught his eye. In the
amber light, objects in the room took on a strange sepia tone. Eerie
shadows danced on the wall and played across the open closet door

in the corner. His heart pounded, but he kept walking. Closer and closer to the door at the end of the hall.

Four feet away. Three feet. Two feet.

By then he was certain someone was in the bedroom. They knew he was coming. They'd been watching out the window. Someone. In the bedroom. With a knife, waiting to stab him. The hair on the back of his neck stood up. His skin tingled. Someone was in the house. Someone lurking behind him. Creeping. Creeping. Ready to grab him around the neck. He stole a quick glance over his shoulder. Another step and he could stand it no more.

"AAHHHH!"

Shouting at the top of his voice, he charged forward and jumped through the doorway. One arm protecting his face, the other with the flashlight raised over his head ready to strike whomever awaited him.

But no one was there.

An embarrassed grin spread across his face. He stood listening to the sound of the waves crashing on the beach outside. Finally, he lowered the flashlight and shone it across the room.

The mattress and boxed springs had been moved from the bed frame. They lay to the side, one corner resting on the floor, another propped in the air at an angle against the frame. The dresser still sat along the wall, but the things on top of it had been moved. Some of them lay on the floor. The blue vase was on its side. And the book was missing.

Connolly moved from the door to the dresser. The light flashed across the top. Next to the vase there was a gap in the clutter where the jewelry box had been. Why would someone take it? He had opened it and looked inside. There was nothing in it. A couple of photographs. A cheap watch. That was about it.

At the far end of the dresser the beam of light fell on the carpet below. His heart jumped.

There on the floor was the book. He knelt on one knee and turned to the front to check for the inscription, then flipped through the pages with his thumb. They fanned by until he reached the picture that was stuck inside. He took it out and held it under the light.

The woman in the photograph was much younger. But her hair was still curly. And those dark eyes gave her away.

"Inez Marchand," he whispered. "And I'd bet a lot of money that's good ol' Harold Schnadelbach standing beside her."

He stuck the photo in the book and closed it.

The night sky was ablaze with stars as Connolly crossed the bridge from Dauphin Island back to Cedar Point. He lowered the window and let the damp night air blow through the car. His skin grew tacky and moist. He propped his elbow on the window ledge and pointed the car toward Mobile.

Forty minutes later he was back in town. Dauphin Island Parkway came to an end at the Loop. Connolly slowed the car to check for traffic then made the turn onto Government Street. He glanced at his watch; it was after midnight.

As he drove toward Tuttle Street, he thought of Barbara and the house. He didn't want her to sell it. In spite of all that had happened, there were some good memories in that place. He didn't want to lose them. But he didn't want to go back there either.

Instead of driving to the guesthouse, he kept going. A few blocks farther, he turned onto Ann Street. As the car rounded the corner, he saw it. A white sign with neat black letters and the realtor's logo. For Sale. He had tried to imagine what it would feel like, seeing the sign in the yard and knowing the house was for sale. But nothing prepared him for the sense of sadness that swept over him.

Connolly stared at the house as the car rolled past. In his mind he saw Rachel on a tricycle, pedaling up the sidewalk. The car parked in the driveway. A child's swimming pool in the backyard. Toys strewn around it. He heard her giggling. Laughing. Splashing in the water.

All at once, the car jerked to a halt against the curb, slamming Connolly's chest against the steering wheel and his mind back to reality. The house was dark. The yard, empty. In the glow of a streetlight he could see Barbara's car parked at the end of the drive. Limbs from an overgrown wisteria bush sprawled across the hood. He sat there a moment, staring at the house. Remembering.

Twenty-seven

*I*t was two in the morning when Connolly returned to the guesthouse. He collapsed across the bed and fell asleep with his shoes still on his feet.

Sometime later he was awakened by the cell phone. Groggy and disoriented, he squinted against the glare of sunlight through the bedroom window as he tried to remember where he was. By the time he found the phone, the caller had hung up. He laid it on the nightstand and buried his face in the pillow.

A few minutes later he opened one eye wide enough to see the clock. Ten. In the morning. He rolled to a sitting position and rubbed his eyes. The screen on the cell phone blinked with a message telling him he'd missed a call. He picked up the phone and pressed a button to check the number. The digits appeared on the screen. It was a local number, but he didn't recognize it.

"Probably just a wrong number."

He tossed the phone on the bed and kicked off his shoes, then started toward the bathroom. After ten minutes in the shower his mind began to work again.

Edwin Marchand was lying. Inez was too. The dead man in the house wasn't who his fingerprint records said he was. Bobby Junkins was dead, whoever he was, and Stephen Ellis was Inez Marchand's son. Connolly dried himself with a towel as he walked to the bedroom.

"But somehow, Henry thinks it's a good idea to charge Dibber with murder." He stared at himself in the mirror as he knotted his tie. "I don't like it when people lie to me."

From the bedroom he walked to the kitchen and heated a cup of instant coffee in the microwave. While he waited for it, he checked the bread box. Behind a loaf of bread he found a bran muffin. There was a spot of mold on top. He pinched it off, then took a bite. It was a little dry but not that bad. He leaned against the counter and ate it between sips of coffee.

By eleven o'clock Connolly was on his way down the driveway. Ten minutes later he turned the Chrysler off Old Shell Road onto Upham Street. Near the middle of the block he came to the Marchands' house. He slowed the car and peered around the bushes. A pickup was parked near the garage. It looked like the truck he'd seen Edwin in before. Connolly turned the car from the street and started toward the house. Gravel thrown up by the tires dinged against the tailpipes as the car rolled to a stop between the garage and the house.

Through a side window he could see Inez in the kitchen. He stepped from the car and tapped on the window. The sound startled her. She looked up from the sink. Connolly called to her through the glass.

"I need to talk to your husband."

She glared at him, arms folded across her chest, an angry look on her face.

"I ain't got nothin' to say to you."

"Your husband. Edwin. I want to talk to Edwin."

Just then, someone tapped Connolly on the shoulder. He turned to see Edwin Marchand standing behind him. Marchand had a serious look on his face.

"What you want with me?"

Connolly was startled but gathered his composure.

"I talked to Hodges."

"Who's he?"

"The detective in this case."

"What case?"

"The dead man they found at the beach house."

Edwin turned away and started toward the garage.

"I already told you." He gestured over his shoulder. "That's her beach house. You'll have to talk to her about it."

Connolly called after him.

"Hodges found your prints in the house."

Edwin stopped and turned back.

"My prints? Where?"

"In the beach house."

Edwin shook his head.

"That's a lie. I ain't never been in that beach house. I haven't seen that beach house. I don't even know where it is. If my life depended on it, I couldn't take you there."

"FBI matched the prints."

Edwin gave him a puzzled look.

"Prints?"

"Fingerprints."

One corner of Edwin's mouth turned down in a sarcastic smirk.

"Now how's the FBI gonna have my fingerprints?"

Connolly shrugged.

"I don't know. Ever been in the army?"

Edwin shook his head.

"No."

"Ever had a pistol permit?"

"Mister, I'm telling you. I ain't never been checked for nothing."

"Your employer, maybe?"

Edwin's voice grew more adamant.

"I ain't never been arrested for nothing. I ain't been checked for nothing. I ain't never had nobody take my fingerprints for nothing. Who'd you say told you this?"

"Brian Hodges."

"And he's ..."

"He's a detective. With the sheriff's department."

Edwin's eyes lit up, as if he'd thought of something. Connolly kept talking.

"He's handling this case. The dead man they found at the beach house. I talked to him. To Hodges. The other day. They checked the house for prints. They found yours. He has a report."

Before Connolly finished, Edwin started toward him. Connolly moved aside, unsure what was about to happen, but Edwin stepped around him and kept going toward the house. Connolly watched as Edwin reached the door, jerked it open, and went inside. The door slammed closed behind him.

Through the window Connolly saw him standing in the kitchen. Inez turned from the sink to face him. Edwin shouted at her, flaying the air with his arms as he spoke. From the look on Inez's face, she was shouting back. The sound of their voices drifted across the yard, but Connolly couldn't understand what they were saying.

After a moment Edwin left the room and disappeared from sight. Inez moved to the sink. Connolly could see her lips moving as she washed a plate, then rinsed it under the faucet. As she moved the plate to the drain board, she glanced out the window. Her eyes met Connolly's. An angry scowl came over her face. She set the plate aside and reached for the edge of the window. In one quick motion she snatched the cord and lowered the blinds.

Connolly turned away and walked to the Chrysler.

Twenty-eight

Since the day Carl Landry showed up in the office, Connolly had talked to every person associated with Dibber's case—except one. Nick Marchand. Something about the thought of going to the nursery and talking to Nick made Connolly want to put it off. Now he was the last man on the list.

From the Marchands' house Connolly drove across town to Moffatt Road then headed west. Twenty minutes later he came to Wilmer, a rural community in the northwest corner of the county. Downtown Wilmer consisted of an oversized convenience store named West End Market, a post office, and an automotive repair shop.

About a mile past the store Connolly rounded a curve in the road and came to a large wooden building designed like a traditional barn with canvas awnings all the way around. Beneath the awnings were potted flowers and garden plants. Sacks of fertilizer and topsoil were stacked on pallets to one side. Out front a yellow sign with blinking lights spelled the name. Southern Nursery Supply.

Connolly turned the Chrysler off the road and brought it to a stop in front of the building. As he stepped from the car, a woman came from the corner of the building.

"May I help you?"

"I'm looking for Nick Marchand."

Her countenance dropped.

"He's probably in the barn."

Connolly gave her a puzzled look.

"The barn?"

The woman gestured over her shoulder.

"In back." She nodded toward the opposite end of the building. "Gate's over yonder."

The woman moved past a table of plants and disappeared inside the building.

Behind the flower shop the nursery covered a hundred acres that fronted on the highway and spilled over rolling hills lined with rows and rows of trees and shrubs in black plastic pots. A fence ran along the highway. From the parking lot Connolly could see the gate fifty yards down. He walked to the car and drove in that direction.

A sign on a fence post said Private, but the gate was open. Connolly turned the Chrysler from the pavement and let the car roll down a farm road that cut through the property. On either side, sprinklers sprayed water in lazy circles that kept the plants moist and the road muddy.

Not far from the gate, the road turned left and descended a low hill. Up ahead he could see it rising toward a barn on a hill in the distance. Connolly continued past the rows of shrubs and trees up the hill and brought the car to a stop near a blue and white Ford tractor. He got out of the car and walked around the corner of the barn.

Twenty yards away was a pile of empty plastic sacks and cardboard boxes surrounded by steel drums arranged in a circle ten feet across. Charred and rusted, the drums looked as though they had endured several years of trash fires. A young man was bent over the pile. He was dressed in blue jeans and a white T-shirt. His skin was pale. His eyes, hollow and lifeless. A three-day growth on his face left him looking scruffy and unkempt. He glanced up as Connolly rounded the corner, startled by his sudden appearance.

"Who are you?"

Connolly moved closer.

"Mike Connolly. I'm looking for—"

The young man turned away. He took a cigarette lighter from his pants pocket and flicked a button on the side. A flame appeared at the end of the lighter. He leaned over a barrel and touched the flame to one of the boxes. When the box caught fire, he grasped it by the corner and moved it around the pile, spreading flames all the way around. The plastic sacks caught fire. Black smoke billowed into the air. Soon the entire pile was ablaze.

The young man turned to Connolly.

"You looking for something?"

"I'm trying to find Nicholas Marchand."

The young man turned his head to one side and yelled.

"Hey, Nick!"

A large door along the back wall of the barn slid open. A man appeared in the opening. Dressed in blue jeans and a work shirt, he wore tan boots and a baseball cap. He was older than the other man, maybe late thirties. He glanced at the fire as he started from the barn. The young man turned to him.

"This guy wants to talk to you."

The young man picked up a cardboard box that had fallen off the pile and threw it in the fire, then moved away. Nick came to a stop in front of Connolly. He shoved his hands in his pockets and waited. Connolly gave him a polite smile.

"You're Nick Marchand?"

"Yeah."

Connolly moved to shake hands then thought better of it.

"My name is Mike Connolly. I represent a man who's accused of stealing a jet ski from your mother's beach house."

Nick nodded. Connolly continued.

"When's the last time you were down at the beach house?"

Nick shrugged.

"I don't know. Two or three weeks before the storm."

"Did you see anyone down there then?"

"Nope."

"Looks like someone has been living down there. Is that where you live?"

"I stayed down there some."

"Anybody else stay down there with you?"

"A few friends. Off and on. Over the years."

"Anybody with you the last time you were there?"

"I don't remember."

This was proving more difficult than Connolly had imagined.

"Look, I'm not trying to make trouble for anyone." He gestured with his hands as he spoke. "I'm just trying to defend my client." An acrid odor wafted through the air. Connolly's nose wrinkled. He glanced around. "What's that smell?"

Nick nodded over his shoulder toward the barn. The door slid shut.

"Ahh ... stuff we put on some of the bushes. Helps them grow. Makes them tolerate the weather a little better."

Connolly wiped his hand over his face.

"What a smell."

Nick grinned.

"Yeah."

Connolly picked up the conversation.

"They found a dead man in the house. Did you know him?"

Nick shook his head.

"Nope."

"Ever seen him before?"

"Nope."

"They say his name is Bobby Junkins. That name mean anything to you?"

Nick shook his head again.

"Don't mean nothing to me."

"What about Stephen Ellis?"

Nick's eyes darted away. He twitched his head to one side and shrugged. Connolly pressed the question.

"You know anybody by that name?"

"Nope." Nick's eyes went cold. "Never heard of him. Got no idea why he'd be in that house."

Connolly struggled to keep the conversation going.

"Anything else missing from the house besides the jet ski?"

Nick took a deep breath.

"I don't know." He sighed. "Hard to tell. The place was so broke up by the storm."

"You filed a report with the Dauphin Island police department."

"That was Mama's idea."

"You didn't file the report?"

Nick shook his head.

"Nah."

"You've been down there since the storm?"

"Rode by it."

"Didn't go in?"

"No."

"Does the name Harold Schnadelbach mean anything to you?"

Nick's eyes darted away again.

"Nope."

"Ever hear of Billy and Frieda Ellis?"

"Nope."

"Know anybody in Lawrenceville, Georgia?"

"Nope."

"Anything at all that you've thought of that might explain why this man was in your mother's beach house?"

"Nope."

Connolly glanced away. He took a deep breath then let it slowly escape.

"Your father says he never went to the beach house."

"Ahhhh ... I don't think he did."

"Your mother?"

Nick looked away once more.

"She went down there a time or two."

"Why did they buy the house?"

Nick shrugged.

"I don't know. You'd have to ask them."

"When did they buy it?"

"I don't know. You'd have to ask them that too. They've had it ... since I was a kid."

"Did they ever rent it out?"

"I don't think so." Nick glanced over his shoulder. "You about through with this? I got things I need to do."

"I guess." Connolly ran his fingers through his hair. "This is hard to get a handle on."

"Yeah. Tell me about it."

Nick turned away and started toward the barn. Connolly walked to the car. He lingered a moment, watching Nick as he slid open the barn door just wide enough to squeeze through then disappeared inside.

Connolly opened the car door. He got in behind the wheel and reached for the door handle. That same acrid odor he'd smelled before wafted through the air.

Twenty-nine

As Connolly drove through the nursery toward the highway, he glanced in the mirror. Behind him someone came from the barn and threw two more boxes on the fire. Smoke and ash rose into the sky.

At the gate he turned left and started toward Mobile. Around the curve past the nursery, the West End Market came into view. He glanced at his watch. It was one o'clock.

"No wonder I'm hungry."

West End Market had a lunch counter. He'd eaten there before. Fried food. Hot and greasy. He turned off the highway into the parking lot at the store and let the car coast past the gas pumps. It rolled to a stop under an oak tree on the far side of the building. He stepped from the car and went inside.

To the right of the door was a counter. Behind it plate-glass windows gave the clerks a wide view of the gas pumps and the parking lot outside. A few feet down the counter was an ice cream freezer. Past it was the lunch counter. The smell of cigarette smoke and hot grease filled the air. A line of customers stood at the cash register by the door waiting to pay. Connolly stepped between them and made his way to the lunch counter.

A warmer with a glass front sat atop a waist-high stainless steel counter. Inside, a lamp cast a red glare across metal trays filled with fried potatoes, fried catfish, fried chicken, and fried pickles. Grease and condensation fogged the corners of the glass.

Behind the counter was a deep fat fryer. A woman stood at the fryer, her back to Connolly. Dressed in blue jeans and a green T-shirt, she seemed oblivious to all but the sound of sizzling grease. She lifted a basket from the fryer, let the grease drip for only a moment, then dumped the contents on a tray. Connolly wasn't sure, but it looked like fried potatoes. She sprinkled something over it and shoved the tray into the warmer.

Their eyes met. She acknowledged him with an arched eyebrow.

"What'll you have?"

Connolly pointed to the warmer.

"Is that catfish?"

"Snack or meal?"

"Catfish."

She sighed and rolled her eyes. Her voice had a disconcerted tone.

"You want the snack box or the meal?"

"Meal."

She took a waxed cardboard box from beneath the counter.

"Drinking anything?"

"Coca-Cola."

She reached into the warmer with a pair of metal tongs and filled the box with fish, fried potatoes, and a fried pickle. She closed the lid on the box and handed it to him, then turned to get the Coke.

Connolly joined the line at the cash register and paid for the food, then took a seat at a table in the corner as far from the door as possible. He pulled a stack of paper napkins from the dispenser on the table and laid them to one side, then opened the box and began to eat. The store was busy. People moved in and out. Connolly was hungry. He concentrated on eating.

A few minutes later he heard a familiar voice. He glanced up to see Toby LeMoyne standing at the counter.

Toby was a deputy sheriff. Tall and athletic, he had broad shoulders and muscular arms that bulged beneath the sleeves of his shirt. His size and physique were intimidating, but he had a kind face and a smile that lit up the room. Connolly had known Toby since he first became a deputy.

The clerk handed Toby a brown paper sack. He took it from her and crossed the room toward a cooler along the wall. A moment later he slid into the seat across from Connolly. He set the sack on the table and twisted the top off a bottle of Milo's tea.

Connolly wiped his fingers on a napkin.

"You come for the grease or the calories?"

Toby opened the sack and took out a hamburger.

"Best hamburger in the county. What brings you out here?"

Connolly took a bite of fish.

"Witnesses."

Toby smiled.

"What poor, misunderstood crook are you trying to set free on society today?"

"Dibber Landry."

Toby nodded.

"I heard about that. Looting houses on Dauphin Island or something."

"That's what they say."

Toby chuckled.

"Looting during a hurricane. Couldn't wait for it to blow over." He shook his head. "Some people will do anything."

"Yeah."

Connolly took another bite of fish. Toby took a drink of tea.

"Saw you coming out of that nursery down there. They got something to do with your case?"

Connolly nodded.

"A guy that works there. Nick Marchand. It was his mother's house."

Toby shook his head again.

"Those are some strange people."

"Yeah."

"All those trees and bushes, and you never see nobody around there."

"Is it like that all the time?"

Toby nodded.

"Yeah." He took another bite of hamburger. "First big case I ever worked on was out there. Old man that owned that place got shot. Just about the time I came on the force. Everybody seemed to know who he was. I'd never heard of him."

"What was his name?"

"Givens. Earl Givens."

A bite of fish stuck in Connolly's throat. He began to choke. Toby's eyes grew wide.

"Mike?"

Toby slid off the bench and jumped to his feet. In one quick motion he slipped his arms around Connolly's chest and lifted him from behind the table. He placed his fist just below Connolly's ribs and gave a sharp squeeze. The fish shot from Connolly's mouth and splattered on the floor.

Connolly took a deep breath. Then another. Toby eased him down to the bench.

"You all right?"

Connolly nodded.

"Yeah." He wiped his mouth on a napkin and took another deep breath. "Thanks."

Toby chuckled as he moved around the table and took a seat.

"You were turning blue."

"I felt blue."

"Man, that's scary." Toby pointed to the Coca-Cola. "Take a drink."

Connolly sipped the drink. Toby looked concerned.

"Maybe you shouldn't eat any more of that fish."

"Maybe so."

Connolly took a napkin from the table and stooped to wipe the fish from the floor. A young boy with a broom and a dust pan nudged him aside.

"I got it."

Connolly returned to his seat. The young boy scooped up the fish, wiped the spot on the floor with a damp cloth, and turned away. Connolly took another sip of Coca-Cola.

"What was the old man's name?"

"Givens." Toby wiped his mouth. "Earl Givens."

Connolly nodded.

"How long ago was that?"

Toby shrugged.

"Early eighties. Maybe. About the time I came on the force."

"What happened to him?"

"Somebody shot him."

"Who did it?"

Toby shrugged again.

"Never found out. I think it's still an open case."

"Never solved it?"

"Everybody had their theories, but we never found enough to charge anybody with it."

"Who was the detective?"

"Clyde Ramsey."

"Clyde Ramsey," Connolly repeated. "Name sounds familiar."

"He's retired now. Lives in midtown. Not too far from you."

"Yeah? Where?"

"Crenshaw Street, I think. Up there by the Loop." Toby took a drink of tea. He started smiling before he'd finished. "Hodges is working your case, ain't he?"

Connolly nodded.

"Yeah. Why?"

"He married Clyde's daughter."

Connolly frowned.

"You're kidding?"

"No, I'm not." Toby laughed. "It's not that uncommon. Lots of us are married to officers' children."

"Lots of us?"

"Yeah. Merris' father was with the Prichard police. The guy who relieves me is married to a girl whose father is with Mobile. We're all pretty tight."

Connolly shrugged and took another drink of Coca-Cola.

"You been patrolling out here a long time."

"Yeah. They try to rotate us around the county, but I get sent out here every few months."

Connolly grinned.

"Are they still mad about that Agostino thing?"

Toby smiled.

"I don't think so. At least, they don't mention it anymore."

"So, what goes on out there at that nursery?"

"Hard to say."

Connolly gave him a questioning look.

"Hard to say?"

Toby smiled.

"Rumors all over the county about a meth lab. Super lab. Big operation. Nobody's been able to find it yet. If that's what they're doing at that nursery, you better watch out."

"Stinks out there."

"I know. Love to get a look inside that barn. Haven't found a reason for a warrant. But I'm looking."

"Yeah?"

"Yeah." Toby grinned. "They don't keep sending me out here because they're mad at me. I know this place. You better be careful."

Thirty

When Connolly finished lunch, he walked to the front of the store and asked to see a phone book. He jotted down Clyde Ramsey's address on a napkin and stepped outside. As he crossed the parking lot, he stuffed it in his pocket. 4405 Crenshaw Street. He knew about Crenshaw Street. His childhood home was on Crenshaw Street. His mother had left them on ... He brushed away the memory and thought about his conversation with Toby. Earl Givens was Nick Marchand's grandfather. Didn't take a genius to figure out Inez Marchand was Inez Givens. Whatever doubt he'd had about her connection to Stephen Ellis evaporated.

Crenshaw Street intersected Airline Highway near the Loop, a few blocks from Government Street. The drive from Wilmer took almost an hour. Connolly steered the Chrysler down the street and checked the house numbers. Clyde Ramsey's house was in the middle of the fourth block.

Like all the others in that part of town, the house was a 1920s bungalow with white siding and metal awnings over the windows. A small patch of grass separated it from the sidewalk by the street. Beside the house was a driveway that led to a garage in back.

Connolly parked in front and walked to the door. He pressed the doorbell and waited. After a moment the door opened part way. A slender man dressed in khaki pants and a wrinkled white shirt appeared. He had snow-white hair cut in a flattop and a two-day growth of white stubble on his face.

"Yes?"

"I'm looking for Clyde Ramsey."

"You've found him."

"My name is Mike Connolly. I'm an attorney. I was wondering if I could talk to you a minute."

"What about?"

"A case you worked on."

"Been a long time since I worked on any case. I don't remember much of that stuff anymore."

"If Toby LeMoyne is right, you'll remember this one."

A smile came to Ramsey's face.

"Toby LeMoyne. Haven't heard that name in years. You know Toby?"

"Yes."

Ramsey pushed the door open wide and stepped aside.

"Come on in. Have a seat. Maybe I'll think of something that can help you."

Connolly stepped inside. The room was dark and cool. Ramsey closed the door and switched on a lamp.

A sofa sat along the wall by the door. Two chairs sat facing it across a cluttered coffee table. At the far end of the room was a spinet piano. It sat to the left of a brick fireplace that looked as though it hadn't been used in years. Newspapers were stacked on the sofa. One of the chairs held a stack of magazines. The other, a worn sofa pillow in a silk case.

Ramsey stepped to the sofa and scooped up the newspapers.

"Have a seat." He dropped the papers on the floor by the piano bench. "Sorry about the mess. I'm here by myself. Not much reason to clean the place up."

Connolly took a seat on the sofa. Ramsey sat in the chair with the silk pillow.

"So, how's Toby doing?"

"He's fine. Had lunch with him a little while ago."

Ramsey crossed his legs.

"I haven't seen him in years."

"He said he worked with you when he first came on the force."

Connolly was about to mention Hodges, then thought better of it. No point in telling everything he knew. Besides, Ramsey seemed pleased at the mention of Toby. Better to leave well enough alone.

"We worked a few cases. He was a young recruit when they sent him out to me." Ramsey chuckled. "Didn't know much about anything. But he was a good guy. Smart. Caught on pretty quick."

"I was wondering if you could tell me something about a man named Earl Givens. Used to own a nursery out at Wilmer."

A somber look came over Ramsey's face.

"Earl Givens." He propped his elbows on the arms of the chair and laced his fingers together in his lap. "That was a tough case."

"Toby said it was his first."

Ramsey managed a thin smile.

"Yeah. Probably was."

"What do you remember about that case?"

Ramsey shifted positions in the chair.

"Not much. They called me one morning." He twisted sideways in the chair and crossed his legs the opposite way. "Hired help found the old man in a barn out there. Deputies secured the scene. I went out. Got there ... middle of the morning. Something like that. The old man was lying on the ground. Best I can remember, the coroner said he'd been dead since sometime the day before."

"What happened to him?"

"Somebody shot him in the head. Never could figure out who."

Just then the phone rang. Ramsey left the room to answer it. While he was gone, Connolly glanced around. The mantle above the fireplace was lined with vases and bowls. Connolly stood and moved across the room to look at them. One end of the mantle held a number of red pieces. On the other were several cobalt blue vases.

To the left of the mantle, the top of the piano was covered with framed photographs. Connolly turned from the mantle and picked up a photograph of a woman sitting at a table. She wore a blue suit with a corsage pinned near her lapel.

Ramsey entered the room and moved behind Connolly.

"That's my wife, Eva."

"She's a pretty lady."

"Yes. She was."

"Is she deceased?"

"Yes." Ramsey took the picture from Connolly. "She died year before last." He returned the picture to its place on the piano. As he set it there, Connolly's eyes fell on a blue vase behind the picture. He hadn't noticed it before. Cobalt blue, it had a wide mouth at the top and curved to a stem that had a clear bubble in the middle. For a moment Connolly's mind dropped out of the conversation. He hadn't seen a cobalt vase in years. Now he'd seen several in a matter of days. Two that were alike. Two that weren't cheap either.

Ramsey seemed not to notice Connolly's distraction. He continued to talk about his wife as he moved to a chair and took a seat.

"It's for the better."

Connolly's mind engaged the conversation again. He turned away from the piano. Ramsey gestured for him to sit on the sofa.

"Alzheimer's," he explained. "She couldn't remember a thing."

Connolly returned to the sofa.

"Do you have any notes on the case?"

Ramsey looked puzzled.

"Case?"

Connolly nodded.

"Givens."

Ramsey shook his head.

"All that stuff's downtown somewhere. I guess. Might not even be a file on it anymore. That was a long time ago."

"Mr. Givens had a grandson. Nick."

Ramsey nodded. His eyes seemed to look right through Connolly.

"What about him?"

"His mother is Inez Marchand."

"Yeah."

"Was she also known as Mary?"

Ramsey stared at him a moment.

"Yeah," he said, finally. "Why?"

"Just curious."

"About what?"

"Everything."

"What kind of case are you working on?"

"Murder."

"You think this has something to do with your client?"

"I don't know."

"What's your client's name?"

"Dibber ... Dilbert Landry."

Ramsey chuckled.

"Funny name."

"How many times was Givens shot?"

"Twice. Once in the stomach and once in the head."

"What did they shoot him with?"

"Thirty-eight. Shot him in the stomach first. Then the head."

"How could you tell that?"

"Shot to the head hit him right between the eyes."

"How did you know that was the second shot?"

Ramsey looked at Connolly.

"Educated guess. Average layman couldn't hit a man between the eyes like that with a pistol. And besides, why shoot him in the stomach if you've already shot him in the head?"

Connolly nodded.

"Any idea who killed him?"

Ramsey shifted in his seat again.

"Not really."

"But you had a theory."

Ramsey gave him a look.

"Why are you interested in this case?"

"Earl Givens had a daughter. Inez Marchand. She owns a beach house on Dauphin Island. After the hurricane some of the neighbors down there found a dead man in that house. My client is accused of killing him."

"You think this old case has something to do with that one?"

Connolly shrugged.

"I don't know. Right now, I'm looking for anything I can find."

Ramsey's face turned to stone. He laid his hands along the armrests of the chair.

"So, you're just out here stirring up anything you can find. Looking for something to talk about in court besides the truth. Like every other defense lawyer I've ever known." He stood. "I think I've said about all I have to say about this."

He moved across the room toward the door. Connolly hesitated then stood as well. Ramsey opened the door.

"I can't help you any further."

Connolly stepped outside. He heard the door close behind him as he crossed the porch.

Mrs. Gordon was right. This was a strange case. He'd seen cases where a witness had refused to talk, but not every witness. Inez. Edwin. Nick. None of them wanted to talk about the dead man in the beach house. Now an eighty-something retired detective didn't want to talk about a twenty-year-old unsolved case.

Connolly shook his head.

"It's like every secret in the world has converged in this one case."

He opened the car door and got in the Chrysler.

Thirty-one

*F*rom Ramsey's house Connolly drove down Crenshaw Street. Seeing the houses again took him back—way back. The green house on the left. Jeff Berry lived there. And next to him was Russell Gray. Down the street on the right, Scott Darnell. Memories flooded his mind. Baseball games in the street. Secrets shared in the quiet of a hot summer night. Memories made bittersweet by the turn his life took that day on the back porch.

When he and his brother walked away from the house the last time, he had vowed never to return. But it was a vow his heart wouldn't let him keep. Over the years he had driven down the street many times, looking at the houses, remembering the people he had known, and thinking of what might have been. After he and Barbara married and moved to the house on Ann Street, he drove that way every morning to the office. Just to drive by the house. Hoping with some childlike hope that his mother might be there. But that was a long time ago. It had been years since he was last on the street.

At the corner he slowed the car almost to a stop. There was no traffic on the cross street. He lifted his foot from the brake pedal and let the car roll through the intersection. And then he saw it. His heart skipped a beat.

A little cottage with white clapboard siding and a patch of lawn in front. An oak tree grew near the corner by the driveway that led to a garage in back. He slowed the car and brought it to a stop across the street.

That lawn had seemed as big as the world when it was his turn to cut it. Now, it was not even the size of the waiting area in front of Mrs. Gordon's desk. To the left of the house, vines and thorns wound around the trunk of the oak tree and up through its branches almost to the top. A dead limb from the tree lay on the roof. Another lay near the porch. Trash littered the steps. He should have kept going. There was no reason to stop. No reason at all. Just an ache somewhere deep inside that needed to see the place one more time. He switched off the engine and stepped from the car.

A warm breeze brushed across his face as he crossed the street toward the garage. From the end of the house he could see through a window to the room that had been their dining room when he was a boy. The walls were bare. A water stain marred the wall to the left. A table sat in the center of the room. It looked like the one they had used, but it was covered with boxes and papers. He stared through the window a moment then continued up the driveway.

The garage had wooden siding that matched the house, but years of neglect had taken a toll. The exterior that had once been white was now green with mildew. Doors across the front sagged in the middle, and a limb had knocked a hole in the roof. Connolly grasped the handle on one of the doors and pulled. The door scraped across the concrete as he forced it open. Light streamed in through the open doorway. Connolly's mouth fell open in disbelief.

Parked in the garage was a 1941 Ford. Painted black, it had chrome trim and chrome hubcaps. It was covered in dust, but even so he could see the car was in great shape. His eyes were wide with amazement.

"This is not possible," he whispered.

Connolly stepped inside the garage and moved around the car. He wiped away the grime from the rear window and peered inside. The seats looked the same as the last time he'd ridden in the car. They had gone to the drugstore the afternoon before his mother left. A candy wrapper was still tucked in the crease of the seat. He cupped his hand against the glass to shade his eyes from the glare and glanced toward the front seat.

Over the back of the seat he could see the key still in the ignition. He moved to the driver's door, pulled it open, and took a seat behind the steering wheel. A metal tag dangled from the end of the key chain. He held the tag in his hand and rubbed it clean with his thumb. Beneath the dust and dirt he saw the green letters and read the name. Service Cleaners and Laundry.

On the seat beside him was a pocket-sized package of King Edward cigars. The cigars inside were covered with mold but he knew in an instant whose they were. He ran his fingers over the steering wheel and swallowed hard to keep from crying.

"This is not possible," he whispered again.

After a few minutes he stepped from the seat and closed the car door. He glanced around the garage. The neighborhood might have changed, but that garage still looked the same as he'd always remembered it. He sniffed the air. It smelled the same too. He glanced around once more, then moved past the car.

A brown lump of something on a shelf to the right caught his eye. Beneath the cobwebs and dust he found a baseball glove with a ball stuck in the web. He picked it up with his left hand. It was mildewed and stiff, but he could read the initials written on the leather at the heel of the palm. MC.

Tears welled in his eyes and rolled down his cheeks.

The ambulance came that day. It took them awhile, but they finally arrived. In the rush of tending to his father, the driver had pushed him aside. The radio on the porch was still on. Across town the Mobile A's were playing the Birmingham Barons at Hartwell Field. They'd just finished a game of catch and sat on the steps. He was holding the glove and ball in his hand as they loaded his father on the stretcher. When they lifted him up to put him in the ambulance, Connolly could see he was already dead. He ran into the garage and hid behind the car. As he stumbled past the rear bumper, he threw the glove on the shelf. It was the last time he'd touched it.

A voice interrupted his thoughts.

"What are you doing out here?"

He wheeled around to see a frail old woman standing in the doorway.

"What are you doing in my garage?" She glared at him. "I oughta call the law."

Her wrinkled face was twisted in a scowl. Her voice was rough and gravelly. She sounded angry, but Connolly didn't feel threatened.

"I'm sorry." He laid the glove on the shelf and wiped his eyes with the back of his hand. "I used to live here."

"Ain't nobody ever lived here but me." She pointed her finger at him and gestured with a wag toward the street. "Now you get outta here. This here's my garage. And I don't allow nobody in here."

All of five feet tall, she had a petite frame, and when she pointed her finger at him, he could almost count the bones in her hand. Her hair was long and gray and pulled in a bun behind her head that stretched her forehead tight against her scalp. She wore a long-sleeved blue cotton dress that fell below her knees and buttoned up the front all the way to the collar. Deep lines creased her face, and her skin looked tough and leathery. And she smelled like alcohol. Cheap liquor. Night Train, to be exact.

Years had passed since the day he and Rick hitchhiked to Bayou La Batre, but not so many that he didn't know who she was.

"Mama."

The scowl on her face changed to a puzzled frown.

"Mama?" The puzzled look became a blank, lifeless expression. "I ain't got no children."

She turned away and started toward the house. He watched as she climbed the steps and disappeared through the back door.

For a while he stood in the garage and waited, hoping she would come out again. Hoping she would tell him why she left. Hoping she would fill in the blank spaces of the past fifty years. But after a few minutes he knew she wouldn't. He closed the garage doors and walked down the driveway to the Chrysler.

Thirty-two

Connolly glanced back at the house as he placed the key in the ignition. Through the front window he could see his mother staring at him. Their eyes met. She turned away. He started the car and drove down the street.

From Crenshaw Street, Connolly headed toward the office. Buildings and houses passed him on either side, but his mind was lost in a fog of memories and emotion. In spite of what she'd said, he was sure she was his mother. Her voice. The look in her eye. The way she walked. She was his mother all right. But how could it be?

In the years since she left, he'd passed that house a hundred times and never once thought she might be living there. If he'd thought about it, even considered the possibility, he would have stopped. He would have banged on the door. Would have charged in and demanded some answers. Yet just then, when she was right there in front of him, he couldn't think of a thing to say. Except to call her name.

A car horn blared behind him. Startled, he glanced around to find he was stopped at the traffic light at Water Street. The car horn blared again. Connolly turned the steering wheel hard to the left, made a U-turn in the intersection, and started up Government Street in the opposite direction. He intended to drive to the guesthouse and collapse on the sofa in the living room, but by the time he reached Tuttle Street, he knew that was a bad idea. He'd sit there until the sun went down, and by then he'd be depressed and sorry and anything could happen. What he needed was some answers, and there was one person left alive who could give those to him.

Connolly pressed the gas pedal. The Chrysler sped through the intersection at Tuttle and continued west past the suburbs to Irvington. There, he turned south and descended into the broad expanse of savannah marsh that lay along the coast below Mobile. Thirty minutes later he reached Bayou La Batre.

A rough and tumble fishing town, Bayou La Batre was home to a large fleet of shrimp boats and a dwindling oyster business. Tucked along a broad bayou, the town lay hidden beneath towering cypress and sprawling oaks, concealed from view and shielded from the ravages of time. Life there was an odd and intriguing mixture of ritual, superstition, and debauchery.

At the drawbridge Connolly turned south and drove along the bayou. To the left, rows of shrimp boats lined the docks at the fish houses up and down the meandering, murky stream. Two miles down the bayou he came to a large mailbox that dangled from a wooden post at the side of the road. A driveway ran from the road at the mailbox to a house in the midst of a grove of pecan trees. The house had jalousie windows shaded by large aluminum awnings that once had been painted green and white. Below the windows azalea bushes sprawled in every direction and scrubbed against the walls of the house.

Oyster shells crunched beneath the tires as the car rolled up the driveway toward the house. Connolly brought the car to a stop near a picnic table ten yards from the side door. He slid from the Chrysler and made his way up the steps.

At the top of the steps Connolly peered through the screen door to the kitchen inside. A metal table with a red Naugahyde top and four matching chairs sat to the left. Beyond the table near the door to the hallway was a gas stove. To the right of the stove was a refrigerator. Cabinets covered the wall to the right, with a window in the middle and a sink below. On the stove was a skillet. Behind it was a pot with something inside already boiling. Uncle Guy stood at the sink.

Now he spent most of the day napping, a luxury he had only recently allowed himself. In the sixth grade he dropped out of school to work an oyster skiff. It was backbreaking work, lowering the tongs, grappling them full of shells, hauling them aboard, then shucking them for the meats while he rested. At the age of fifteen he left the skiff and took a job as a deckhand on a shrimp boat. By twenty-one he was a boat captain and spent the next fifty years piloting shrimp boats. It was a hard life, but he enjoyed working and it was a life that favored him.

When Connolly's mother left them, Connolly and his younger brother crammed what they could in a pillowcase and hitchhiked to Bayou La Batre. Guy and his wife, Ruby, raised them as their own. It was Guy who paid for Connolly to attend college and Guy who pointed him toward law school.

Connolly opened the screen door. As he stepped inside, Uncle Guy wheeled around. The old man looked startled at first, but his eyes sparkled when he saw Connolly.

"Hey. Didn't expect to see you today." He grinned at Connolly. "You're just in time for supper."

Connolly caught the screen door and pulled it closed.

"Great."

Guy wiped his hands on a dish towel and threw his arms around Connolly in a bear hug. Connolly slipped an arm around the old man's waist and rested his head on his shoulder. The feel of that shoulder, the faint smell of sweat and aftershave lotion. Like a thousand times before, the world seemed to melt away.

After a moment Guy pulled back. He turned aside and rubbed his eyes as he started toward the refrigerator.

"You don't come down here often enough."

Connolly took a seat at the table.

"Been busy."

Guy opened the refrigerator and stooped to look inside.

"A man needs to be busy." He took a pan of fish from the shelf and turned to Connolly. "Mullet all right with you?"

Connolly smiled. Mullet was his favorite fish.

"Where'd you get them?"

"Caught them last night."

Connolly raised an eyebrow.

"You caught them?"

Guy cut his eyes at him.

"I ain't that old."

Connolly chuckled.

"Where'd you go?"

"Little River." Guy closed the refrigerator and set the pan on the counter. "They were jumpin' everywhere. Could have had a boat-load but I didn't feel like cleaning 'em."

The thought of Guy in a boat, throwing a cast net, made Connolly smile. An old man, still enjoying the things that had occupied his entire life. The fish sizzled in the pan. Steam rose from the pot on the back burner. Grits. They always ate grits with mullet. Connolly pulled his tie loose from his collar and leaned back in the chair.

In a few minutes the fish were done. Guy took plates and bowls from the cabinet. He filled the bowls with grits and the plates with fish then brought them to the table. He returned to the refrigerator for a jug of tea and snagged two glasses from the dish drainer by the sink. When everything was ready, he took a seat across from Connolly. They ate in silence. Connolly was on his third piece of fish before he realized he'd had fish for lunch.

Guy paused and took a drink of tea.

"You working, or just come to see me?"

Connolly wasn't sure where to begin. He took another bite, then a drink of tea. Guy stared at him from across the table.

"Well, what's the matter?"

Connolly took another sip of tea. Guy grew impatient.

"Set that glass down and talk to me."

Connolly took another sip then set the glass on the table.

"I went by the house on Crenshaw Street today."

Guy sighed and leaned back in his chair.

"You stop?"

"Yeah."

"Was she there?"

The question startled Connolly.

"How did you know she was there?"

"It's her house."

"You mean she's been there all this time?"

"Not all of it."

"How long?"

"I don't know."

"Well, when was the last time you talked to her?"

"She called me from a pay phone in Chiefland, Florida, about two weeks after you and Rick came down here."

"That's the last time you talked to her?"

Guy nodded.

"She called here one other time. Ruby talked to her."

"When was that?"

"About the time you were taking the bar exam."

"And that's it?"

"You think I been keeping something from you?"

"I don't know how she could be living there and I not know it. Has she been there all this time?"

Guy sighed.

"Off and on, I think."

Connolly stared at him. Guy shrugged.

"I rode by there a time or two. Place was in bad shape. At first I thought it was empty, but then I noticed a light on in back, and one other time I saw her out there by the garage."

"It was her?"

"It was her." Guy wiped his chin with his napkin. "Look, I know this is tough for you, but—"

Connolly struck the table with his fist. Years of emotion boiled to the surface.

"Why? Why did she leave us like that? Why didn't she come looking for us?"

"I don't know."

"Daddy left us. She left us."

Guy stood and took his plate from the table. He walked across the room and set it in the sink.

"There's a little more to the story than that."

Connolly propped his elbows on the table and rested his forehead in his hands.

"More than what?"

Guy leaned against the counter, his arms folded across his chest.

"John didn't leave. He had a heart attack."

Connolly pushed his chair away from the table and leaned back.

"I know."

Guy shook his head.

"No, you don't. Not all of it."

Connolly frowned.

"What do you mean?"

"I mean … the man you know as your father. John Connolly. He isn't your father. Not biologically."

Connolly felt confused.

"What are you talking about?"

"When your mother married John, they moved up to Mobile, met new people, found a life she hadn't known before. She and John got to running with some folks who liked to go out at night. Started going to places. Radio Ranch. Ivey's Supper Club. Bunch of places I don't even know."

Connolly frowned.

"Radio Ranch?"

"It was a club on Dauphin Island Parkway. Nice enough place. I mean, you didn't have to worry about a fight breaking out or anything." Guy shifted positions. "She met this guy there. A surveyor. Worked for the railroad. Had a room at a house on Claiborne Street. They met. First one thing and then another and then ..."

Connolly had a sinking feeling in the pit of his stomach.

"She got pregnant."

Guy nodded.

"With you."

"Who was he?"

"I don't know."

"Did she tell Da ... did she tell her husband?"

"Eventually."

"What'd he say?"

"He moved out. Elizabeth moved in with us down here. Stayed a few months. John came and got her about the time you were born."

Connolly shook his head.

"The things you don't know."

"Your mother was a mixed-up woman. Been that way all her life. I mean, she's my sister and I love her, but she has a strange way."

Connolly stared at the floor.

"She smelled like Night Train."

"I don't doubt it. She always liked to drink. Used to sneak around and drink when we were in school. Then it got a hold of her, and she couldn't get rid of it."

"Sounds familiar."

"Runs in the family. Did you try to talk to her?"

"Yeah."

"What'd she say?"

"I said I used to live there. She said nobody ever lived there but her. I told her she was my mother. She said she didn't have any children. Then she just walked away. Went inside."

Guy wiped his hands on the dish towel and threw it on the counter.

"Well, there's one more thing."

"What?"

"After you and Rick had been down here awhile, I went to court in Mobile and got custody of you. She found out about it, and from what I hear, she didn't like it." He looked away. "Wasn't much she could do about it."

Connolly frowned.

"You took us from her?"

Guy looked him in the eye.

"I wasn't about to let her take you off. She was riding from truck stop to truck stop. Hopping around with who knows what. You can hate me for it if you want to. I did what had to be done."

Guy pushed away from the counter and started down the hall. Connolly heard the recliner open in the living room. He took one more sip of tea and rose from the table. He crossed the room with his dishes and laid them in the sink.

What a day. Nick Marchand. Nearly choked at lunch. Clyde Ramsey. His mother. Now all of this. He wiped his hands on the towel and walked to the living room.

Guy sat in the recliner with his eyes closed. Connolly took a seat on the sofa.

"I don't hate you."

Guy responded without opening his eyes.

"It was a tough time. I didn't know what to do. She run off with that truck driver—"

"Who was he?"

"Harley Mullins."

"You knew him?"

"Nah." Guy shook his head. "Never met him. She told me who he was when she called that time from Chiefland. Harley Mullins from Okahumpka, Florida. Met him at a truck stop in Loxley."

"What was she doing there?"

"Where?"

"The truck stop. In Loxley."

"I don't know. I imagine she'd been off with that bunch she used to hang around with. They liked to go to the speedway over in Pensacola. Probably coming back from there and stopped to eat." Guy sighed. "I don't know. That's what I figure happened."

Connolly crossed his legs and leaned his head against the back of the sofa.

"We got hungry."

"I know you did. I was worried. I didn't know she was gone, but I knew what she was like."

"Rick cried himself to sleep that night."

Guy took a deep breath. Connolly glanced at him. The old man's eyes were open now, and wet.

"You did the right thing. Coming down here."

Guy closed his eyes. Connolly closed his and folded his hands in his lap.

"So, what about Rick? Who was his dad?"

Guy took a deep breath.

"John. But he gave you his name."

"His name?"

"John Michael Connolly."

Connolly's eyes popped open. No one had ever called him by his full name. He never even used it himself. All his life he'd thought of himself as Mike. But his full name was John Michael Connolly Jr. A smile broke across his face.

"I guess he did."

Guy reached behind him and turned off the lamp.

"Name's all that matters." He settled back in the chair. "The rest don't mean much."

Thirty-three

The following morning Connolly awakened to the glare of sunlight streaming through the front window. To the left, Guy lay snoring in the recliner. Across the room beneath the window was a table with pictures of Ruby, Connolly, and Rick. The one of Connolly was made when he graduated from college. The one of Rick was taken when he was still in high school. The night before a dance. Wearing a green leisure suit with a paisley shirt. Connolly chuckled to himself.

Sleeping on the sofa left his neck stiff. He stood and rubbed it as he leaned over and kissed Guy on the forehead. The old man gave a faint smile and turned his head. Connolly crossed the room to the hall. As he rounded the corner by the kitchen, Guy called to him.

"Connolly."

Connolly stepped back into the room. Guy looked up at him.

"Whatever she did, she did it because of her. Not because of you."

"Sometimes that's not easy to remember."

"I know. But it's true. She was like she was before you ever came along."

Connolly nodded.

"And something else." Guy lifted an eyebrow. "She's still your mother."

"I know."

Guy closed his eyes. Connolly crossed the kitchen and stepped outside.

By seven that morning Connolly was back at the guesthouse. He showered, changed clothes, and headed downtown. It seemed like years since he'd been to the office, but instead of going there he drove behind the courthouse to St. Pachomius Church. He parked the Chrysler out front and made his way up the steps to the sanctuary.

Inside, the air was cool and refreshing. Morning prayers had ended. The sanctuary was empty and quiet. He took a seat on a pew near the front and pulled down a kneeler. Leaning forward, he rested his head against the back of the next pew. With his eyes closed he could see in his mind his mother standing in the doorway at the garage. He could hear her voice. "Nobody ever lived here but me." The sound of those words made his soul bristle.

The pew beside him creaked. He opened his eyes and glanced to the right. Father Scott sat next to him.

"Missed you this morning."

Connolly sighed and slid back in the seat. Father Scott smiled.

"You look tired."

Connolly laid his hands in his lap.

"Feels like I've been on a long trip."

"What's up?"

Connolly didn't know where to begin.

"You ever feel like sometimes the world just turns inside out? Like you go around a corner thinking everything is one way. Then, wham! Nothing's what you thought it was."

Father Scott grinned.

"Raisa call you?"

Connolly shook his head. He hadn't thought about her in ... a day or two. That whole thing seemed a distant memory.

"No." Connolly sighed again. "Not that."

"You still working on that case about that dead body in the beach house?"

Connolly nodded. Father Scott crossed his legs.

"I read about it in the paper. Mentioned you."

Connolly smiled.

"Strange case. It's like all the secrets in the world converged on this one case."

"They ever figure out who he was?"

Connolly nodded.

"Sort of."

Father Scott frowned.

"Sort of?"

Connolly grinned.

"Matched his prints to an arrest record from Georgia. Said he was Stephen Ellis. DA brought his father down here to see the body. We go over to the morgue. Father looks at the body. It's not Stephen. Records are all confused. It's Stephen's best friend. Bobby."

"Bet he was relieved."

"Stephen's dad?"

"Yeah."

"Yeah, but that's a strange deal too. Turns out, Stephen's father isn't really his father. He's just the husband of the woman who raised him. She's not his mother either." Connolly glanced over at Father Scott. "Is this making any sense?"

Father Scott chuckled.

"Actually, yes. I've been down these rabbit holes before." Father Scott shifted positions on the pew. "So where is he?"

"Stephen?"

"Yeah."

"I don't know. No one knows. Or, at least, no one's talking about it—which isn't anything new for this case. But that's not the end of it."

"There's more?"

"Lots more."

"That why you came in here?"

Connolly looked away. His voice softened.

"Not really." He took a deep breath and let it slowly escape. "I was talking to Toby LeMoyne yesterday. Do you know Toby?"

"We met."

"There's this old case. Might have something to do with this one. We were talking about it. He gave me the name of a guy who knew something about it. Lives on Crenshaw Street. I went to see him yesterday." Connolly looked over at Father Scott. "I used to live on Crenshaw Street."

"When you were married?"

Connolly shook his head.

"When I was a little boy."

Father Scott nodded. Connolly took another deep breath.

"So, I went to see this guy. After I talked to him, I drove down the street. It's the old neighborhood. I hadn't seen it in a long time.

Got down to my old house. Looked like nobody lived there. Grass is all grown up. Place hasn't been painted. So, I stopped and walked up to the garage." Tears welled in his eyes. He glanced over at Father Scott. "His car is still in the garage."

Father Scott frowned.

"Whose car?"

"My dad's." Connolly cleared his throat. "Well ..." He shrugged. "Not exactly my dad."

Father Scott looked puzzled. Connolly wiped his eyes.

"While I was in the garage looking at the car and trying to figure out why it was still there, this woman came out of the house. Told me to get out." Tears ran down Connolly's cheeks. He looked over at Father Scott again, his voice a whisper. "She was my mother."

Father Scott looked surprised.

"Your mother?"

Connolly's voice was little more than a breath.

"Yeah."

"I thought she was dead."

"I did too."

They sat in silence a moment. Then Connolly began again.

"I went down to see my uncle last night. Asked him about her. He knew she wasn't dead. Hadn't seen her in a while but knew she was alive. Then he told me the man I knew as my father wasn't really my father." Connolly looked over at Father Scott once more. "My mother had an affair."

Connolly turned away. Father Scott put his hand on Connolly's shoulder. Connolly wiped his eyes again.

"I don't know what's going on."

"Did your uncle tell you about your father? Your biological father."

"Not really. I mean, he doesn't know much about him."

"Give you a name?"

Connolly shook his head.

"Doesn't know what it is." Connolly turned to Father Scott. "What is going on? Why is this happening? Why wouldn't she talk to me?"

"What did she say?"

"Told me to get out. Said she didn't have any children. Said no one had ever lived there but her."

"What did you say?"

"I couldn't say much of anything." An angry scowl came over Connolly's face. "I hate that woman."

"I know."

"I wanted to ..." Connolly leaned forward, his hand balled in a fist. "She left us there." He pounded his fist against the back of the next pew. "She didn't care whether we lived or died."

Father Scott leaned closer.

"That's what has to come out."

Connolly glared at him.

"What?"

"The bitterness."

The glare on Connolly's face became a scowl.

"Bitterness? She was wrong." Connolly's voice grew loud. "I wouldn't treat anybody like that. We could have died, and she wouldn't have cared."

"She was wrong. But this isn't about her." Father Scott pointed at Connolly. "It's about you."

"Me?"

"You can't stay there."

"Can't stay where? What are you talking about?"

"You're still right there at that same spot."

"What spot?"

"That night, when you realized she wasn't coming back. That next morning, when you had to get up and take care of your brother. You're still right there at that moment."

Connolly looked away. Father Scott leaned toward him.

"You can't stay there. You've got to move on."

"I want her to talk to me."

"I know. But this isn't about her."

Connolly's voice took on a sarcastic tone.

"You mean it's about me learning to forgive?"

"That might be part of it. But listen to me. You are at a critical point. Everything you've experienced in the last three or four years has worked to bring you to this point. This opportunity."

Connolly's forehead wrinkled in a frown.

"Opportunity? For what?"

"So you can close the door on who you used to be."

Connolly felt puzzled.

"I'm not sure I follow you."

"You've held on to what your mother did to you and what she did to your brother. In many ways you went on. Went to school. All of that. But emotionally, spiritually, you held on to what she did, and you've been waiting for her to come make it right. And you've been waiting for a chance to bust her with it."

Connolly had a determined look. He jabbed the air with his finger.

"And now I can."

Father Scott's voice softened.

"And now you must let it go. That thing you've been holding on to. What she did to you. It has tied you to her."

"Tied me to her?"

Father Scott nodded.

"It's like a door, only this one goes both ways. You can always get back to that moment. And she can always get to you."

Connolly gave him a sullen look.

"She doesn't want to have anything to do with me."

"I know, but that's not the point."

"What is the point?"

"You became like her."

Connolly thought a moment then leaned back. A whisper slipped from his lips. Father Scott pressed him.

"If you can get this resolved, you can move on from being a sober alcoholic to a man who used to have a drinking problem."

Connolly gave him an exasperated look.

"But how?"

"Memories."

"Memories?"

"Memories."

Once again a frown wrinkled Connolly's forehead.

"You mean like go back and rebuild my recollection of what happened?"

"No." Father Scott shook his head. "I mean allow the Holy Spirit to use those memories to show you the rest of what was going on."

Connolly felt confused. Father Scott smiled at him.

"If you let Him, He will take you back through the memories you have and show you some things about your past you haven't known before."

Connolly folded his arms across his chest.

"I've already learned more than I wanted to know."

"I'm not talking about new information. I'm talking about new insight."

Connolly gave a sideways glance.

"And this new insight is supposed to help me?"

"The truth shall set you free."

Connolly sighed.

"I don't know."

Father Scott turned on the pew to face him.

"You have to do this. You have to let Him."

Connolly did not respond. Father Scott laid his hand on Connolly's shoulder.

"Come, Holy Spirit. Use Mike's memories to reveal to him the things he hasn't seen about his past and set him free to love and serve You. Amen."

Connolly glanced over at Father Scott.

"That's it?"

"For now."

"For now?"

"He will show you what you need to know."

"With memories."

"Yes. With memories." Father Scott stood. "When they come, don't be afraid."

"But how?"

Father Scott moved to the end of the pew.

"Just follow Him through the memories. You'll know."

"How will I know if I've seen the right thing?"

"Easy." Father Scott smiled. "You'll be free."

Connolly watched as Father Scott started up the aisle toward the chancel railing.

Thirty-four

By the time Connolly left the church, the morning was already hot and humid. Sweat trickled down his back as he walked down the steps toward the car. He thought of what Father Scott had said. It had been a long trek from the gin bottle and Marisa. Living from drink to drink. Then living from no to no. Most days had been a battle. Often he could only say to himself, "Not today." Maybe it was time. Maybe he could get free from the past, once and for all.

At the sidewalk he slipped off his jacket and opened the car door. He dropped onto the front seat and sat sideways with his feet resting on the pavement outside the car. The past two days had been rough. Going to the office was the last thing he felt like doing.

Across the street an inmate from the jail washed the sidewalk outside the sheriff's office. Connolly stared at him and thought of Dibber. A dead body in Inez Marchand's beach house. Inez. Mary Inez Givens Marchand.

The conversation with Clyde Ramsey drifted through his mind. Earl Givens. Murdered. Shot in the head with a thirty-eight. Connolly perked up. Earl Givens. Murdered. They did an autopsy. Morgan would have a report. He swung his feet inside the car.

When Connolly arrived at Mobile General, he found all the spaces near the building were taken. He parked on the far side of the lot and started toward the emergency room entrance. As he stepped away from the car, his cell phone rang. He took it from his pocket and checked the number on the screen. The call was from Mrs. Gordon.

"You coming to the office anytime this week?"

"What's up?"

"I'm working. What are you doing?"

"I'm at the hospital."

The tone in her voice changed.

"What happened?"

"Nothing. I'm at the morgue. I need to talk to Ted Morgan."

"Oh."

"Any calls?"

"Several."

"Any of them important?"

"They seem to think so."

"I'll call them when I get to the office. I'll be down in a little while."

Connolly switched off the phone and stepped through the emergency room entrance. He crossed the waiting area and moved past the receptionist's desk. A little way down the corridor he turned right and passed through the double doors to the morgue. Ted Morgan was seated at the desk in his office. Morgan glanced up as Connolly appeared.

"You back again?"

"Yeah."

"Did the DA's office call you?"

"About what?"

"Junkins' family will be in tomorrow."

Connolly frowned.

"Junkins?"

"Yeah. That dead guy they thought was somebody ... Stephen Ellis. Turned out to be—"

Connolly interrupted.

"Oh. Yeah. Sorry. A lot's happened since then."

"Yeah?"

"Yeah." Connolly stepped from the corridor into the office and took a seat near the desk. "I was wondering if I could ask you about an old case."

"How old?"

"Fifteen or twenty years."

"Got a name?"

"Givens. Earl Givens."

Morgan frowned.

"Name sounds familiar. One of your clients in prison trying to find a way out?"

Connolly shook his head.

"Givens was the victim. He's dead."

"Oh. Who killed him?"

"Not sure. Nobody wants to talk about it. Clyde Ramsey was the detective. You know him?"

"Ramsey? Yeah. I know him. But he's retired."

"I know."

"I always liked him. You talk to him?"

"Yeah."

"How's he doing? I heard his wife died not too long ago."

"Yeah. Alzheimer's. He's all right. You remember this case?"

"Maybe."

"Got a file on it?"

"File that old would have been closed a long time ago."

"They never solved it. Ramsey says it's still open."

Morgan rolled his chair around to a row of file cabinets along the wall behind the desk.

"Well ..." The latch on the bottom drawer clicked as he pulled it open. "If it's still active, it might be in here. Got a few old ones down here." He leaned over the drawer and thumbed through a row of manila folders. "Earl Givens." He took the file from the drawer. "April 23, 1985." Morgan glanced through the file as he scooted the chair toward the desk. A smile broke across his face. He looked up at Connolly. "I remember this guy." He looked back at the file. "The underwear robbery."

A frown wrinkled Connolly's forehead.

"The what?"

Morgan cackled.

"Somebody killed him and left everything except his underwear."

"What are you talking about?"

"I went to the scene." Morgan laid the file on the desk. "A farm ... no. A nursery. Out near Wilmer or someplace like that. He was lying facedown in this old barn. Fully clothed. Had his wallet in his hip pocket. Some change in a front pocket. Keys. Watch was still on his wrist. Nothing missing. Even found his cap right there by the body. Brought him down here to do the autopsy and found out he didn't have on any underwear." Morgan chuckled. "I called it the underwear robbery."

Connolly scowled.

"You're sick."

Morgan shrugged.

"Clyde didn't think it was funny either."

"Anything interesting besides the missing underwear?"

Morgan picked up the file.

"Not that I recall." He glanced over the pages in the file as he flipped through. "Looks like everything else was normal." A few pages further he paused and scanned down the sheet. "Adrenaline was high. Nothing too special about that." He glanced at Connolly. "Yours would be elevated if someone was pointing a gun at you."

Connolly nodded. That had happened a time or two. Morgan turned to the next page. His eyes brightened. He tapped the file with his finger.

"Now, this was something I was never quite sure of."

"What's that?"

"There were traces of prolactin. And the lab found phenylethylamine."

"What does that mean?"

"He was excited."

"I thought you said that was normal."

"I said the elevated adrenaline was explainable."

"And this isn't?"

Morgan shifted positions in the chair.

"No. It's explainable."

Connolly waited a moment.

"Well?"

Morgan looked uncomfortable.

"Both of these are present during ... arousal."

Connolly felt his forehead wrinkle again.

"Arousal? You mean sexual arousal?"

Morgan nodded.

"Yeah."

"You mean he was having sex when he was shot?"

"Maybe. He might just have been aroused."

"Did you—"

Morgan cut him off.

"Yes. I checked. No traces of semen on his clothes. No traces of—"

"But his underwear was missing."

"Yes."

Connolly gave him a sarcastic look.

"Doesn't that strike you as odd?"

"Not really. You'd be surprised what people wear under their clothes. And what they don't. But that doesn't matter. We would have known it if he'd been engaged in that kind of activity."

"Even back then?"

Morgan gave him a look.

"It was the eighties, Mike. Not the dark ages. We didn't have all the DNA tests we have now, but we could detect the presence of semen on his clothing or skin. Believe me. It isn't that difficult to find."

"Did you check his clothing?"

Morgan glanced at the file and shrugged.

"Doesn't say."

He fell silent as he continued through the file. Then, something caught his eye on the back page. Connolly saw the look.

"What?"

Morgan closed the file.

"Nothing."

Morgan scooted the chair to the file cabinet and opened the drawer. He slipped the file in place and shoved the drawer closed.

Connolly couldn't let it pass.

"I saw the look on your face. What did you see on that last page?"

Morgan rolled the chair back to the desk. He swiveled around to face Connolly and folded his hands in his lap.

"Not everything in that file pertains to him."

"What do you mean?"

"I mean, there are things in our files that aren't open to the public."

"There was someone else present?"

"Maybe."

"Like who?"

"Can't say."

"Can't say, or won't say?"

"Can't."

Connolly thought for a moment.

"A minor."

Connolly stared at him, waiting for an answer. Morgan lifted an eyebrow.

"Can't say."

Connolly persisted.

"Wouldn't be a minor now."

"No. But I can't tell you about him without a judge's okay."

Connolly didn't need to see the file to know what it meant.

"Thanks."

He stood and started toward the door.

Thirty-five

*F*rom Mobile General, Connolly drove to Clyde Ramsey's house on Crenshaw Street. As he reached to ring the doorbell, a gray Buick appeared in the driveway past the end of the porch, backing toward the street. Ramsey sat behind the steering wheel. He glanced at the porch. Their eyes met. The car came to a stop. Ramsey glared at him through the driver's window.

"I told you, I got nothing else to say to you."

Ramsey turned aside. The car started down the driveway. Connolly stepped from the porch.

"I know about the boy."

The car came to a stop. Ramsey glared at him again. Connolly came across the lawn and stood a few feet away.

"You interviewed him."

Ramsey turned in the seat to look out the back window. The car started down the driveway once again. Connolly called to him.

"I know he was there when the old man was killed."

The car rolled a little farther then came to a stop. Ramsey stared through the windshield at Connolly.

"You just won't leave well enough alone, will you?"

Connolly stepped to the driver's door.

"I need to talk about this case. I know he was there. I know you interviewed him. I just want to talk about it."

Ramsey turned off the engine and leaned away from the steering wheel. He sighed. His shoulders slumped. Anger seemed to evaporate. A faraway look came in his eyes. He turned to Connolly.

"He needed killing."

Connolly glanced down at the tops of his shoes, unsure what to say. Ramsey opened the door and stepped from the car.

"Every day." He slammed the car door shut. Connolly jumped. Ramsey's eyes were on fire again. "Every day! That kid went out there after school. Every day." He took a deep breath and lowered his voice. "Do you know what I'm saying?"

Connolly nodded. Ramsey banged his fist against the car door.

"The old man …" Ramsey looked Connolly in the eye. "When he told me …" Ramsey clenched his teeth. He took another deep breath and let out a long, slow sigh. "If the man hadn't been dead already, I would've killed him myself."

"Nobody knew what was going on?"

Ramsey nodded.

"His mother knew."

"Inez Marchand?"

Ramsey nodded again.

"He'd done the same thing to her when she was a kid."

Connolly felt sick to his stomach. Ramsey continued.

"Nick tried to tell her, but she wouldn't listen. Then I think one day she saw something in his clothes …" Ramsey sighed again. "It was …" He glanced away. The tone of his voice dropped. "He needed killing."

"So, Inez killed her own father?"

Ramsey fell silent. Connolly tried again.

"You interviewed Nick?"

Ramsey didn't respond. Connolly tried another question.

"No one was ever prosecuted?"

Ramsey sighed again. The muscles along his jaw flexed.

"A boy's not supposed to be in that position." Ramsey took a deep breath and leaned against the car. "The kid already had the pain of what the old man did to him. If the case went to trial, he'd have to tell a courtroom full of people about it. And he'd have to live all his life knowing …"

Ramsey's voice trailed away. He folded his arms across his chest. Connolly stuck his hands in his pockets.

"So, you convinced them to let it go."

Ramsey's eyes brightened. A grin lifted the corners of his mouth.

"The district attorney and I went back a long way. He didn't have much choice."

Ramsey crossed his feet. Connolly frowned.

"Is this something I want to know about?"

Ramsey shrugged.

"It's been a long time. He's dead now. I don't think this part of the story matters much." Ramsey shifted positions against the car. "The DA back then was a guy named Lem Covan. You remember him?"

"I actually tried a case or two against him before he retired."

Ramsey nodded.

"His daddy was Harley Covan."

Connolly nodded.

"Harley E. Covan. They tell me when he was DA he would just tell the judge which ones were guilty and the judge would send them to prison."

Ramsey chuckled.

"Not far from the truth." He moved his hands to his side. "Harley was a good guy, but he loved to gamble. Poker. Craps. Roulette. Only thing was, he was afraid to fly. He'd get in a boat and ride fifty miles into the Gulf to fish, but he wouldn't get near an airplane. Which meant he'd never go to Las Vegas or any of the usual places where gambling was legal. Instead, he'd drive to some rug joint in Biloxi or Panama City or some place like that."

Connolly shook his head and smiled.

"The DA in an illegal casino."

"Yeah." Ramsey paused for a moment as if thinking then continued. "So good ol' Harley was over in Biloxi one night in the back room at this club having a big time when the sheriff raided the place. New guy. Hadn't been sheriff very long." Ramsey chuckled. "Didn't stay sheriff very long either. Not after he did that raid. They came in, scooped up everybody. Took them off to jail. Seized a truckload of machines, tables, all that."

Connolly finished for him.

"And Harley E. Covan."

Ramsey grinned and nodded.

"And Harley Covan. District attorney from Mobile."

"What happened?"

"I got a call from my brother about three o'clock that morning. He was a deputy over there. Told me they had Harley in one of their interview rooms. Said they'd let him go and forget the whole thing if I came and got him."

Connolly nodded. Ramsey's eyes sparkled.

"I went over and got him. Far as I know, no one ever found out about it." He gave Connolly a smile. "Except me and Harley."

"Did you have to explain all this to Lem?"

"About the raid?"

"No. About the kid. Nick. And not prosecuting his ..."

Ramsey shook his head.

"I just told him to tell Harley I was cashing in my Edgewater chit."

"Edgewater?"

"That was the name of the place. The Edgewater Club."

Connolly grinned.

"And they decided not to prosecute Inez."

Ramsey looked down at the grass.

"Well, the case ... the case just ... faded away."

Connolly nodded.

"Well, it might be on its way back."

Ramsey looked up. His eyes were alert.

"What do you mean?"

"You remember I told you I was working on a murder case?"

"Not this one."

"No. Her son."

A frown wrinkled Ramsey's forehead.

"Nick? Nobody said he was charged with anything. I just saw him the other day. He didn't say anything about—"

"Not Nick. She had another son."

"Another one?"

"Before Nick. She went off to Atlanta. Met a guy. Got pregnant. Had a little boy."

Ramsey looked away. Connolly continued.

"This guy in Atlanta, the one she met, was a writer. It was the sixties. She got all swept up in it. Got pregnant. Not long after that, he was killed in a plane crash. She left the baby with some friends and moved back to Mobile."

"I thought you were defending somebody over that guy they found in her beach house."

Connolly nodded.

"I am."

Ramsey looked away again.

"I don't know anything about all that."

"When's the last time you saw Nick Marchand?"

"Uhh ... it's been awhile."

"When?"

"I can't remember."

"You just said you saw him—"

Ramsey cut him off with an angry retort.

"I said I can't remember." He opened the car door and got in behind the steering wheel. "I have to go. I was on my way to the bank." He started the engine. "I'll see you later."

Ramsey backed the car down the driveway. The car disappeared up the street. Connolly walked toward the Chrysler.

Thirty-six

Connolly stood by the Chrysler and stared down the street long after Ramsey's car disappeared from sight. In the distance he could see the corner of the front porch at his mother's house, two blocks away. Part of him wanted to drive by one more time. Part of him wanted to run away. He checked his watch. It was after noon. He needed to get to the office. He got in the car, turned it around in Ramsey's driveway, and headed downtown.

A parking place was open on Dauphin Street near the office building. He parked the car and rode the elevator to the third floor. Mrs. Gordon came from the copier room as he started down the hall.

"You finally decide to come to work?"

Connolly ignored her question.

"Where are those messages?"

"On your desk."

He brushed past her and continued down the hall. She called to him as he walked away.

"What's got you so aggravated?"

He stopped and turned to face her.

"There are maybe three or four people who could bust this case wide open. And not one of them wants to talk about what they know."

"Dibber?"

"Yeah."

Mrs. Gordon dismissed him with the wave of a hand.

"Relax. Carl sent us another payment on the fee. At least you're making money."

Connolly turned away, shaking his head.

"They can't pay enough for this one."

He hung his jacket on the coatrack and took a seat behind the desk. A stack of phone messages awaited him. He picked them up and sorted through them. As he finished his third call, Mrs. Gordon appeared at the door.

"There's a call for you on line two. Somebody named Tiffany. I think it's that girl you saw a few days ago."

Connolly picked up the phone. Tiffany wasted little time with formalities.

"Tinker wants to see you. Come to The Pig tonight around eight."

"Is he gonna show this time?"

"Come around eight."

The line clicked and went dead. Connolly hung up the phone. Mrs. Gordon was still in the doorway. She gave him a puzzled look.

"What was that about?"

"One of her friends wants to talk."

"And you're going to meet them?"

"Yeah."

Mrs. Gordon turned away.

"Maybe it wouldn't be so bad to have Hollis around after all."

Connolly leaned back in his chair and rested his head against the wall. He heard Mrs. Gordon scoot her chair across the floor. Then the click of her fingers on the keyboard. And then he was asleep.

Late that afternoon Connolly walked to the courthouse and made his way to the district attorney's office on the fourth floor. Juanita looked over the counter at him as he stepped from the elevator.

"Yes?"

"I was wondering if Gayle Underwood could see me."

Juanita turned away.

"I'll check."

Connolly backed away from her desk. In a moment she called to him.

"Ms. Underwood will be right—"

Before Juanita could hang up the phone, the door near her desk opened. Gayle Underwood appeared.

"Mr. Connolly. Come on back."

She held the door for him then led him down the hall.

"You caught me at a good time. Judge Cahill had something going on this afternoon. We didn't have a docket." She guided him to a small conference room a little way down the hall. "What's on your mind?"

"I hear the Junkins family are coming to town."

"Yes. Did we call you about that?"

"I don't know. Haven't gotten that far in my phone messages. Ted Morgan told me."

"We're meeting with them tomorrow around two. I think Judge Cahill will be upset if you don't meet with us."

Connolly chuckled.

"Judge Cahill wants you to think he'll be mad."

Gayle frowned.

"I don't like it when he shouts." She pointed to a chair. "Have a seat."

Connolly sat across from her at the table.

"I was in Cahill's court one day. He had a man in there on a domestic abuse case. The guy had gotten into a fight with his wife. Hit her. Cahill doesn't like those cases at all. The guy didn't really understand what was going on. He made some offhand remark, and Cahill exploded. Gave him sixty days in jail. Huge fine. Walter cuffed him and took him out. As soon as they were gone, Cahill chuckled and called the next case."

"He's out of control."

Connolly shook his head.

"Not really. I asked him if he was going to leave the guy in there for sixty days. He laughed and said he'd give him a week to cool off and see what they could work out." Connolly chuckled. "He usually gets to the right result."

"You seem to get along with him."

"I like him. He tells me what he thinks. I tell him back."

Gayle nodded.

"What could I do for you?"

"I was wondering if we could talk about a case. An old case."

She looked puzzled.

"What case is that?"

"Earl Givens."

"You represent Mr. Givens?"

"Mr. Givens is dead."

Gayle looked confused.

"What kind of case is this?"

"Murder."

"Murder?"

"Yeah."

"Well, if he's dead, isn't the case over?"

"He was the victim."

"Oh. I don't think I can talk about someone else's case."

Connolly laced his fingers together and rested them on the table.

"This case was never solved."

"We have a file on it?"

"I'm sure you do."

"Earl Givens?"

"Earl Givens." Connolly grinned. "You know his daughter."

"I do?"

"Yes."

"Who is she?"

"Inez Marchand."

Gayle's eyes opened wide.

"Interesting. And you think the two cases are related."

"Maybe. Think you could find the file?"

"I don't know. Might take awhile. They keep some old files up here, but to tell you the truth, I'm not sure where they are."

"Think you could call me and let me know what you find?"

She shrugged.

"Maybe."

"I can go to Judge Cahill for it."

"Think he'll give it to you?"

"I'm entitled to any information that tends to exonerate my client. He'll make you look for it."

"And you think this old case will exonerate your client?"

"I think it might. Wouldn't look too bad for you either. If you solved it."

"Is this just a hunch, or do you have something specific in mind?"

Connolly stood.

"Take a look at it, and let me know what you think."

Gayle stood. Connolly stepped into the hall. She walked with him as far as her office.

"Tell me something." There was a twinkle in her eye. "What if Henry decided to charge your client with the old case?"

Connolly chuckled.

"Not even Henry's that crazy."

She glanced at him with a playful smile.

"Really?"

Connolly grinned.

"Givens was killed in 1985. My client would have been ... about fifteen at the time."

They reached the door to Gayle's office. She paused there.

"I'm not so sure Henry would see that as a problem."

Connolly laughed.

"You're learning fast, Ms. Underwood."

He stepped to the end of the hall and walked out to the lobby.

Thirty-seven

*J*uanita was gathering her purse to leave when Connolly stepped from the hallway to the lobby. He avoided eye contact with her and walked to the elevator. As he waited, Henry McNamara appeared beside him.

"Mr. Connolly, what brings you down here?"

"Just checking on a few details. You leaving for the day?"

"It's after five."

Connolly glanced at his watch. He didn't realize it was that late. McNamara folded his hands behind his back.

"How's Mr. Landry?"

"Fine."

"There's a tropical storm out in the Gulf." A cheesy grin spread across McNamara's face. "Too bad he won't be out in time to loot some more houses when it makes landfall."

Connolly smiled.

"That depends on how fast Cahill can get us a hearing."

McNamara chuckled.

"In your dreams."

"We'll see."

The elevator doors opened. They stepped inside. McNamara pressed the button for the lobby.

"You don't really think you can get him off, do you?"

Connolly stared ahead.

"I've got as much in my favor as you have in yours. I'd say that's enough to negate probable cause right there."

"Not in this county."

"Maybe."

"Not in this state."

"You may be right."

The elevator reached the lobby. Connolly stepped out and turned toward the exit. McNamara went in the opposite direction.

From the courthouse Connolly drove to Ann Street. As he rounded the corner, he was greeted by the black and white For Sale sign in the yard at Barbara's house. He brought the Chrysler to a stop and got out. Anger rose inside. He wanted to pull the sign up and fling it across the street. He wanted to shout and cuss and scream. Instead, he pushed the car door closed and walked up the walkway to the front door.

Barbara answered the doorbell with a smile.

"You coming in this time, or just standing on my porch?"

The anger he'd felt before melted away. A grin broke across his face.

"Want to have dinner?"

"Sure." She glanced at the jeans and shirt she was wearing. "I need to shower and change."

Connolly shook his head.

"Not for this place."

Barbara gave him a playful look.

"Where'd you have in mind?"

"The Whistlin' Pig."

The playfulness left her face. Her eyebrows curled in toward each other in a frown.

"The Whistlin' Pig?"

Connolly shrugged.

"Seemed like a good night for barbeque."

"I haven't been to that place in—"

Connolly interrupted her.

"Never?"

"Actually, I think I went there once."

"Yeah?"

"Yeah." She gave him a sly grin. "Bobby Patrino took me there."

The smile left Connolly's face. He felt his body tense.

"Bobby Patrino?"

"Yeah."

"When did you go out with Bobby Patrino?"

"In high school."

Connolly relaxed.

"You want to go? With me?"

"Sure." She closed the door and stepped outside. "Ready?"

Connolly glanced at his watch.

"We don't have to be there till eight."

"You have a reservation at The Pig?"

"No. I have to meet somebody there."

Barbara's smile lost some of its luster.

"I thought you wanted to see me."

"I do. I do. It's just, I had to go there anyway, and I thought ..."

She took his arm.

"Relax. I'm not upset."

They walked across the porch and down the steps. Halfway to the car Connolly stopped.

"I'm sorry. If you don't want to go ..."

"Don't be silly. I never should have said anything. I'd love to go."

She tugged on his arm. He resisted.

"No. Really. I didn't mean to ..."

She nudged him in the side.

"Mike. Get in the car."

They walked past the For Sale sign without any mention of it. Connolly opened the car door for her. When she was seated, he moved around the rear bumper and got in behind the steering wheel. She caught his eye with a wry smile.

"So, what do we do till eight?"

Connolly shrugged.

"We could cruise around town."

Her smile grew more playful.

"And then what?"

"Park in the shadows some place."

She leaned toward him.

"We wouldn't have to go to some side street for that."

Connolly started the car.

"Let's go to a movie."

"A movie?"

"Yeah. It's six now. We could find one at the Roxy. It'll get out around eight."

Barbara laughed.

"The Roxy's closed."

"Closed?"

"Been closed for years."

"Well, we could ..."

"Let's go to your place."

"My place?"

"Yes. Your place."

"You sure?"

"Sure I'm sure. Let's go to your place."

"Okay."

Tuttle Street was only a few blocks away. They reached the guesthouse in less than five minutes. He ushered her inside and closed the door.

"You want something to drink?"

She wandered toward the living room.

"What do you have?"

He opened the refrigerator and looked inside.

"Well ... there's water, some soured milk. A little orange juice that's been in here ..." He opened the carton and smelled inside. "Awhile. There's Coca-Cola ... and a few bottles of ginger ale." He took a bottle from the shelf. "I'm having ginger ale."

Barbara called to him from the living room.

"Okay. I'll have some too."

Connolly filled two glasses and brought them to the living room. Barbara stood near the window across the room. He handed her a glass and gestured toward the sofa.

"Let's sit over here."

Barbara took a sip from the glass. A puzzled look came over her face. She held the glass at arm's length and gave it a look.

"What is this?"

"Ginger ale."

"I know. I mean, what kind is it? This is better than I remember ginger ale being."

"Boylan."

"Boylan? Never heard of it."

"Bottled in New Jersey."

Connolly took a seat on the sofa. Barbara sat next to him.

"How'd you hear about it?"

"Buie Hayford."

"Buie?"

"Yeah."

"What's Buie doing now? I haven't heard about him in years."

"Right now I imagine he's doing his best to explain his way out of some criminal charges."

"Oh?"

Connolly took a sip.

"He was up to his neck in that stuff with Raisa and those women."

She turned to look at him.

"He was behind that?"

"He and Perry Braxton."

She nodded.

"I think I knew that and tried to forget about it."

"Not a bad idea."

Barbara took another sip of ginger ale.

"How's Dibber?"

"Dibber's looking a little better."

"Think he can get out of it?"

"Maybe." Connolly shifted positions on the sofa. "Are you really going to sell the house?"

Barbara sighed.

"I was hoping we could get through the evening without talking about that."

"Are you?"

"A young couple looked at it today."

"Were they interested?"

"I think so."

"I don't like it."

"You don't have to like it. It's my house."

"I know it's your house, but it's my memories."

She gave him a kind look.

"Is that what you're running from?"

"What?"

"Memories."

"I'm not running from anything."

"Oh? Then why won't you come past the porch?"

"If I go in there, I might not come out."

She grinned.

"That would be so bad? Trapped in the house with me?"

"Not with you. With who I used to be."

"I don't think it works that way."

"I don't want to find out."

"Well, I know it's hard, but I think it's the right thing to do."

Connolly sighed.

"Maybe so."

They sipped their drinks in silence. A moment or two passed. Connolly glanced at her.

"There's something else I wanted to ask you about."

"Okay."

"I had to go over on Crenshaw Street to see a man about Dibber's case. Retired detective."

Barbara's face turned serious.

"And you drove by the house."

"I stopped."

She looked surprised.

"You stopped?"

"Yeah."

"Anybody living there?"

Connolly nodded. He took a sip of ginger ale.

"The car was in the garage."

"The car? Your father's car?"

"Yes."

"You're kidding."

"My baseball glove. Rick's old bicycle. Just like we left it."

"Who's living there?"

Tears welled up in Connolly's eyes. He took another sip. Barbara's face softened. Her voice became a whisper.

"Your mother was there."

Connolly nodded. Tears rolled down his cheeks. Barbara set the glass on the coffee table and moved closer to him.

"I had no idea she was alive."

"Good." He took a deep breath. "I thought I was losing my mind."

"Did you tell Uncle Guy?"

Connolly nodded again.

"I saw him last night. Spent the night down there."

"What did he say?"

"He wasn't surprised. Said he'd driven by there a time or two. Thought she might be there."

"Has he talked to her?"

"I don't think so."

"Did you?"

"I tried."

"What did she say?"

"She said I couldn't be her son. She never had any children."

Barbara leaned against him. She gripped his thigh with her hand and gave him a squeeze.

"You're sure it was her?"

Connolly set the glass of ginger ale on the end table by the answering machine. He slipped his arm around her shoulder and pulled her closer. Her hair brushed against his cheek. The smell brought back memories. Good memories. He breathed it in and rubbed his face against her. She pulled away and turned to look at him.

"What are you doing?"

"Smelling your hair."

"Smelling my hair?"

"Yes."

"Why?"

"Because I like the way it smells."

"I thought we were talking."

"We are. I was just smelling your hair."

She stared at him a moment.

"You're strange sometimes, you know."

"You've told me that before."

She smiled and leaned against him once more. Her voice became serious again.

"What are you going to do?"

"I don't know. I'm thinking about going back over there."

"Want me to go with you?"

"Not yet."

Thirty-eight

A little before eight, Connolly and Barbara left the guesthouse and drove to the Loop. The Whistlin' Pig was located on Holcombe Avenue, three blocks off Government Street in a 1940s-era restaurant building. Made of poured concrete, the walls had curves with rounded glass blocks in place of the corners. The exterior was painted gray with molded aluminum trim around the roof that gave it the look and feel of a diner, which it once had been. Above the building was a sculpted pig about the size of a Volkswagen. Painted pink, it had a curly tail that spun lazily around. Its mouth was puckered as if it were whistling, and smoke drifted from its nostrils. Higher still, above the pig, neon letters spelled out the name. The Whistlin' Pig.

Connolly turned the Chrysler into the parking lot and brought it to a stop in a space alongside the building. He came around the car and opened the passenger door for Barbara. She glanced around and took a deep breath.

"Smells like a barbeque place."

Connolly grinned. Together they walked to the door and went inside.

A counter with stools ran the length of the wall opposite the door. Booths lined the front wall by the windows. Tables were arranged in the space between. Connolly guided Barbara to an open booth. They sat across from each other. He took a menu from behind the napkin holder and handed it to her.

"Need one of these?"

"Might be interesting reading."

In a few minutes Tiffany appeared. She glanced at Barbara then turned to Connolly.

"Who's she?"

"Don't worry about it. Is he here?"

"Yeah. But we thought you was coming by yourself."

Connolly scanned the room.

"Is he coming to the table?"

"No."

She gestured over her shoulder.

"He's in the bathroom."

Connolly nodded.

"Okay. Let me know when he comes out."

"He wants you to come in there."

Connolly gave her a look.

"He wants to meet in the bathroom?"

"I put a sign on the door. People'll think it's out of order. He just went in there when you drove up."

Connolly glanced at Barbara.

"I'll be back."

He slid from the booth and crossed the room to a hallway near the end of the counter. The men's room was on the left. A sheet of notebook paper was taped to the door with the words Out Of Order scrawled across it. Connolly pushed the door open and stepped inside.

Three wooden toilet stalls lined the wall to the right. Doors on the stalls were closed, but from what he could see beneath them, there was no one in the room. He walked to the sink and turned on the water to wash his hands. Behind him he heard a toilet seat rattle.

Connolly turned off the water.

"Tinker? You in there?"

A voice spoke to him from the stall on the end.

"Yeah."

Connolly turned around and leaned against the sink.

"Tiffany said you wanted to talk."

"Yeah."

"Come on out."

"No way. We'll do our talking like this."

"Be easier if I could see you."

"No, sir. Better for both of us if you don't."

"Well ... okay. What'd you want to talk about?"

"You was out at the nursery yesterday. Asking a bunch of questions."

"Yes."

"Tiff says they got Dibber charged with killin' that man."

"You know something about it?"

"I know a lot about it."

"Where's Stephen Ellis?"

"You was real close to him when you was out there."

"He's alive?"

"Noooo. That boy's dead and gone. But you was real close to him."

"Come on out. Let's do this face-to-face."

"I told you, I ain't doin' it like that. Look, here's the deal. Nick's got this meth lab goin'. He's in with a bunch of guys in a big way. That guy you're looking for showed up. Nick was worried he was gonna blow everything. And then his friend started mouthin' off. He got on everybody's nerves. So, after they done Stephen ..." Tinker paused. Connolly heard him take a drag on a cigarette, then he continued. "After they done him, Tony did the other guy too."

"Why'd they leave him in the beach house?"

"Wasn't goin' to. But some of them neighbors came around while we ... while they was loading up and everybody got scared. So, they just left him in there. Storm was comin'. Nick figured the whole place'd get washed away. Even if it didn't, he didn't think nobody'd be able to pin it on him."

"Even though it was his mother's beach house."

"Nick never was too bright when it come to stuff like that."

"Nick shot Stephen?"

Just then the door to the hallway opened. A man appeared. Connolly jerked around, startled. The man stepped inside.

"Sign says this thing's out of order. Does it work?"

"Uhhh ... I don't know about the toilets. I just washed my hands." Connolly heard Tinker latch the door to the stall. He shuffled his feet to cover the sound and moved around the man. "I guess if it doesn't work, you'll find out pretty soon."

The man chuckled.

"I reckon so."

Connolly opened the bathroom door and stepped into the hallway. He walked to the dining room and slid into the booth across from Barbara. Two glasses of iced tea sat on the table. He picked up the one on his side and took a drink.

Barbara took a sip from her glass and smiled at him.

"Everything okay?"

"I guess."

"Was he in there?"

"Someone was."

"Tell you anything?"

"A little. We got interrupted."

"I saw that guy go in there. Trouble?"

"I don't know."

Connolly watched the hall. In a few minutes the man appeared near the counter. He crossed the room to a table and took a seat. A woman and two children sat with him.

Connolly took another sip of tea.

"I think it's all right."

"You're going back in there?"

"No."

A waitress appeared at their table, an older woman with jet-black hair and heavy makeup.

"Ready to order?"

Connolly scanned the room.

"Where's Tiffany?"

"She's not working tonight. I saw her in here awhile ago, but this is her night off. What'll you have?"

Connolly looked at Barbara.

"Pork sandwich."

The waitress scribbled the order on her pad and nodded to Connolly.

"And you?"

"I'll have the same."

The waitress stepped away. Connolly glanced out the window. Across the parking lot he saw the yellow Caprice he'd seen before. A woman sat in front on the passenger side, but Connolly couldn't see her face. The car drove from the lot and turned left. In the distance he saw the taillights glow red as the car slowed then made a right at the next corner.

Thirty-nine

After dinner Connolly and Barbara walked outside to the Chrysler. He opened the passenger door for her. She glanced at him as she slid onto the seat.

"What do you think?"

Connolly was puzzled.

"About what?"

There was a twinkle in her eye.

"Think she's home?"

One side of his mouth turned down in a grimace. He closed the door and walked around the rear bumper to the driver's side. The car keys jingled in his hand as he reached for the door and pulled it open. He dropped onto the seat with a heavy sigh.

Barbara glanced at him.

"We could ride by and see."

Connolly put the key in the ignition and turned it. The car came to life. He laid his arm along the top of the seat and twisted around to look out the rear window. A pickup truck turned from the street into the parking lot behind them. Connolly waited for it to pass then backed the Chrysler away from the building.

Barbara gestured with a nod.

"Let's go see."

Connolly turned to face forward.

"Not tonight."

A block beyond the Loop, Connolly cut across to Airline Highway. In the glow of the lights from the dash he saw Barbara smile. A little way down Airline, he turned onto Crenshaw. Two blocks past Clyde Ramsey's house, Connolly slowed the car.

"Okay. You wanted to see it." He pointed to the house in the middle of the block. "There it is."

Shadows from the streetlight played across the lawn then disappeared only to appear again on the side of the house. Barbara leaned close to Connolly and looked out the car window.

"Oh, Mike," she whispered. She stared past him at the house. "Are you sure someone lives there?"

Connolly nodded. Barbara turned to look at him.

"And you're sure she's your mother?"

"Yeah." He mumbled. "It's her."

Through the front window by the porch Connolly saw a light in a room at the back of the house.

"There." He pointed. His voice was tense and quick. "See that light?"

Barbara turned to look.

"Where?"

"In the—"

"I see it." She sounded surprised at first, then her voice dropped off. "Or is that the light from the neighbor's—"

Inside, someone moved past the light. A moment later it went out. Barbara leaned back to her side of the front seat. She propped her elbow on the armrest. Connolly took his foot from the brake. The car started forward. He glanced at her.

"What?"

She cocked her head toward him with a look that said he was supposed to know what she was thinking. He threw up his hands.

"What?"

"You can't let her live like that."

He gave her an angry frown.

"What do you mean?"

"She's your mother, Mike."

"She didn't worry about me and Rick."

"Mike ..."

His voice grew louder.

"We ate out of a can for two days."

"But ..."

Connolly slapped the steering wheel.

"No! I listened to Rick cry himself to sleep. I had to ..." His voice broke. He swallowed and tried again. "I had to get him up for school." Tears in his eyes made it difficult to see. "We ate sardines for breakfast." Tears rolled down his cheeks. "You're supposed to have pancakes or eggs or something." His voice fell to a whisper. "We had sardines and pimento cheese. On stale Graham crackers." He wiped his eyes with his hands and took a deep breath. His voice became resolute. "She didn't care about us. Why should I care about her?"

By then the car was creeping through the intersection at the next block. Barbara slid across the seat next to him and put her arm across his shoulder.

"Pull over."

Connolly shook his head. Barbara insisted.

"Pull over." She pointed with her free hand. "There's a spot. Pull over. Right here."

Connolly guided the car to the curb and took it out of gear. He leaned his head back against the seat. Tears rolled down his cheeks. Barbara squeezed him closer and ran her other arm around his waist.

"You can't keep hating her." She rested her head on his chest. "Whatever she did, it wasn't because of you."

"It was us she went off and left."

"That was because of who she was. Not because of you. Not Rick. I never met her, but I'm sure she was that way before you came along."

Connolly sighed.

"Came along is right."

Barbara lifted her head.

"What do you mean?"

"John Connolly isn't my father."

Her eyes were wide.

"What are you talking about? Who told you that?"

"Guy."

"Guy? When?"

"Yesterday. Day before. Whatever day it was I was down there."

"Well, who did he say is your father?"

Connolly gave a heavy sigh.

"My father was a surveyor for the railroad. My mother met him at a club. Had an affair with him. Not long after she married my ... whatever he was." He turned to look at her. "What do you call the man you've thought of as your father all your life, and then after all these years you find out you aren't his son?"

Barbara smiled.

"How about 'Daddy'?" She stared at him a moment. "How'd Uncle Guy know all this?"

Connolly slid lower in the seat.

"Daddy found out about the affair and left. Mama was pregnant with me. She moved in with Uncle Guy. Daddy came back right before I was born."

"He came back."

"Yeah."

"He was a good father."

"Yeah." Connolly took a breath. "He was a good father."

They sat there awhile. Neither one said a word. Finally, Connolly glanced at Barbara.

"We stopped on a dark street after all."

She smiled.

"I know. But I didn't get a kiss."

"We can fix that."

He pulled her close and pressed his lips to hers.

Forty

At two the following afternoon Connolly returned to the district attorney's office. Juanita stared at him from behind her desk. Connolly smiled at her as he approached.

"I'm here to see Gayle Underwood. We're supposed to meet with a family."

Juanita mumbled something as she turned away to dial Gayle's number. Connolly couldn't understand what she said.

"Excuse me?"

"I said you're down here enough they need to give you an office."

Connolly nodded and smiled, but the look on her face was unsettling. He moved away and wandered to the far side of the room. In a moment the door near Juanita's desk opened. Gayle appeared. She caught Connolly's eye.

"Come on back. They're in the conference room on the corner."

He followed her down the hall to the same room where they'd met with Billy Ellis a week earlier.

From the hall Connolly could see a man and woman standing with their backs to him, facing the wall opposite the door. The man was dressed in a dark-gray business suit. The woman wore a navy blue dress and two-inch pumps. They turned toward the door as Gayle and Connolly entered. Gayle stepped to one side.

"Mr. and Mrs. Junkins, this is Mike Connolly."

The man stepped forward.

"Hadley Junkins." He shook hands with Connolly. "This is my wife, Flora."

Flora nodded. Connolly gave her a tight-lipped smile.

"I'm sorry we have to meet under these circumstances."

Flora's eyes were cold.

"You represent the man who killed our son?"

Connolly nodded.

"I represent the man they've accused of it. Yes, ma'am."

Gayle gestured toward the chairs around the table.

"Why don't we have a seat." She pulled a chair away from the table and offered it to Flora. "Have a seat."

Hadley and Flora sat beside each other on the far side of the table. Connolly sat opposite them, his back to the door. Gayle moved to the end of the table.

"Henry will be here in a minute."

She pulled out a chair and took a seat. Flora looked at Connolly.

"How do you do it?"

"Do what?"

"How do you defend those ... people?"

The look in her eye made him feel self-conscious.

"Well ... for one thing, there's usually a question as to whether the person the police arrested actually committed the crime they've charged him with."

"You think that's the case with our son?"

"There's little doubt the man in the beach house was murdered. But the only connection between him and my client is that they were both supposedly in the beach house."

"And that isn't enough?"

"Not to prove murder."

Hadley cleared his throat.

"They don't have the weapon?"

"No."

"But they have prints."

"Yes. They have prints. But that only shows my client was present. He and several others."

Henry McNamara entered the room.

"I see you all are getting acquainted." He pulled a chair from the end of the table to Connolly's right and took a seat. He glanced at Connolly. "Don't let me stop you."

Connolly nodded. He turned to Hadley.

"Mr. Junkins, where do you live?"

"Savannah."

Connolly pointed to Flora.

"The two of you are married?"

Flora sighed and leaned away. Hadley nodded.

"Yes."

"How many children do you have?"

"Three."

"One of them is named Bobby?"

"Yes."

"Do you know a man named Stephen Ellis?"

"Yes."

"How do you know him?"

"He and my son are friends." Hadley folded his hands together and rested them on the table. "They met in college."

"Met in school. Remained friends after school?"

"Yes."

"When's the last time you saw your son?"

"About three weeks ago."

"Where was he?"

"At our house. In Savannah."

Connolly scribbled a note to himself.

"Was he living with you?"

"No. He lives in Atlanta."

"When's the last time you saw Stephen Ellis?"

Hadley hesitated.

"I ... I don't know ..."

Flora answered for him.

"It's been years."

Connolly turned to her.

"He didn't come around regularly?"

"He was our son's friend. Not ours."

Hadley spoke up.

"He and Bobby got into some trouble in college. We tried to tell Bobby to stay away from him."

Connolly nodded.

"That was some time ago?"

"Yes. Fifteen or twenty years ago, I suppose."

"Did they get into any trouble since then?"

"Not that I'm aware of."

"What does your son do in Atlanta?"

"He works for a freight forwarding company. They have a warehouse near the airport."

"Did he come down here with Stephen?"

Hadley glanced away.

"I don't think I can say."

Flora spoke up.

"Yes."

Connolly turned to her.

"He did?"

"Yes."

"How do you know?"

"He told me."

"Stephen told you?"

"No. Bobby told me."

"Did he say why they were coming?"

Flora rolled her eyes.

"Something about Stephen wanting to find his mother."

"He knew who she was?"

"I guess so. You could never tell. Stephen always had this story—"

Hadley interrupted.

"He said his father was a writer. Said they made one of his books into a movie."

"When did he tell you this?"

Flora spoke up.

"Long as we've known him. Talked about it all the time. I think he told us about it the first time we met him." She glanced at Hadley. "You remember that?"

"Yes." Hadley nodded. "At the Pitty Patt, in Quitman."

Connolly smiled.

"The Pitty Patt?"

"A restaurant," Hadley replied. "Cafe, actually. Just outside Valdosta. We all went there to eat."

"All of you?"

"Yes. Bobby, Flora. Me. Billy and ..."

Flora rolled her eyes again.

"Frieda."

Hadley smiled.

"Yes. Frieda."

Connolly looked at Hadley.

"Frieda and Billy were both there?"

"Yes."

"And you're sure Stephen told you about his father. His biological father. With both of them present?"

"Yes."

"Any idea how he found out? About his father?"

Flora cocked her head to one side.

"Is it true?"

Connolly nodded.

"I think so. Do you know when Stephen and Bobby came down here?"

Hadley answered.

"About three weeks ago."

"I thought you didn't know."

"I didn't say I didn't know. I said I couldn't answer." Hadley sighed. "I guess it doesn't matter now. Bobby was in Savannah for the weekend and told us they were going. They left that following Monday."

"Bobby was in Savannah the weekend before he left to come down here?"

"Yes."

"Was Stephen with him?"

"No."

"But they were traveling together? To come down here."

"Yes."

"Did Bobby call you at any time during the trip?"

"No."

Flora interrupted.

"Yes."

Hadley looked surprised.

"He did?"

"Yes."

Hadley frowned.

"You didn't tell me."

Flora shrugged him off.

"I forgot." She looked at Connolly. "They were supposed to be down here a week. Bobby should have been back by the following Sunday. Took the week off. Supposed to be back at work that next Monday. He called me Saturday afternoon. Just to check in. Said they found her. Stephen's mother. And they were staying over." She gave a dismissive roll of her hand. "Something about the beach being nice and Stephen wanted a few more days with her."

"Was that it?"

"I think so."

"So, Stephen was just trying to find his mother. His biological mother?"

"Yes."

Hadley interrupted.

"No."

Flora looked at him. Connolly glanced in his direction.

"No?"

Hadley took a deep breath.

"There was a little more to it."

"Okay."

Hadley took another deep breath.

"The woman who raised him. I can't ... Frieda. She told him about the books and the movie and his father. The man he knew as his father ... Mr. Ellis—"

Flora interrupted.

"Billy."

Hadley nodded.

"Yes. Billy. He didn't want Stephen to know the story. But she told him. And, before she died ... She died ... last year some time. Anyway, before she died, she started talking to Stephen about the father's estate. Told him about all the money he made. Told him he was entitled to part of the guy's estate. The father. The biological father. The writer."

"Frieda told Stephen that he was entitled to his father's estate?"

"Yes."

"Where did that estate go? Who has it?"

"From what I understand, most of it went to the man's wife."

"The writer's wife?"

"Yes. But his mother—Stephen's biological mother—received a percentage. A small percentage. I think she received this while he was still alive."

"While Stephen—"

"No. The writer. While he was still alive. I think he gave her an interest in the royalties from his works. Sounded like a way to give her some support. I don't know."

Deep furrows wrinkled Connolly's forehead.

"How do you know this?"

"He asked me about it." Hadley glanced around the table. "I'm a lawyer. Stephen called me at my office. Asked me if there was any way to get part of it."

"And you told him …"

"Whatever I said to him would be protected by attorney-client privilege." Hadley sighed. "But it would be my opinion that under Georgia law he could probably find a way to have his claim heard in court."

Connolly leaned away from the table. He stroked his chin with his fingers and smiled. A few pieces of the puzzle slid into place.

Forty-one

*L*ater that afternoon Connolly drove to Mobile General and once again made his way to Morgan's office. Brian Hodges stood alone in the corridor. Connolly leaned through the doorway and glanced inside. Gayle Underwood sat across from Morgan's desk with Hadley and Flora Junkins. Connolly turned to Hodges.

"Is Ted around?"

Hodges shrugged.

"Haven't seen him."

Connolly started toward the autopsy suite.

"I'll see if I can find him."

Just then Morgan came around the corner.

"I'm right here. Everybody ready?"

Connolly nodded.

"I think so."

Morgan stepped through the doorway to his office. Connolly stood in the hall near Hodges. Morgan glanced at Hadley and Flora.

"Mr. and Mrs. Junkins?"

"Yes."

"I'm Ted Morgan. The county coroner." He acknowledged Flora with a nod and shook Hadley's hand. "Are you ready for this?"

Hadley rose from his chair.

"If we must."

Flora didn't budge. Her eyes filled with tears. Connolly caught Morgan's attention with a nod.

"You don't need her, do you?"

Morgan shook his head.

"No. Mrs. Junkins, you can wait here if you like."

Morgan turned toward the door. Hadley followed him out.

Gayle came behind. Hodges and Connolly lingered in back. As they started up the hallway, Flora bolted from the office.

"Wait."

Connolly and Hodges stepped aside to let her pass. She caught up with Hadley and took his arm. Gayle moved next to Connolly.

"See me before you leave."

"Sure."

Morgan led them to the cooler at the end of the hall where the bodies were kept. As before he checked his notes, opened one of the doors, and pulled out a corpse. He lifted the sheet from the face. Hadley leaned over and took a look. He gasped and covered his mouth with his hand. Flora peeked from behind his shoulder. Their reaction left little doubt the body was that of Bobby Junkins.

Morgan took Hadley and Flora back to his office. Gayle went with them. Hodges and Connolly walked outside and stood in the shade of the building near the entrance to the emergency room. Connolly slipped off his jacket and leaned against a post that held the awning near the door.

"I talked to Edwin Marchand."

Hodges jerked his head around, a puzzled look on his face.

"Who?"

"Edwin Marchand."

Hodges nodded.

"Not much of a talker, is he?"

"Had a lot to say about one subject."

"What was that?"

"His fingerprints."

A cold look came over Hodges.

"That client of yours is guilty, and you know it. He needs to take a plea and put an end to all this." He gestured over his shoulder. "You saw those people in there. Haven't you caused enough trouble?"

"Edwin's rather adamant about those prints."

A frown wrinkled Hodges' forehead.

"What do you mean?"

"Says he's never been in that beach house."

"And you believe him?"

"Says he's never even seen it. Where'd those prints come from?"

"FBI."

"No. I mean, how did the FBI come to have his prints on file?"

"I don't know. Military records, I imagine."

"Edwin says he's never been in the military."

Hodges shrugged.

"I don't know."

Gayle came from the building. Connolly continued talking as she approached.

"Says he's never been fingerprinted by anybody."

Hodges' face was flush.

"Look, all I know is we lifted some prints. Sent them to the FBI. They came back with a match."

Connolly glanced up. Gayle was staring at Hodges. She had a quizzical look.

"Whose prints?"

Hodges turned away.

"I gotta go."

He took a step toward the sidewalk. Connolly answered the question.

"Edwin Marchand's."

Gayle frowned at Connolly.

"Edwin Marchand's?"

Hodges stopped a few steps away. Connolly gestured toward him with a nod.

"He says the FBI matched a set of prints from the beach house to Edwin Marchand."

Hodges shoved his hands in his pockets. Gayle turned to him.

"This is the first I've heard of this, Brian. What's this about?"

Hodges turned to face her.

"Nothing."

"The report you sent me didn't say anything about Edwin Marchand."

"I talked to him."

"What did he say?"

Hodges shot an angry look at Connolly then glanced back at Gayle. Connolly answered for him.

"Said he'd never been in the house. Says he's never even seen the house."

Gayle pressed the issue with Hodges.

"This isn't in the file. Can he account for his time?"

"I don't know."

"What do you mean you don't know?"

Hodges' voice took a sharp tone.

"I mean, I don't know."

"Don't you think you better find out?"

Hodges gave her a sullen look.

"Maybe you better talk to Henry."

He turned aside and walked away. Gayle stared after him a moment then glanced at Connolly.

"Walk me to my car."

They crossed the parking lot together. Gayle looked grim.

"That was rather unpleasant."

"I don't think Edwin Marchand was involved in this."

"No." She nodded over her shoulder. "In there."

Connolly smiled.

"Guess that's why Henry stayed at the office."

She sighed.

"I guess so."

"You wanted to talk."

"Yeah."

Connolly waited for her to continue. Sweat trickled down his back with each step. He tried again.

"You want to talk later?"

"I took a look at that file you mentioned. There's one or two things in it you might be entitled to know."

"Henry actually wants to follow the rules?"

They reached a dark-blue Ford sedan. She glanced over at him.

"I didn't ask Henry."

Gayle opened the trunk and took out a briefcase. She removed a file from the case then slammed the trunk lid closed.

"There it is."

The file made a slapping noise as she dropped it on the trunk lid. Connolly looked at it, then at her.

"Earl Givens' file?"

"Yes."

"The DA's file?"

"Yes."

"You would let me see the file?"

A sly grin turned up one corner of her mouth.

"It's on the trunk." She took a cell phone from her pocket. "I'm going to step over here and return a few phone calls."

She walked around the car and leaned against the front fender. Connolly heard her phone beep as she pressed some numbers and placed a call. He opened the folder and began to read.

The file contained the usual documents. An incident report from the officers who responded. Toby LeMoyne had signed it. Statements from several of Givens' employees. A diagram showing the location of the body. Near the back was a copy of the coroner's report. Connolly flipped through it. There was nothing in it that Morgan hadn't told him already, until he turned to the last page. And then he saw what had caught Morgan's eye when they were talking in the office. On the last line of the report was a note indicating a copy had been sent to Amelia's House, a center that specialized in counseling minors who had been sexually abused.

"I was right," he whispered.

Connolly closed the file. Gayle glanced in his direction, then closed her cell phone and slipped it in her pocket.

"See enough?"

"Yeah."

"Anything in there you want?"

"The coroner's report."

"Okay. Anything else?"

"Do you have the pistol?"

"Inventory says we have it and the bullets they took out of the victim. I went over there to look. The bullets are there, but I couldn't find the pistol."

Connolly pointed to the file.

"Think you could get someone to compare the bullets in our case to the ones from this one?"

"Not without asking Henry."

Connolly turned away, thinking. Gayle picked up the file and put it in the briefcase.

"You want me to ask him?"

Connolly shook his head.

"Not yet."

She opened the trunk, placed the briefcase inside, and closed it.

"Well, just let me know. I think it might be a good idea to do it anyway."

She walked around to the driver's door and opened it. Connolly was still standing by the rear bumper, staring at the pavement. She paused and turned to him.

"You all right?"

Connolly lifted his head and smiled.

"Yeah. I'm fine."

Forty-two

The information in the DA's file on Earl Givens had confirmed what Connolly already knew. Clyde Ramsey had talked to Nick about what happened at the barn the day Givens was shot, and he had uncovered a family secret. But what stuck in Connolly's mind had nothing to do with Ramsey or Givens or any of that. What stuck in his mind was the exchange he had heard between Gayle and Hodges about Edwin Marchand's fingerprints. She didn't know Edwin had denied being in the beach house.

Hodges' response kept playing through Connolly's memory as he drove away from the hospital. "Maybe you better talk to Henry."

Hodges and McNamara.

"They could mess up a one-car funeral procession."

Hodges had given him a copy of a report on the fingerprints from the house. He had said it came from the FBI. Connolly had glanced at it the day Hodges gave it to him, but he hadn't given it much of a look. Gayle gave him one also, but he hadn't done anything with it either.

As he drove past the Port City Diner, he began looking for a parking space.

"Papers," he mumbled. "Why do these things always involve so many papers?"

He parked the car near Royal Street and walked back to the office building. Mrs. Gordon came from the hallway as he entered. She glanced at him as she took a seat at her desk.

"Who are you?"

Connolly gave her a smile.

"Hello, Mrs. Gordon."

She glanced at him, then turned to the work on her desk.

"How do you know my name?"

Connolly paused as he reached the hallway.

"Any messages for me?"

She finally lifted her head to look at him.

"They're on your desk."

He started toward his office. She called after him.

"You keeping up with your time in this case?"

He called back to her.

"My time?"

She scooted her chair away from the desk to see down the hall.

"I assume you've been off grasping at one more sliver of hope for Mr. Landry?"

He turned to her from his office doorway.

"Yes."

"Give me your time so far. We need to update his bill before you have the preliminary hearing."

"Before the hearing? Have they set a date for it?"

"Not that I know of. But we need to bill them before that happens."

"You think it's hopeless?"

"Hope is your department. I'm just the secretary. Give me your time so I can add it to the bill. I'm sure you've done more than they've paid for."

"I thought you said we were making money on this case."

"Give me your time."

Connolly chuckled.

"Okay."

Connolly tossed his jacket across a chair by the door as he stepped to the filing cabinets on the far side of the room. He opened a drawer and took out the large brown shuck that held the notes and documents he had collected in Dibber's case. He laid it on the desk and pulled a file folder from the back. Inside he found the reports Hodges had given him. The first page was an incident report. The second was a diagram of the bedroom indicating the location of the body and other items in the room. The third page was a memo from Hodges to the file that summarized information he had received regarding fingerprints collected at the beach house. That memo indicated what Hodges had told him. The FBI had matched prints from the house with prints from Dibber, Stephen Ellis, Inez, Nick, and Edwin. Three other sets were unidentified.

He laid the memo on his desk and took out a second file. In it were the reports he'd received from Gayle. He leafed through them and found her copy of Hodges' memo. That memo indicated the FBI had matched prints for Dibber and Nick. Six others were found to be from different people, but those were unidentified. Connolly stared at the pages and ran his fingers through his hair.

It was not uncommon to see preliminary results. Finding a match for Stephen Ellis' prints had taken awhile. Nothing unusual about that. All Hodges had to do was prepare a memo to update the information and send it on to Gayle. But why did he react the way he did when she asked him about it? Had he not talked to Edwin Marchand? Connolly remembered Hodges' comment outside the hospital.

"Doesn't say much, does he?"

Hodges was right. Edwin didn't have much to say. Which meant they had talked. So, why had he argued with Gayle about it? And why had he suggested she talk to Henry McNamara about it?

Connolly took a seat at the desk and leaned back against the wall. He closed his eyes and played a mental game with himself.

Suppose Edwin was telling the truth. He'd never been inside the beach house. That would mean either Hodges was lying or the FBI made a mistake. The FBI had been known to make mistakes, but Hodges' reaction left Connolly suspicious. Why would Hodges lie?

"Same reason everyone else does."

To cover up the truth. To keep someone from knowing what really happened.

"To protect someone."

If Hodges was lying, then the prints belonged to someone else. Someone he didn't want known. Someone who didn't want anyone to know they had been there. Someone who wasn't supposed to be in the beach house.

Connolly folded his arms in his lap.

Who could that be? He'd talked to everyone who knew anything about this case, and none of them had told him about anyone who would have meant anything to Hodges. Hodges didn't know the Marchands. They weren't his friends. Tinker and the men who worked for Nick spent most of their day strung out on meth. Hodges was like all detectives. He worked a case until he arrested someone, and then he wasn't interested in cute theories about it. He wasn't creative, but he wasn't using drugs either. And even if he was, McNamara wouldn't go along with it. McNamara dreamed of being an FBI agent, or district attorney, or governor, or something more than his current job. He wasn't very creative either, but he wasn't corrupt. Whatever it was Hodges found in that house, whatever he did with it, had to be something McNamara wouldn't question. Something that would pique McNamara's interest.

Connolly's eyes popped open.

"An informant." He rocked forward in the chair. "Someone in that house was working for the sheriff's department."

And he knew how to find out. He grabbed his jacket from the chair by the door and started up the hallway.

Forty-three

The drive from downtown to The Whistlin' Pig took ten minutes. Connolly parked in back near a Dumpster and entered through the kitchen door.

To the left was a large stainless steel sink. A gray-haired man was bent over it scrubbing pots and pans. His black rubber apron was splattered with grease and bits of food. Steam rose around his arms. Water from the sink sloshed over the edge and splashed on the floor at his feet as he turned a pot over and rinsed it under the faucet. At the end of the sink next to the door was a dishwashing machine. It made a swishing noise as water circulated through it. Racks of clean dishes sat at the end of the machine.

Across the room a waitress stood at the pickup window waiting on an order. She smiled at Connolly as he entered the kitchen. Another waitress at a drink machine behind her glanced in his direction then moved away. A customer at the counter looked up.

Between the door and the pickup window, a stainless steel table filled the middle of the room. Above it pots and pans hung from a rack suspended from the ceiling with chains. A white plastic ice chest sat in the center of the table. Splotches of barbeque sauce covered the lid, but beneath the greasy red smears was the word *chicken* written in black letters. At the far end of the table was a second chest. Across the side of it was the word *pig*. Women with sauce-stained aprons ringed the table arranging food on plates. One side worked the pork. The other side worked the chicken.

Between the table and the pickup window was a woman wearing blue jeans and a pink T-shirt. She shouted commands above the chatter of the women and the banging of pots and pans. She glanced in Connolly's direction. He crossed the room toward her. She paused between orders.

"We take sales calls in the mornings."

She reached past him for a plate of food. Connolly moved aside.

"I'm not a salesman."

The woman set the plate on the ledge of the pickup window.

"Order up!" She brushed past him to the table with an order ticket. "Two chicks—off the bone! One pig and a fry!" She laid the ticket on the table and glanced at Connolly. "Health department finds out you're back here we're in big trouble."

A woman at the end of the table collided against Connolly's shoulder.

"Out of the way!"

Connolly moved to the side. The woman in the pink T-shirt scowled at him.

"What do you want?"

"I'm looking for Tiffany. Have you seen her?"

"Not yet."

"Know where I could find her?"

She nodded toward the far side of the room.

"Ask Eric. And then get out of my kitchen."

She nudged her way past him.

"Order up." She snatched another order ticket from the pickup window and shouted to the women in the kitchen. "Three pigs on a bun! Two fries!"

Connolly moved out of the way.

At the far end of the kitchen to the right, a young man tended a wood fire in a barbeque pit built inside a red brick fireplace that covered most of the wall. A white cord dangled from earphones in his ears and ran down his back to an iPod clipped to his belt. Chickens cut in quarters lay on the grill from one side to the other. Flames crackled beneath them. Smoke rose into the chimney above. With a long-handled meat fork and the flick of his wrist, he worked his way across the grill flipping the meat. Grease dripped on the fire below. Flames leaped up around the meat. He shifted the fork to his left hand, took a garden hose from a hook at the corner of the fireplace, and sprayed the grill with a fine mist. Steam boiled up the chimney. The fire died away.

Connolly crossed the kitchen to the barbeque pit and tapped the young man on the shoulder. He glanced to one side to see who was behind him. Connolly pulled one of the earphones loose and leaned closer.

"Are you Eric?"

"Yeah."

"I'm looking for Tiffany. Have you seen her?"

Eric shook his head.

"Ain't seen her all week."

"You know where she lives?"

He nodded.

"Staples Road."

"You know the house number?"

He shook his head.

"Nah, but you can't miss it. 'Bout the third house on the right. Bad shape. But it's got a yellow door."

Connolly handed him the earphone and took a step away, then turned back.

"If you talk to her, don't tell her I asked."

The young man nodded.

"No problem."

Eric put the earphone in his ear. Connolly backed away. Eric jabbed a chicken quarter with the meat fork and took it from the grill.

Forty-four

Staples Road intersected Dauphin Island Parkway at the Food World shopping center about ten miles south of town in an area that had once been a nice middle-class neighborhood. Most of the people who first lived there were employed at Brookley Air Force Base, a large complex built during World War II on the southern edge of Mobile. When the base closed, the neighborhood began to struggle. Workers lost their jobs. Businesses closed. Many of the houses fell into disrepair.

Eric's description proved accurate. Connolly found Tiffany's house without any trouble, a wooden-frame structure with asbestos siding. A window on one end was broken, the missing pane replaced with unpainted plywood. In front a tired and dilapidated stoop sagged over a faded yellow door that was rotten and crumbling at the bottom. Beside the door was a large picture window with a crack through the middle. On the far side of the house a bulldog strained at the end of a chain that was fastened to the base of a pine sapling.

Connolly turned the Chrysler off the street and brought it to a stop partway up the drive. He came from the car and walked to the front door. There was no doorbell. He rapped on the side of the house with his fist. In a moment the door opened and Tiffany appeared, dressed in blue jeans and a green T-shirt. She gave him a blank stare.

"You got Dibber out yet?"

"We need to talk."

Tiffany moved aside. Connolly stepped through the doorway to the living room. To the left was a sofa beneath the window in front. At the far end of the room was a television. A recliner sat in the corner across from it, the upholstery ripped and torn. Opposite the door was a dining area. To the left of it was a kitchen. A hall opened to the right.

Tiffany shuffled across the room and sat in the recliner. Connolly took a seat on the sofa. She looked at him with the same blank stare.

"So, what you want to talk about?"

"Dibber said you told him Nick Marchand kept his money in that beach house and that's why he was down there during that storm."

"What if he was?"

"Was he?"

"What if he was?"

"He said you were working for Nick. Buying money orders for him."

"Maybe."

"Did you send Dibber into that house?"

She didn't respond. Connolly kept going.

"He said he went in there because you told him there was money in there."

"He didn't find no money."

"How do you know that?"

"He told me."

"You've been back to that house since all this started."

She stared at him a moment.

"He didn't know where to look."

"And you did?"

"Maybe."

"What were you looking for when you went back down there?"

Her eyes blinked.

"Who said I was down there?"

"Me."

"You?"

"Yeah."

She nodded her head. Connolly felt uncomfortable. He glanced through the doorway to the dining area. An assortment of bottles and containers were scattered across the table. An acrid odor drifted through the house.

"What were you doing when I drove up?"

"Huh?"

"What were you doing when I drove up?"

"Cooking."

"Cooking?"

"Yeah."

"Supper?"

"Yeah." She had an odd smile. "Supper."

"Did you know the dead man?"

"Seen him a time or two."

"See anybody else?"

"Lots of people."

"Ever see anyone they might have called Steve?"

"Yeah."

"What about somebody else? Somebody—"

Just then the front door opened. A man entered. He looked across the room at Tiffany.

"Whose car is that—" Then he noticed Connolly sitting on the sofa. "Who are you?"

Connolly smiled. The voice.

"Hello, Tinker. I'm Mike Connolly."

Tinker had a nervous grin.

"I guess you caught the voice."

"Yeah."

"What you doing here?"

"Talking. Have a seat. You can join us."

Tinker glanced at Tiffany then back to Connolly.

"I don't think she'll be with us much longer."

Tiffany's eyelids fluttered closed, popped open, then closed again. Her neck relaxed. Her head rested against the back of the chair. Tinker smiled.

"It's all right. She'll be awake in a little while." He pulled a chair from the dining table and sat facing Connolly. "What you want to talk about?"

"The other night, before we were interrupted, you told me some things about Stephen Ellis."

Tinker nodded. Connolly continued.

"Tell me what happened to him."

Tinker slipped off the chair and walked down the hall. Connolly could see him checking each of the rooms. He returned a moment later and took a seat again.

"Sorry. Had to check. Make sure nobody was listening."

Connolly nodded.

"Where is Stephen Ellis?"

Tinker shook his head.

"I tell you what, they'll know where it came from." Tinker took a pack of Camel cigarettes from his pocket, stuck one in his mouth, and lit it. "Actually ..." He paused to take a long drag on the cigarette. "... he's not there no more. Not all of him anyway."

"Not all ..." Connolly felt his stomach turn over. "You mean ..." He swallowed hard to keep from vomiting. "What did they do with his body?"

A grin broke across Tinker's face. He shook his head again.

"I'd love to tell you, but I can't."

"All right. Never mind about that for now. You were telling me what happened. Start from the beginning."

Tinker took another drag on the cigarette and nodded.

"We ... they ... was all down at Dauphin Island. Nick, Pete, Tony—"

"Pete?"

Tinker nodded.

"Works for Nick." He took another draw from the cigarette. "Nick and Steve got to arguin'. Something about some guy that died and money he'd made off a movie. I'm not sure. I was a little tight, if you know what I mean. Next thing I knowed, Nick pulled out a pistol and shot him in the head."

"He shot Stephen?"

"Yeah. Little while later that guy that was with him come in. He seen Steve sprawled across the bed all dead and everything, and he started hollerin' and screamin'."

"Across the bed?"

Tinker nodded.

"In that first bedroom. You been down there?"

"Yes."

"In that first bedroom." Tinker stuck the cigarette in his mouth. He continued to talk with it hanging off his bottom lip. "Right there by the kitchen. Nick was in there when Steve come in. Steve started in on him as soon as he come through the door. They got into it. Nick was settin' on the bed. Steve went in there. Nick had this pistol in his pocket. They got to arguing. Steve turned around to leave. Nick pulled out that pistol and popped him in the head. He collapsed on the bed." Tinker chuckled. "Nick had to jump out of the way."

"Then the other guy came in?"

Tinker took another long draw on the cigarette and nodded.

"He saw Steve laying there. Blood everywhere. Started scream-ing. Runnin' around. Ended up in the back bedroom. Yellin' and throwin' things. Tony got enough of it. Went back there and shot him."

"What happened after that?"

"Nothin' right then. Next day Nick took me and Tony down there to clean the place up. Put Steve in a blanket, loaded him in the truck. Threw the mattress in there. Everything else we could get out of that first room."

"You saw all this?"

"Well ... I ... uhh. I don't know if I should say I saw it. I'm just tryin' to help Tiffany."

"Tiffany?"

"She said if I told you what happened, she could get them off her back."

"Get who off her back?"

"Nick. He's been after her since that guy broke in the house."

"After her? For what?"

"He thinks she put him up to it. The guy they arrested for tak-ing that stuff from the house."

"Nick thinks Tiffany put him up to looting the house?"

Tinker nodded.

"To steal his money."

Connolly frowned.

"Whose money?"

"Nick's."

"Did she?"

Tinker glanced across the room at Tiffany.

"Can't say."

Connolly paused a moment, thinking, then continued.

"Tell me who else was around."

"What do you mean?"

"How many times have you been to the beach house?"

Tinker shrugged.

"I don't know."

"Ten?"

"Yeah."

"A hundred?"

"I don't know. Maybe."

"In all those times you were down there. Before the hurricane. Before Stephen was shot. Before this other guy was shot. At the nursery. Whatever. Who else have you seen down there?"

"Well ... they was Nick's mama. Pete. Tony."

"Anybody else?"

Tinker glanced across the room toward Tiffany then turned back to Connolly.

"I don't think so."

"No one else? A girlfriend. A neighbor. Someone from one of the other houses down there."

A frown wrinkled Tinker's forehead.

"One time we come down there, there was this—"

"At the beach house?"

Tinker nodded.

"Yeah. There was this car parked down there. We was in Nick's truck. He just kept on going. Had this look on his face like ... I can't describe it. Just this look. He seen that car and just kept going. Turned around at the end of the road."

"You mean, he saw this car at the beach house, and he didn't want to stop?"

"Yeah."

"Did he say why?"

"Didn't say nothing. I asked him about it. He didn't say a word. Just kept drivin'."

They sat in silence, each one looking past the other. Finally, Connolly spoke.

"Now, about Stephen Ellis."

Tinker shook his head.

"I can't tell you no more about him. If I do, they'll know exactly where it come from."

"Well, that leaves us with a problem."

"What's that?"

Connolly gestured with a nod toward Tiffany.

"To help her, you'll have to testify."

Tinker jerked the cigarette from his lips. His eyes were open wide.

"Testify? You mean like in court?"

"Yeah."

Tinker shook his head.

"I ain't testifyin' in no court." He laughed. "Nick would kill me."

"You have to. No other way for them to know what happened."

A knowing smile came over Tinker. He stood.

"Wait right there." He pointed to Connolly. "Wait right there. I got something may do the trick."

Tinker scurried down the hall. Connolly heard him open a drawer then slam it shut. A moment later he was back.

"Here." He held out his hand. In it was a red plastic prescription bottle about two inches long with a white cap on top. "That'll prove it."

Connolly hesitated. Tinker gestured with his hand.

"Go on. Take it. Open it up."

Connolly took the bottle.

"What's in here?"

"Open it and see for yourself."

Connolly held the bottle away from his body and twisted the cap off. A vile odor rushed out. He tipped it toward him to see inside. A lump of something filled the bottle to the rim. Connolly frowned at Tinker.

"What is it?"

Tinker grinned.

"His finger."

Connolly's chin dropped.

"His finger? Whose finger?"

"That guy's. The one you was talkin' about. Steve."

Connolly looked inside the bottle once more. As he stared at it, he could see the fingernail surrounded by swollen, putrid flesh. He twisted the cap back on the bottle and did his best not to vomit.

Tinker cackled.

"You don't look so good."

"I don't feel so good."

"You're white as a ghost. You gonna hurl?"

"I hope not."

Connolly thrust the bottle toward Tinker. Tinker backed away, gesturing with both hands.

"No, no, no. You keep it. Better it goes to court than me."

"It's not much good without you."

Just then the sound of a baby's cry came from somewhere down the hallway. Tiffany shifted positions in the chair.

"You got to do it, Tinker." Her eyes were open. "I need you to."

Tinker's shoulders sagged. He dropped onto the chair across from Connolly. Tiffany moved past them and disappeared down the hall.

Forty-five

It was almost dark when Connolly left Tiffany's house. Holding the medicine bottle at arm's length, he made his way down the steps and started across the grass toward the Chrysler. Halfway to the car he heard a noise from the edge of the yard. Out of the corner of his eye he saw the bulldog rise from his resting place near the pine sapling. The chain rattled as the dog moved. Connolly glanced in that direction. The dog gave a low growl then charged toward him. Near the corner of the house, the dog reached the end of the chain. Its head jerked up as its paws sailed into the air. The dog crashed to the ground on its back. In an instant it jumped to its feet and charged again, straining against the chain, barking and growling.

Connolly opened the car door with his free hand and slid past the steering wheel onto the front seat. He pulled the door closed and moved the bottle to his other hand to take the keys from his pocket. When the engine came to life, he backed the car away from the house. As the car turned toward the street, he glanced at the bottle. In the sunlight he could see the lines and swirls of skin pressed against the red tint of the bottle. A finger. A human finger. Rotten flesh. In his hand, inches away. His stomach rumbled.

At the street he stopped the car and opened the ashtray on the dash beneath the radio. He stood the bottle upright inside the tray and pushed the tray closed against it, lodging the bottle between the end of the tray and the dash. He jiggled it once or twice to make sure it wouldn't fall then turned the car into the street.

That bottle gave him a serious problem. If it really contained a finger, he couldn't keep it. And he couldn't just throw it away. A finger was part of a human body. He was supposed to take it to Ted Morgan. The coroner was the official custodian of human remains, especially remains that arose under suspicious circumstances. But Morgan would want to know where it came from and how he got it, and then there would be an investigation.

A grin spread across Connolly's face. He could take the finger to McNamara. The look on McNamara's face might be worth the trouble it would cause.

Whatever he did with it, that finger was going to cause problems for Dibber. Morgan would identify the person from whom it came. Might take a few days, but he'd find a way to identify it. And when he found out it belonged to Stephen Ellis, McNamara would charge Dibber with another count of murder. Never mind that he didn't have the whole body, or a cause of death. He would charge Dibber and sort out the details later. Any momentum pushing this case toward an amicable resolution would be wiped away, and it would happen as a result of evidence Connolly was compelled to disclose. Evidence with a negative impact on his own client.

At Government Street a stalled car blocked traffic in the right lane. Connolly brought the Chrysler to a stop and checked the mirror. A line of cars moved past him to the left. While he waited for traffic to clear, he glanced at the bottle. For the first time he noticed the name of the pharmacy across the top of the cap in blue letters. Embry's. A drugstore on the corner near St. Alban Cathedral. He turned the bottle and gave it a closer look.

A label had been attached to the side. Most of it had been peeled away leaving a thin film of glue underneath that was tacky and smeared, but one corner of the label was intact.

Connolly checked the traffic in the mirror again, then moved around the stalled car. At the corner he made the turn onto Government Street and steered the car into the parking lot in front of Zippadelli's Market, a neighborhood grocery store at the Loop. He brought the car to a stop beside the building and took the bottle from the ashtray.

In the corner of what remained of the label, he found a number. It had been a long time since he'd been to a drugstore, but he was sure the number on the label was the number for the prescription that had once filled the bottle. With that number the pharmacy could give him the name of the person to whom the bottle belonged. A glimmer of hope flashed through his mind. Just as quickly, it vanished.

Connolly shook his head in disbelief.

"No way. It can't be that easy."

Holding the bottle in his right hand, he stepped from the car and walked inside the grocery store. A clerk stood at the cash register. Connolly caught her eye.

"Do you have a phone book I could use?"

The clerk nodded over her shoulder.

"Zippy has one in the back."

Connolly walked past her down an aisle to the butcher shop in the back of the store. Andy Zippadelli saw him coming.

"Hey, Mike. You decide to cook tonight?"

Connolly acknowledged him with a smile.

"I need to use your phone book."

"Sure."

A telephone hung on a post at the end of the meat case. Zippy took the phone book from a shelf on the post above the phone and handed it across the counter to Connolly.

"You need the phone?"

Connolly shook his head.

"No. Just a number."

Across the aisle from the meat case was a stack of Coca-Cola cartons. Connolly set the book on top of the cartons and flipped through the pages until he located the listing for Embry's Pharmacy. He set the bottle on the book, took the cell phone from his pocket, and punched in the numbers. A friendly female voice answered the phone. Connolly took a breath and began.

"I need to get a prescription refilled."

"Yes, sir. Do you have the number?"

Connolly picked up the bottle and read the numbers from the label.

"934275."

He heard the clerk typing the numbers on a keyboard.

"Mr. Marchand?"

Connolly felt his heart jump.

"Yes."

"This is your wife's prescription."

Connolly's heart jumped again, but his mind raced ahead.

"This one's for Inez?"

"Yes, sir."

Now he needed to end the call, without raising her suspicions.

"Is that a problem?"

"No, sir, but it's expired."

"Oh."

"We can call her doctor and see if they'll authorize it."

"No. That's okay. I thought this was mine."

"Okay. I can look right here and find that for you if you—"

He cut her off.

"That's okay. I'll call you back."

Connolly pressed a button to end the call and slipped the phone in his pocket. He handed the phone book across the meat case to Zippy. Zippy nodded toward the bottle.

"You need some help?"

Connolly shook his head.

"No. I'm fine."

Zippy returned the phone book to the shelf.

"Sure I can't interest you in a nice steak?"

Connolly's stomach rumbled.

"Not tonight, Zippy. I think I'll just have vegetables."

A customer came to the meat case. Zippy wiped his hands on a towel and turned away.

From Zippadelli's, Connolly drove to the guesthouse. In the kitchen he found a Ziploc bag in the drawer by the sink. He put the bottle in the bag, sealed it, and carried it to the refrigerator. Inside the freezer compartment a box of ice cream sat next to the ice maker. Beside it was a bag of broccoli and a carton of fish. He pushed the fish aside and set the bag with the bottle against the freezer wall, as far from anything else as possible. Satisfied it was safe, he closed the freezer, opened the door beneath, and took out a bottle of Boylan's.

Across the hallway in the living room, he slipped off his jacket and threw it on a chair, then collapsed on the sofa. With his feet propped on the coffee table, he twisted off the cap from the bottle and took a long drink.

The law required him to take the finger to Morgan. And that's what he would do. He would take the finger to him and whatever happened after that would happen. He would take the finger over there and give it to Morgan. No explanation. Just give it to him. Set it on the desk. Walk away. He would do it.

Right after he talked to Hodges.

Forty-six

The following morning Connolly left the guesthouse at sunup and drove downtown to St. Pachomius Church. He took a seat near the back of the sanctuary and waited. Sunlight streamed through the stained-glass windows, sending shafts of red, blue, and green light dancing across the pews in front of him. Before long, others began to file in and take a seat. After awhile Father Scott moved across the chancel to the pulpit. The sound of his voice rolled down the chancel steps like water. As Connolly listened, tension he'd felt from the day before began to melt away.

When the service was over, Connolly stepped outside and walked across the street to the sheriff's office. Hodges had just arrived. He glanced up as Connolly appeared in the doorway.

"You're out mighty early." Hodges set a styrofoam coffee cup on the desk and moved around to his chair. "Something we need to talk about?"

Connolly leaned against the door frame.

"Yesterday, when Gayle Underwood asked you about Edwin Marchand."

Hodges took a seat.

"She shouldn't have brought that up in front of you."

"Maybe so. But the thing is, that was the first time she'd heard about Edwin Marchand. Until yesterday afternoon she had no idea Edwin Marchand's prints were in that house and no idea what he'd said about it."

Hodges took the lid off the cup of coffee and poured in a packet of cream.

"That's her problem."

"Yeah, well, I spent some time thinking about it."

Hodges shot Connolly a look.

"You solving her problems now?"

"I'm looking out for Dibber Landry. And if she didn't know about Edwin Marchand, I have to ask myself what else she doesn't know about."

Hodges smiled.

"You don't have time for me to tell you all that." He took a sip of coffee. "But that's not anything for you to worry about. Dibber's got enough to keep you busy."

"Well, that's just it. See, it is my problem."

"Oh?"

"I went back and checked the reports."

"What reports?"

"When I met with her and Henry, they gave me a copy of your report about the fingerprints. The report you gave them. It's not the same as the one you gave me."

"They gave you a copy of my report?"

"Yes."

"When?"

"The first time we met. Right after I took Dibber's case. A day or two after you arrested him."

Hodges shrugged. He looked up from his coffee cup.

"She never asked for an update."

"Maybe. But you never followed up with Edwin Marchand either."

"I talked to him."

Connolly shook his head. Hodges cocked his head to one side.

"You calling me a liar?"

"Edwin Marchand denied being in that house. He denied ever being there. He denied ever seeing the place. If you had a report from the FBI that said his prints matched prints that were in the house, his denial would have made him a suspect in this case."

"So?"

"He was never a suspect in this case."

"How do you know that?"

"Because I know you arrested Dibber from the records on the jet ski he sold the pawnshop. Not the fingerprints. If you'd done an investigation, you would have had seven other potential suspects."

Hodges' forehead wrinkled in a frown.

"Seven?"

"Your report says there were prints from Dibber and seven other people found in that house."

Hodges sighed.

"Whatever."

"Who are you protecting?"

"I'm not protecting anyone. And if I was, what makes you think I'd tell you?"

"This is a capital murder case. I'm entitled to know the names of any witnesses you know about who have anything to say about what happened in that house."

"Says who?"

"The Rules of Criminal Procedure and about a million court decisions."

"You're entitled to evidence that tends to exonerate your client."

"I'm entitled to know the names of the people who were present in that house. You can't protect someone just because they're undercover."

Hodges smiled again.

"You think we had somebody undercover?"

"I think you're looking for a meth lab somewhere in the county. I think you think somebody is running one out at that nursery."

"And you think we had someone on the inside."

"Yes."

"And I lied about those being Edwin Marchand's prints to conceal that person's identity."

"Yes."

Hodges took another sip of coffee.

"Well, maybe we have somebody in there, and maybe we don't. Either way, I'm not giving you any more names."

Connolly turned away.

"We'll see about that."

Forty-seven

From the sheriff's office Connolly returned to the guesthouse. He took the medicine bottle from the freezer and carried it to the car. Minutes later he turned into the parking lot behind Mobile General Hospital and hurried inside.

As Connolly came through the double doors at the end of the corridor, he saw Ted Morgan in the autopsy suite. His assistant stood nearby. A corpse lay on the autopsy table.

Connolly entered the room. Morgan looked puzzled.

"Mike? You want to help me with this one?"

Connolly reached across the cadaver and took Morgan's wrist. He placed the medicine bottle in Morgan's palm and squeezed his fingers closed around it. Morgan frowned.

"What's this?"

Connolly looked him in the eye.

"Someone gave this to me. I'm giving it to you. I don't ..." He let go of Morgan's hand and took a step back. "That's all I can say. It was given to me; now I'm giving it to you."

Connolly turned away and started toward the door. Morgan called after him.

"But what is it?"

Connolly tossed a wave over his shoulder but did not reply. As the double doors banged closed behind him, he heard Morgan gag. A smile broke across Connolly's face.

Down the corridor a little farther, Connolly took the cell phone from his pocket. He checked to make sure he hadn't missed any calls then pressed a button to turn it off. The screen on the face of the phone went blank. Lights that illuminated the keys went out. He slid the phone into his pocket.

For the next thirty minutes Connolly drove the city streets, aimlessly wandering from block to block. He was relieved to be rid of the bottle and the finger, but he knew there would be trouble. Morgan would call the district attorney's office. Someone there would put enough of the circumstances together. They would find McNamara. And McNamara would find him. He would shout and scream and demand an explanation. Whose finger was it? Where did it come from? How did you get it? All questions Connolly didn't want to answer. Better to avoid them. At least for now.

Before long Connolly found himself at the Loop. Crenshaw Street was just ahead. The street sign loomed ahead, and seeing it put him at war with himself. Part of him wanted to drive by his mother's house for another look. Part of him wanted never to return there again. While the argument raged in his mind, he made the turn at the corner. A moment later he was there. In front of his mother's house. He slowed the car to a stop and stared out the window.

In his mind he imagined knocking on her door. No. Kicking it down. Barging in the house, demanding an answer. Or sitting on the steps until she came out. But that might take a long time. From the look of the yard, she hadn't been outside in quite a while. The grass was almost knee high in places. Not really grass anymore, just weeds. Barbara was right. The lawn needed to be mowed.

"But not by me," he mumbled.

He moved his foot from the brake and rested it against the gas pedal. The car picked up speed as he drove away.

From Crenshaw Street, Connolly cruised through midtown, trying to think of something to do without putting himself in a place where anyone could find him. When nothing came to mind, he gave up and decided to have an early lunch. He drove out Government Street toward the suburbs. Oak trees and stately homes gave way to strip malls and fast-food restaurants. A few miles farther he came to Crumley's Truck Stop.

The truck stop had a garage with three service bays on one side and a cafe on the other. A pile of used tires lay at one end of the building. A fishing boat was parked in one of the service bays. Another was full of cardboard boxes. The one bay that was empty looked as though it hadn't been used in a long time. Rows of trailer trucks lined the far side of the parking lot. Six rusted and faded fuel pumps stood between the highway and the building. The pavement around them was stained with diesel. But the cafe was open and that was all Connolly cared about. He parked the car and went inside.

Two men sat at the counter near the cash register. From the logo on their shirts, Connolly was sure they were truck drivers. Empty tables filled the room beyond the counter. Booths lined the opposite wall. Connolly took a seat at a table as far from the door as possible and sat with a view of the gas pumps through the front window.

A waitress appeared before he was settled in place.

"What could I get you to drink?"

Connolly hadn't seen her coming. The sound of her voice caught him off guard. He glanced up at her.

"Tea."

"You want a menu?

"What's the special?"

Her gray hair was pulled behind her head in a bun with a pink ribbon tied around it. Thick makeup left a line below her jaw and flaked along the creases that crossed her face. She'd seen a lot of life, most of it the hard way. But her eyes were kind. She gave him a wry smile.

"Meat loaf. But you don't want it."

Connolly smiled back.

"What do I want?"

"Fried catfish."

Connolly shook his head.

"Had that the other day. Not in the mood for it right now. What else?"

"Fried chicken."

Connolly nodded.

"Okay. Fried chicken."

"You get two sides with it."

Connolly shrugged.

"I'll let you decide."

The waitress disappeared.

In a few minutes the two men at the counter left. Connolly had the dining room to himself. He watched the parking lot through the window.

Outside a boy pedaled past on a bicycle. A baseball glove dangled from the handlebars and flopped from side to side with the pumping motion of his legs. Connolly wondered why he wasn't in school then couldn't remember if school had started yet. While he wrestled with that thought, a truck turned off the highway with a flat tire. Blue smoke rose from the flapping rubber as the truck came to a stop a few feet beyond the fuel pumps. The driver stepped down from the cab and stood staring at the wheel. The boy on the bicycle returned and coasted to a stop beside the truck. He said something to the driver. The driver said something back then kicked the tire and walked away. Connolly could see his lips moving as he walked toward the building. It wasn't something the boy should have heard.

The boy shifted his weight to the opposite foot. The bicycle rocked to one side. Connolly's eyes fell on the baseball glove once again. A smile crossed his face.

As a boy, baseball had been his only dream. Every afternoon when his father came home from work, they would stand in the backyard of that house on Crenshaw Street and pitch the ball, sometimes until it was too dark to see. Just the two of them. He could still hear the sound of the ball against his leather glove.

A screeching sound jerked Connolly from the memories. In the lot out front an old man was dragging a large floor jack across the pavement. One hand tugged at the handle of the jack. The other struggled to hold a pair of wooden blocks. The blocks were stained with oil. Their edges scuffed from use and neglect.

About the time the old man had the jack positioned under the truck, the waitress appeared at Connolly's table with a plate of fried chicken, mashed potatoes, and green beans. She set it on the table with a glass of tea.

"That what you wanted?"

Connolly smiled up at her.

"That's perfect."

She stepped away. He laid a napkin in his lap and began to eat.

Outside, the driver of the truck with the flat tire passed the window. He stopped when he came to the Chrysler and moved around it, looking. Leaned forward, cupped his hands against the glass, and peered inside. Ran his hand over the door and tugged at the handle. When it didn't open, he moved to the back and ran his fingertips over the fender. Connolly took the napkin from his lap and laid it on the table. The man stared at the car. Connolly moved his legs from beneath the table to stand. The man outside turned away and started across the parking lot toward the truck. Connolly moved his legs back under the table and put the napkin in his lap.

When he finished eating, Connolly walked outside to the car. By then the truck with the flat tire was gone. The boy on the bicycle was nowhere to be seen. The parking lot was quiet. He backed the Chrysler away from the building and started toward town.

Forty-eight

On the ride back to town, Connolly turned on his cell phone. A message on the screen told him he'd missed five calls, all of them from Mrs. Gordon. Word was out about the finger. McNamara was looking for him. He switched off the phone and tossed it on the seat.

The highway into town took him past a row of 1950s-era motels. A little farther the motels gave way to a shopping center and a string of automobile dealerships. Just past the car dealers was a large billboard sign that pointed the way to Hank Aaron Stadium, home of the BayBears, the minor league successor to the team Connolly and his father had enjoyed at Hartwell Field years ago. A message beneath the sign announced an afternoon game.

Connolly glanced at his watch. It was twelve forty-five. Fifteen minutes till the first pitch. He changed lanes and turned the Chrysler from the highway to the drive that led to the stadium. He found a space near the main gate and parked the car. As he switched off the engine, he glanced through the windshield.

Across the way a father and son walked toward the gate. They were smiling and laughing in the hot summer sun. Connolly felt a sense of loneliness wash over him. He leaned back in the seat and watched as they moved out of sight. Memories tumbled through his mind. Fear rose inside him. He'd spent a lifetime trying not to remember. But the memories kept coming.

The sound of his father's voice in the morning. His hand shaking him awake. The three of them at breakfast around the kitchen table. Connolly, Rick, their father. The last good-bye as they hurried off to school. Connolly held each memory in his mind, savoring, searching. The kitchen table. The chairs. Rick. Their father. Connolly felt himself surrender to the warmth of the moment. Instead of pushing the memories aside, he searched them, indulging those moments from the past in a way he'd never been able to before. No longer tethered by fear or guilt, his eyes scanned the room, taking in each detail. The smile on his father's face. The handles on the cabinet doors. Canisters on the counter-top. The laughter in their voices.

Then the room went silent. Everyone tensed. And he saw her.

Leaning against the doorway to the hall, bleary eyed, disheveled, she had a blanket wrapped around her shoulders. The look on her face hit him hard, and for the first time he realized she hadn't been there even when she was there.

Their father was the one who got them up each morning, fixed them something to eat, packed their lunches, sent them off to school. He was the one who helped them with their homework and projects. And he was the one who tucked them in at night. His father. Not his mother.

She had been gone long before she left with that truck driver.

More images ran through his mind, flowing freely now. Ball games in the street, his father watching from the porch. The three of them in front of the television, their mother nowhere in sight. Then Uncle Guy and the words he'd said days ago.

"He came back right before you were born."

He came back. Not for her. Not for anyone else. He'd come back for him.

Connolly wiped his face.

"It's not her I miss." He gave a heavy sigh. "It's him."

Sweat trickled down his back. He lowered the windows. A breeze blew through the car, and with it came images of his mother.

Kneeling in the bathroom by the toilet. She glanced up at him, haggard and pale. Her voice, gravelly and rough.

"Get Mama a towel."

He'd handed it to her, but he'd wondered why she was always so sick.

That image of her faded away, replaced by another, then another. He sat in the car, staring past the windshield, watching each memory as it passed through his mind. And with each one came the realization that what he'd felt she'd done to him wasn't about him at all. Guy had said it. Barbara and Father Scott, too.

Hearing it from them hadn't seemed to help much at the time. But sensing it now in his spirit, it seemed more real. Something had happened to make her the way she was long before he'd been born.

She'd been unfaithful to her husband, which led to an affair, which led to him. And then she'd been unfaithful to him and Rick. Connolly chuckled to himself. Not anything new. Just more of who she already was.

Sometime later he was jerked back to the moment by the sound of a baseball striking a car in front of him. The ball hit the trunk lid and bounced into the air. He watched as it took two bounces toward the Chrysler then dribbled to a roll. He stepped from the car and glanced around. There was no one in the lot but him. He picked up the ball and spun it around. His fingers found their place against the seams. It felt good in his hand. He smiled and glanced around again, then drew the ball down toward his waist, kicked one leg up, and stepped forward as if to deliver a pitch.

Just then the crowd inside the stadium roared in response to a play. Connolly laughed. He stood there a moment, feeling the ball, listening.

From the stadium he drove back to the guesthouse and changed from a suit to a pair of worn blue jeans, a faded T-shirt, and the scuffed Topsiders. On the way out he grabbed a baseball cap from the closet near the door.

Outside he crossed the garden behind the main house to a shack on the far side of the property. He found a lawn mower and a gas can, loaded them in the trunk of the Chrysler, and headed down the driveway.

In a few minutes he was back at the corner near his mother's house. He sat there a moment, the Chrysler idling, the sun beating down on him through the windshield. Weeds in the front yard swayed in a gentle breeze, but the air was hot and humid. In no time at all he'd be sweating from every pore in his body. Sweating. For her. The woman who'd abandoned him. And his brother. Anger rose inside him. He turned the steering wheel to the right. She didn't deserve it. Didn't deserve his help. Didn't ... He slapped the steering wheel.

"It's not just her house." He straightened the steering wheel and moved his foot from the brake pedal. "It was his house." He sighed.

"And it was my house." The Chrysler started down the street. "And she's trapped. So trapped in who she was she doesn't even know it."

The car rocked to one side as Connolly turned from the street to the driveway. He touched his foot against the gas pedal. The car lurched forward and came to a stop near the garage. He opened the door and got out. He didn't check to see if she was watching. Didn't knock on the back door and ask for permission. Instead, he lifted the mower from the trunk, filled it with gas, and gave the starter cord a pull. The engine sputtered to life.

Sweat ran down his face and into the corners of his eyes as he pushed the mower into the tall weeds near the back steps. By the time he reached the bushes on the far side, his shirt was soaked. As he made the turn at the edge of the yard, he glanced at the house. His mother stood at the window in the corner where his bedroom had been. Their eyes met. She turned away.

Loneliness struck deep in his soul. Memories of the first night he and Rick had been there by themselves came pouring out. He shoved the mower across the yard, and let the memories pass through his mind. He'd seen them a thousand times before, but this time he didn't indulge them. Whatever she was, she was that and more long before she gave birth to him. The memories evaporated. The loneliness vanished.

Before long his body settled into a rhythm. He pushed the machine across the yard without any need of conscious thought. His mind was free to wander. His thoughts drifted from the yard to Dibber and Tiffany.

Dibber and Tiffany. A strange pair. Dibber was at least ten years older than she. A waitress at a barbeque joint. Making the run for Nick each week to buy money orders with money he made selling drugs. Money laundering in its most basic form. Money from the sale of crystal meth Nick and the boys cooked in that barn at the nursery. The same barn where his mother shot his grandfather. If Dibber's case went to trial, there would be a lot to tell a jury, but Connolly wasn't sure how he'd ever get them to see that it helped their case. Dibber would come off looking like one of them.

The backyard didn't take long. He moved to the front. As he worked his way toward the street, Dibber and Tiffany vanished from his mind. He wasn't thinking of anything. Then an image of Gayle Underwood flashed through his mind. The sound of her voice. Always a hint of laughter, even when she was serious. Even when she was talking to Hodges outside the hospital. The conversation played through his mind. She'd sounded like that was the first time she'd been told about Edwin and the finger-prints. She must have seen a report. She did see a report. She told him the prints weren't on—

Just then the front door opened. His mother appeared with a glass of ice water. He switched off the mower and crossed the lawn to the steps. She handed him the glass then turned away.

"Don't cut down my flowers."

Connolly chuckled as he took a drink of water and crunched a piece of ice between his teeth.

When he was a boy, he and Rick took turns mowing the lawn. Rick always did a neat job. Trimmed around the trees. Put every-thing in order. Connolly mowed down everything in sight. When it was his turn, she always reminded him not to cut the flowers. He'd wondered why, since she never worked in the yard. Come to think of it, he didn't know how any of the flowers got there in the first place. He turned to ask her, but she was already closing the door. He drained the last drops from the glass then set it on the top step and started the mower.

Forty-nine

By the middle of the afternoon Connolly was back at the guesthouse. It wasn't yet five o'clock. No telling what McNamara might do to find him. Connolly hurried to the shower, changed clothes, and drove to Barbara's house.

The realtor's sign was still in the yard. He parked across from it and sat there, staring at the black letters. The thought of selling the house, of never being able to come back there, left him feeling empty. After a moment he opened the car door and stepped outside. He thumped the sign with his finger as he walked past it to the front porch. Barbara greeted him at the door.

"Take the afternoon off?"

"No."

"Mrs. Gordon called here looking for you."

"I'm sure she did."

"Said you had a call you needed to return."

Connolly grinned.

"Can't be everywhere at once."

"Are you avoiding someone?"

"Something like that."

Barbara stepped onto the porch and pulled the door closed. She cut her eyes toward the steps.

"We could sit out here, but I think we'd be a little warm."

Connolly glanced around. The steps were in the sun.

"I think you're right."

"Want to come inside?"

Connolly leaned against a post.

"Not today."

"You really have a problem with that, don't you?"

"I really don't want to go back to who I was."

She moved closer and slipped her arms around his waist.

"You aren't who you used to be."

He slid his hands across her back.

"Maybe not."

She leaned against him and rested her head on his chest.

"We could go over to your house."

"We could walk around back and sit out there."

She raised her head and smiled.

"Okay."

Together they walked around the house and sat on the back steps in the shade. For a long time neither one said a word. Then Connolly took her hand.

"Are you really going to sell this house?"

"I'm really going to sell it."

"Anyone made an offer on it?"

"Not yet."

"What's the realtor say?"

"She says it'll sell."

He stared across the backyard.

"You remember the time we put dish detergent in Rachel's pool?"

"I remember the time you put it in there."

Connolly chuckled.

"We'd been washing the car. She wanted to play in the pool. Seemed like a good idea."

"She had soap suds from head to toe."

"I miss her."

"Me too."

Connolly rested an elbow on his knee and propped his chin in his hand.

"Why'd she have to move so far away?"

"Tallahassee isn't that far."

"Seems like a long way." He sighed. "Have you talked to her this week?"

"Yes."

"How is she?"

"She's fine."

"Everything okay with her job?"

"Yes. It's a good job. Physical therapists make good money these days."

Connolly shook his head.

"Physical therapist. Seems like a title someone made up just to give someone a job."

"They help."

"Oh, I know. Just seems like life has changed so much."

"Not as much as you."

Connolly glanced over at her.

"Me?"

"We've spent more time talking in the last three years than we talked the entire time we were married."

"You think?"

"I know."

"I guess you're right. Maybe we should move to Tallahassee."

Barbara frowned.

"Move to Tallahassee? What for?"

"Start over. Get it right with the grandchildren."

"Grandchild."

"She won't be the only one."

"Probably not."

"Think they'll come back for Christmas?"

"Maybe. Depends on her work."

"Yeah."

Barbara looked at him.

"Are you just filling up the afternoon?"

"What?"

"You've never rambled like this before. Are you just filling up the afternoon?"

Connolly smiled.

"No. Just talking."

"You better call Mrs. Gordon. Where's your cell phone?"

"In the car."

"You didn't answer it when she called."

"I turned it off."

The tone of her voice changed.

"Mike, that poor woman's been scouring the earth trying to find you. She called here twice."

"Couldn't be helped."

"What's going on?"

"Dibber."

"What about him?"

"I think we're about to bust this case open."

"What'll it be this time?"

"I don't know."

"That why you wanted to sit back here?"

"No."

He slipped his arm around her waist and pulled her close. She turned to him. They kissed. After a moment she leaned away. He grinned.

"That's why I wanted to sit back here."

Fifty

That evening, Connolly returned to the guesthouse. He tossed his jacket on the sofa and stepped to the kitchen. As he opened the refrigerator, a car turned from the street and started up the driveway. The beam of the headlights washed across the room through the front window. Connolly recognized the car. He took a bottle of ginger ale from the refrigerator and walked outside. He waited at the end of the driveway as the car came to a stop a few feet away. The door flew open. Mrs. Gordon started talking before her feet hit the ground.

"Where have you been?"

"Around."

"I've been looking for you all day."

"I heard."

"The least you could do was return my calls. Do you know how difficult it is to run an office without being able to reach you? What are you doing?"

Connolly leaned against the Chrysler and took a sip of ginger ale.

"Right now, I'm drinking a bottle of ginger ale. Want one?"

"No," she snapped. "I don't want a bottle of ginger ale. I want to know how soon you can find a replacement."

"A replacement?"

"Yes. A replacement. For me. I quit."

"You quit?"

"I quit."

Her face was red and her eyes flashed, but Connolly had trouble keeping a straight face.

"Quit what?"

"My job."

"Why?"

"I sit at my desk all day deciphering cryptic notes you scribble on the files. I answer calls from people you haven't bothered to contact in weeks. I juggle appointments, court dates, discovery, depositions. And you don't even bother to come to the office. You don't even bother to return my calls. Do you know how long it's been since you spent a day at your desk?"

"I hope you can't remember."

"That's just it. I can't."

"Good." Connolly took another drink. "I'd hate to spend so much time at my desk that either one of us could remember it."

"Where have you been?"

"I wanted to be unavailable."

"Well, you accomplished that. But why me?"

"Why you?"

"Why did you have to be unreachable to me?"

"So you wouldn't have to lie."

"Wouldn't have to lie?"

Connolly nodded. Mrs. Gordon kept going.

"I've lied before."

"I'm sure you have, but it wasn't because I asked you to."

"You didn't come right out and say, 'Tell them a lie.'"

He gave her a deadpan look.

"When did I ever imply you should not tell the truth?"

"What was I supposed to say? 'He's drunk out of his mind right now. Can he call you back?'"

Connolly shrugged and looked away. Mrs. Gordon stepped closer. She looked him in the eye and lowered her voice.

"You asked me to lie when you drank yourself into oblivion and passed out on the floor."

Connolly gave her a sober look.

"I'm sorry."

"I know you are. But why didn't you call me today?"

Connolly took a drink of ginger ale.

"Henry McNamara called?"

"Yes."

"Walter called?"

"Yes."

"Judge Cahill has a hearing set in the morning?"

"Eight o'clock. How'd you know?"

"I went over to Tiffany's house yesterday. Her friend Tinker was there."

"Tinker?"

"The guy I talked to. At The Whistlin' Pig."

"What'd he have to say?"

"He had a lot to say, then he gave me a prescription bottle with a finger in it."

A frown wrinkled Mrs. Gordon's forehead so deep it pushed her eyelids over her eyes.

"A finger?"

Connolly nodded.

"Said it belonged to Stephen Ellis."

"Inez Marchand's son?"

Connolly nodded.

"I took it to Ted Morgan this morning."

"And you didn't want to answer any questions about it today."

Connolly nodded again.

"You really quitting?"

Mrs. Gordon sighed.

"No. But don't do this again." She stepped to her car and opened the door. "I'm the person you call." She got in behind the wheel and glanced back at him. "You understand? Whatever happens, I'm the person you call."

Connolly smiled at her.

"Okay."

She slammed the door closed. He took a sip of ginger ale and watched as she drove toward the street.

Fifty-one

A few minutes before eight the next morning, Connolly entered Judge Cahill's courtroom. Walter, the bailiff, sat at his desk to one side of the judge's bench. He glanced up as Connolly came through the doorway.

"You give up returning calls?"

"Sorry."

"Judge tried to find you yesterday. Wanted to do this yesterday afternoon."

"Is he upset?"

"He's not too happy."

Connolly crossed the room and moved past Walter's desk. He opened the door behind the bench to Judge Cahill's chambers. Cahill stood at the coffeepot. He turned toward the door as Connolly entered.

"Where were you yesterday?"

"Sorry I missed you."

"Walter called your office two or three times. I called myself."

"I was out."

Cahill stirred cream in his coffee and took a sip. He looked over at Connolly and chuckled.

"More like you didn't want anyone to find you."

"How's Henry?"

Cahill took another sip of coffee.

"Henry is Henry. Get a cup of coffee. I'll be out in a minute."

He brushed past Connolly and stepped into his office. Connolly poured a cup of coffee and returned to the courtroom.

Ten minutes later Henry McNamara entered. Gayle Underwood followed a few steps behind. A moment later the court reporter entered. Connolly caught Gayle's attention. She rolled her eyes toward the ceiling. Connolly smiled and turned away.

McNamara's voice boomed across the room.

"I'd turn away too."

He moved past Connolly and took a seat at the counsel's table across from the witness stand. Connolly glanced over at him.

"Good morning, Henry."

McNamara glared at him.

"You think this is funny?"

"I have no idea what you're talking about."

"You think you can just hand Morgan something like that and no one will want to know where it came from?"

"I think anyone who graduated from law school in the last century could figure out where it came from."

"Your client should have—"

The door behind the judge's bench opened. Walter stood as Judge Cahill took a seat at the bench.

"All rise. The District Court of Mobile County is now in session." He paused while Cahill settled into his chair. "Be seated."

Judge Cahill opened the file and looked around the courtroom.

"Walter, where's the defendant?"

"I thought you wanted to talk to the lawyers."

"We have a motion from the State in a capital murder case. I think the defendant has a right to be here." Cahill turned to Connolly. "Mr. Connolly, has your client waived his right to be here this morning?"

Connolly stood.

"No, Your Honor. He hasn't."

Cahill slapped the file closed and spun around in his chair.

"Walter, call me when he gets over here."

Cahill bounded from his chair and disappeared through the door to his office. Walter came from his desk and passed Connolly on his way out. McNamara whispered something to Gayle then left the courtroom himself. The court reporter disappeared through the door behind the judge's bench. When they were gone, Gayle looked at Connolly.

"Henry's upset."

Connolly shrugged.

"It does Henry good to get upset."

"Yeah, but it doesn't do me any good."

"Morgan look at the finger?"

"Yeah."

"Whose is it?"

"Stephen Ellis'."

"The real Stephen Ellis or the other Stephen Ellis?"

Gayle smiled.

"Bobby Junkins had all ten of his fingers."

"You checked?"

"I saw them the other day when we were down there."

"You're sure it was Stephen's finger? The real Stephen?"

"Yes. Checked the fingerprints."

Connolly gave her a sarcastic smile.

"Fingerprints. For the first Stephen Ellis or the second?"

Gayle grinned.

"We got it right this time."

Connolly wasn't so sure.

"Did you get the report yourself?"

Gayle shook her head.

"Morgan."

"Not Hodges?"

Gayle gave him a smirk.

"Not this time."

Twenty minutes later Walter returned with Dibber, handcuffed in front and wearing an orange jumpsuit. Walter guided him to a chair beside Connolly.

"Don't get up without asking me first, understand?"

Dibber nodded. Walter moved away. Dibber leaned toward Connolly.

"What's this about?"

Connolly leaned close to Dibber's ear.

"I gave them a bottle with Stephen Ellis' finger inside."

Dibber blurted out.

"His what?"

Connolly gestured for him to be quiet.

"Not so loud. His finger. I took it to the coroner. They want to know where I got it."

"Where did you get it?"

"Tinker."

"Tinker?"

"Yeah. Any reason why I shouldn't tell them?"

"About Tinker?"

"Yeah."

"What'll they do?"

"Probably arrest him."

"I don't care about Tinker. Will they arrest Tiffany?"

"I don't know."

"What's the choice?"

"Tinker's not my client. Cahill will probably tell me I can tell them where it came from or I can go to jail."

Dibber grinned.

"You ever been in jail?"

"I'm no good to you in there."

The door behind the bench opened. Walter stood.

"All rise."

Connolly and Dibber stood. Judge Cahill took a seat.

"Be seated." He opened the file and glanced around the courtroom. "All right, are we ready?"

McNamara answered.

"Yes, Your Honor. The State is ready."

Cahill turned to Connolly.

"Mr. Connolly?"

"Yes, Your Honor. We're ready."

Cahill leaned over the bench to the court reporter.

"Ready?"

"Yes, Your Honor."

"Very well. We are here on case number 25919197. State of Alabama versus Dilbert Landry. This is a capital murder case, and we are here today on the State's motion for discovery. Mr. McNamara, you have a witness you want to put on?"

"Yes, Your Honor."

"Very well, call your witness."

"Your Honor, the State calls Dr. Ted Morgan."

A deputy near the door led Morgan into the courtroom. When he was seated and sworn, McNamara began.

"Dr. Morgan, we are here on State versus Dilbert Landry. Are you familiar with that case?"

"Yes, I am."

"How are you familiar with that case?"

"I did an autopsy of a corpse associated with that case."

"Now, yesterday, did you receive some material relevant to that case?"

"Yes."

"What did you receive?"

"I received one human finger."

"From whom did you receive that finger?"

"I received it from Mike Connolly."

"Is he here in the courtroom today?"

"Yes."

"Point him out for us, please."

"He's the gentleman seated at counsel's table."

"Let the record reflect that the witness has correctly identified Mr. Connolly."

Cahill cleared his throat.

"So ordered."

McNamara continued.

"Did you do some analysis of that finger?"

"Yes."

"What did you find?"

"I found that it was the index finger from the left hand."

"Whose left hand?"

"You'd have to ask the detective about that."

"The detective?"

"Yes."

"Which detective?"

"Brian Hodges. He did the fingerprints."

"I was under the impression you did the fingerprints."

"No, sir. I called him. He came over and took the prints."

"You didn't request them?"

"I don't have access to that kind of information. I just tell them what I have, and they make those decisions."

"Do you know whose finger it was?"

"Yes. I mean, Detective Hodges told me what the report said."

Connolly smiled to himself. McNamara continued.

"And what did he tell you it said?"

Connolly stood.

"Objection. This is hearsay."

McNamara turned to Judge Cahill.

"The rules allow it if we can produce the witness at trial."

Connolly spoke up.

"The rules allow it at a preliminary hearing. This isn't a preliminary hearing. It's an evidentiary hearing on his motion. He has the burden of proof here, and he can't do it with hearsay."

Cahill's eyes cut McNamara with a look that went straight through him.

"You don't have Hodges here?"

"I can get him."

Cahill threw his hands in the air.

"This is a capital murder case, Henry! Do you have anything else from this witness?"

"No, Your Honor."

Cahill glanced at Connolly.

"Mike, you have anything for him?"

"Just a couple of questions."

Cahill turned to Walter.

"Get Brian Hodges up here."

Connolly spoke up.

"Judge, could I get a ruling on my objection?"

"The objection is sustained, Mr. Connolly. Sustained." Cahill sighed. "Proceed."

McNamara took a seat. Connolly moved in front of the witness stand.

"Dr. Morgan, you said you did an autopsy on a corpse associated with this case."

"Yes."

"That corpse was found in a beach house on Dauphin Island."

"Yes."

"And it is the corpse regarding which Mr. Landry is charged with capital murder."

"Yes."

"Now, since the time you did that autopsy, has anyone come to claim the body?"

"Yes."

"How many people have come?"

"A Mr. Billy Ellis came first."

"And what happened when Mr. Ellis came?"

"Everyone thought the corpse was his son, but when Mr. Ellis looked at the body, he identified it as that of one Bobby Junkins."

"Who else looked at the body?"

"Mr. and Mrs. Junkins."

"And they identified it?"

"Yes," Morgan replied. "They identified the body as being the body of their son."

"Do you know how the body was first identified as Mr. Ellis' son?"

"Fingerprints."

"Who took those fingerprints?"

"I believe they were taken by Detective Hodges."

"And on the basis of those prints, everyone thought the dead man was Stephen Ellis."

McNamara rose from his chair.

"Objection."

Morgan answered anyway.

"Yes."

Judge Cahill glanced at McNamara.

"Overruled."

Connolly continued.

"Did you do any analysis of this finger? Not the prints and all that. But you." He pointed to Morgan. "Did you do any analysis of it?"

"Yes."

"What did you do?"

"The finger was covered with some sort of black substance. We analyzed that. And there was some material under the fingernail."

"What did you find?"

"The black material on the exterior was soot."

"The finger had been in a fire?"

"Yes."

"Were you able to determine anything about the soot?"

"The general composition was consistent with any number of combustible materials. Cardboard, cotton, wood."

"Any kind of plastic residue?"

"None on the finger."

"What about under the fingernail?"

"Under the nail we found a mixture of sulfur, nitrogen, traces of ammonia. Traces of a material used to make gel caps."

"Anything else?"

Morgan shook his head.

"I think that's about it."

Connolly turned to Judge Cahill.

"That's all, Your Honor."

Cahill turned to Morgan.

"You may go." He glanced over at McNamara. "Any other witnesses?"

McNamara stood.

"We call Mr. Connolly."

Cahill's mouth flew open.

"What?"

"We don't need Detective Hodges, Your Honor. We can get what we want through Mr. Connolly."

Connolly spoke up.

"I object, Your Honor. I'm not testifying in a hearing about my own client."

Cahill spun around in his chair.

"Call me when Hodges gets here."

He stepped from the bench and disappeared. Connolly took a seat next to Dibber at the table.

"Nice try, Henry."

"Why don't you just tell us and get this over with?"

Connolly leaned close to Dibber's ear.

"Make it look like we're talking."

"They would make you testify against me?"

"For that, I would share a cell with you."

Dibber chuckled.

Fifty-two

A little before nine that morning, Hodges entered the courtroom. By that time the courtroom was filled with attorneys, spectators, and witnesses for the morning docket. Hodges moved past Connolly to the table where McNamara and Gayle were seated. They huddled together for a moment, then Hodges took a seat in a chair near the rail in front of the audience.

Promptly at nine the door to Judge Cahill's chambers opened. Walter stood.

"All rise. The District Court of Mobile County is now in session. Judge Robert Cahill presiding. Be seated."

There was a rustling noise as everyone took a seat. Cahill opened the file on his desk and surveyed the room.

"We are in the middle of a hearing on a capital murder case. Y'all take a seat and get comfortable. Hopefully this won't take all morning." He turned to McNamara. "Mr. McNamara, I see Detective Hodges is here. Are you ready?"

McNamara stood.

"Yes, Your Honor."

Cahill looked at Connolly.

"Mr. Connolly, are you ready?"

Connolly rose from his chair.

"We're ready, Your Honor."

"Very well. Detective, come on up."

When Hodges was seated and sworn, McNamara began.

"Detective Hodges, Ted Morgan testified earlier that he called you to come to his office yesterday. Do you recall doing that?"

"Yes. I went to the hospital yesterday morning. Dr. Morgan had a severed finger he was trying to identify."

"What did you do?"

"I fingerprinted it."

"You applied the ink and ..."

Hodges nodded.

"Yes. I rolled the prints on a standard print card."

"What did you do next?"

"I e-mailed the print to the FBI."

"You e-mailed it?"

"Yes."

"You can do that with enough clarity to get a match?"

"Yes. Their system is fully automated. I mean, they have the cards somewhere, but all their prints are digitized anyway so it's no big deal."

"Were they able to identify the finger?"

"Yes."

"Whose was it?"

"The finger was that of Stephen Ellis. White male. Age forty-four. Last known address was in Lawrenceville, Georgia."

"Did you inquire as to how Dr. Morgan came to have this finger?"

"He told me he got it from Mr. Connolly."

"The same Mr. Connolly seated at the defense table?"

"Yes."

"Did you attempt to contact Mr. Connolly about the finger?"

"No. I called your office and spoke to you about it."

"Nothing further from this witness."

Cahill nodded to Connolly.

"Mr. Connolly."

Connolly stood and moved in front of the witness stand.

"Detective, this isn't the first set of prints you've lifted in this case, is it?"

"No."

McNamara stood.

"I object, Your Honor. We're here about this finger and how Mr. Connolly came to have it and who gave it to him. We aren't here about fingerprints in general."

Connolly turned to face Judge Cahill.

"This hearing is about a fingerprint from a finger in a case in which this detective matched other fingerprints. Those matches proved to be incorrect. I think I have a right to ask him about that."

Cahill leaned back in his chair and stared at the ceiling.

"Overruled. For now."

Connolly turned back to Hodges.

"Detective, tell us about those other prints you lifted in this case."

"We lifted prints from the beach house. The medicine bottle the finger was in. And we lifted prints from the finger."

"That's it?"

"Yes."

"How many different prints did you find in the beach house?"

Hodges glanced through his file.

"Eight."

"And, how many of those were you able to identify?"

He glared at Connolly.

"Five."

"And who were those five?"

"Your client, Dilbert Landry. Nicholas Marchand. Inez Marchand. Edwin Marchand. And the deceased, Stephen ... I mean, Bobby Junkins."

"Now about the body in the house. You were able to identify prints from it."

"Yes."

"You sent those to the FBI."

"Yes."

"And what did they say?"

"The FBI said he was Stephen Ellis."

"But that turned out to be incorrect."

"They never acknowledged it."

"Do they ever acknowledge that sort of thing?"

"I don't know. I guess so."

"You ever have them tell you in any other case that they made a mistake?"

"No."

"But the dead man wasn't Stephen Ellis, was he?"

"No."

"Who was he?"

"He was Bobby Junkins."

"But his fingerprints on file with the FBI said he was someone else."

"Yes."

"Now, you said you identified prints for Edwin Marchand."

"Yes."

"Did you talk to Edwin Marchand?"

"Yes."

"What did he say?"

McNamara stood.

"Objection, Your Honor. This has nothing to do with my motion."

Cahill spoke without looking up.

"Overruled."

Connolly continued.

"What did Edwin Marchand say?"

"He said he'd never been in the beach house."

"Is that all he said?"

"Yes."

"Did you ask him to account for his time?"

"What do you mean?"

"You had a time of death for the body, didn't you?"

"Morgan said it was about a week before they found it. He couldn't say for sure."

"Did you ask Mr. Marchand where he was during that time?"

"Not really."

"In fact, you knew he wasn't in that house, didn't you?"

"I just tell them what the FBI tells me."

"What did the FBI tell you?"

Connolly stepped to the counsel table as Hodges answered.

"They said ... they were Edwin Marchand's prints."

Connolly took two pages from his file. He crossed the room toward Hodges.

"You recall talking to me in your office about this case?"

"Yes."

"You gave me a copy of a report." He stopped at the court reporter and marked the pages with an exhibit number. "You remember that?"

"Yes."

"I show you what I've marked as Defense Exhibit A. Do you recognize this?"

"It's a copy of a memo to the file."

"You prepared it."

"Yes."

"And what does it say?"

"It says what I just told you. That we had IDs on five of the prints."

"The five you mentioned just now."

"Yes."

"Okay. Take a look at what I've marked as Defense Exhibit B. Do you recognize that?"

"Yes."

"What is it?"

"It's a memo to the file."

"You prepared it."

"Yes."

"What does it say?"

"It says we had IDs on two prints."

"Those were?"

"Dilbert Landry and Nicholas Marchand."

"Can you explain the difference?"

"The difference?"

"Why one copy says one thing and the other copy says something else?"

"I—"

"You know Edwin Marchand's prints weren't in that house, don't you?"

"I know—"

"You know he's never even seen that house, don't you?"

"I—"

"In fact, if this were any other investigation, Edwin Marchand's statement that he'd never been in that house, coupled with the supposed prints you lifted from the house, would have made him a prime suspect, wouldn't it?"

"I don't think—"

"Whose prints were those?"

"Which ones?"

"The ones you said were Edwin Marchand's. What did the FBI report actually show?"

"I can't—"

"You have a file in your lap. You referred to it during your testimony. Look through it and take out the actual report the FBI sent you."

"They e-mailed their report."

"Let me see a copy of that e-mail."

Hodges looked at Judge Cahill. McNamara stood.

"Judge, again, we aren't here on the question of fingerprints in general. We're here about the finger Mr. Connolly gave to Dr. Morgan."

Cahill sat up in his chair.

"I think Mr. Connolly has raised enough of a question about the accuracy of the work on this file. Detective, do you have a copy of the e-mail?"

"Yes."

"Let's see it."

Hodges looked through his file and took out a single page. He handed it to Judge Cahill. Cahill looked at it then handed it to Connolly. Connolly glanced over it then stepped to the court reporter and marked the document. He moved back to the witness stand and handed the document to Hodges.

"Detective, I show you this document that I have marked as Defense Exhibit C. Can you tell us what that is?"

"It's an e-mail I received from the FBI office in Virginia."

"What does it say?"

"It says ..." Hodges took a deep breath. "It says they had a match for three of the prints."

"And what were the names?"

"Nicholas Marchand. Inez Marchand. And ..."

Hodges paused. Connolly prodded him for an answer.

"Go ahead, Detective. Tell us the third name."

"I didn't think it would matter."

"You didn't think it would matter?"

"No."

"That wasn't for you to decide, was it?"

"Everyone knew Edwin Marchand had nothing to do with this case."

"Everyone? How would they know that?"

Hodges looked away. Connolly continued.

"You knew he had nothing to do with this case, didn't you?"

"Yes."

"You knew Edwin Marchand had nothing to do with this case because someone told you he had nothing to do with this case, didn't they?"

"Yes."

"Who told you?"

"My father-in-law."

Connolly froze. He'd expected to hear McNamara object. He'd expected to hear Hodges say the person in question was a confidential informant. He'd expected Cahill to argue with him about it. But he'd never expected the answer Hodges gave.

Cahill glanced down at him.

"Any more questions?"

Connolly looked at Hodges.

"And who is your father-in-law?"

"Clyde Ramsey."

"And the third name on that e-mail was?"

"Clyde Ramsey."

"And you found his prints in the beach house, not Edwin Marchand's."

"Yes."

Connolly stepped away.

"Nothing further, Your Honor."

Fifty-three

Judge Cahill propped his arms behind his head and rocked in his chair. Hodges stood to leave. Cahill stopped him.

"Wait a minute, Detective. Sit down."

Hodges took a seat. Cahill continued to rock in his chair.

"You deliberately mishandled the information in this file?"

"I didn't think it would matter ..."

Cahill's arms fell to his side. He sat up straight and shouted.

"You didn't think it would matter! This is a capital case and you didn't think it would matter!"

Hodges looked deflated. Cahill pressed on.

"Do you know why your father-in-law's prints were in that beach house?"

Hodges did not reply. Cahill's voice grew louder.

"I'm asking you a question. Do you know why his prints were in there?"

"He was, I believe, seeing Mrs. Marchand."

"He was having an affair with Mrs. Marchand?"

"Yes, Your Honor."

"And you covered it up by concealing information in your file?"

"I didn't think it would matter."

"Well, you thought wrong."

Walter was already standing at Cahill's desk with a form in his hand. Cahill took it and filled in the blank spaces with a pen. He found a preprinted stamp on his desk and banged it on the form, then scribbled some more. When he was finished, he signed it and handed it back to Walter.

"Detective Hodges, I find you in criminal contempt of court

and sentence you to five days in the county jail. Walter, take this man into custody. Did you leave a weapon downstairs?"

"Yes, Your Honor."

"You have any weapons on you?"

"No, Your Honor. Honestly, I didn't think—"

"You're in custody, Mr. Hodges. You sure you don't have a pistol on your ankle?"

"No, Your Honor."

"All right. Walter, cuff him and take him to jail."

Gayle stood and began gathering papers from the table where she and McNamara were seated. Cahill glared at her.

"Take a seat, Ms. Underwood. We aren't through here yet."

She slid onto her chair. Cahill shot a glare in Connolly's direction.

Walter came from his desk and placed Hodges in handcuffs. When the cuffs were secure, he led Hodges to the back of the courtroom and turned him over to a deputy. When Walter was back at his desk, Cahill turned to Connolly.

"Now, about this finger."

Connolly stood.

"Yes, Your Honor."

"What do you have to say?"

"I came into possession of a medicine bottle … a prescription bottle. The bottle contained something that appeared to be human remains. I took it to Ted Morgan. That's all I can say."

"You don't know who gave it to you?"

"Any information I may have developed about the contents of that bottle were developed in the course of representing a client. What I may know about that bottle, if anything, is protected by the attorney-client privilege."

Cahill slapped the bench.

"I'm not asking what your client told you! I'm asking about that bottle."

Connolly forced himself not to smile.

"If the court finds that the information I may or may not know about the contents of that bottle did not arise from a privileged communication with my client, then I assert that it is information developed in the course of defending my client. As such it is work product and is not subject to disclosure."

Cahill turned away.

"Mr. McNamara?"

McNamara stood.

"Judge, I'm not asking for what his client said to him. I just want to know where he got the finger. Either he cut it off Mr. Ellis himself, or someone gave it to him. As long as that someone wasn't Mr. Connolly's client, I'm entitled to know who that someone was."

Cahill gave Connolly a look he'd seen many times before.

"Did you get this from your client?"

Connolly glanced over at Walter. A pair of handcuffs lay on the desk in front of him. Walter gave him a smile.

Connolly dropped his gaze to the floor. He shuffled his feet as he thought. If he told them Tinker's name, Tinker would be arrested before sundown. Tinker would be in jail, charged with whatever crime McNamara could dream up. A judge would appoint a lawyer to defend him, and he would be lost as a witness in Dibber's case. If he didn't tell, he'd be spending the night in a cell next to Dibber.

Cahill stroked his cheek.

"Easy way or the hard way, Mr. Connolly."

Connolly looked up.

"I received the finger from a wit ... potential witness."

Cahill shouted.

"What's the witness' name?"

Connolly's eyes were focused on Cahill, but he nodded toward McNamara.

"I'll give them his name and address, but I'm not telling them anything else."

Cahill looked at McNamara.

"Better than nothing."

McNamara sighed. Cahill closed the file and stood.

"You two get together and talk." He started from the bench. "Mike, give him the name and address." He turned back to the others in the courtroom. "We'll take a short recess. I'll be back in ten minutes."

Cahill pushed open the door behind the bench and disappeared into his office. Connolly turned to McNamara.

"You want it now?"

McNamara took out a pen.

"I can't believe you did this." He grabbed a notepad from the table. "What is it?"

Connolly smiled.

"His name is Tinker Johnson."

McNamara laughed.

"Tinker?"

"Tinker."

"Okay. Where does Tinkerbell live?"

"I talked to him at 3965 Staples Road."

McNamara jotted down the address.

Fifty-four

*I*t was midmorning when Connolly left the courthouse and returned to the office. He worked at his desk until noon, then walked up the street to the Port City Diner for lunch. When he finished eating, he returned to his office and spent the afternoon returning calls and working on files.

A little before five he could stand it no longer. He slipped on his jacket and started up the hall with an armful of files. He dropped the files on Mrs. Gordon's desk and straightened his tie.

"That ought to hold me for the rest of the year."

She didn't bother to look up at him.

"Work like that every day and you could make some money at this business."

"Work like that every day and they'll cart me out of here on a stretcher." He opened the door, then turned back to her. "I really didn't mean to make you mad yesterday."

With the flick of her wrist, Mrs. Gordon sent the pen in her hand sailing toward him.

"Get out of here."

The pen struck him on the shoulder and fell to the floor. He stepped to the corridor. The door closed behind him.

From the office building he drove through midtown to the guesthouse. He parked the car at the end of the drive and went inside. It was early, but he was tired. The past few weeks had been draining. Stephen Ellis. Earl Givens. His mother. It was more than he'd bargained for when he first agreed to take Dibber's case.

In the guesthouse he ran a hot bath and sat in the tub reading the newspaper. The water was cold by the time he reached the sports section. He turned on the hot water to warm it up while he read about the Braves and their chase for another pennant. When he finished with the sports section, he threw the paper on the floor and slid low in the tub. Water covered all but his nose and mouth. The heat from the water eased the tension in his neck. He began to relax.

An hour later Connolly climbed from the tub and made his way to the bedroom. He crawled into bed and pulled the covers over his head. In a few minutes he was sound asleep.

Hours later he was awakened by the sound of someone pounding on the door. He flipped back the covers and looked around. The room was dark. The pounding on the door continued. He found his cell phone on the table beside the bed and pressed a button. The display lit up showing the time.

Two in the morning. The pounding on the door grew louder.

Connolly crawled from bed and took his pants from a chair by the door. He slipped them on and started down the hall. By the time he reached the door, they were zipped and buttoned, but his belt dangled loose at his waist. He stood at the door and called out.

"Who is it?"

A voice from the other side answered.

"Tiffany. Let me in."

He unlocked the door and turned the knob. The door opened toward him. Tiffany burst through and pushed her way past him.

"You gotta help me."

"What's the matter?"

She turned to face him.

"They got Tinker."

"Who?"

"The cops. They came to the house and got him."

"When?"

"Tonight."

"Now?"

"No. A few hours ago. I don't know when. They came to the house. Got him. Started going through everything. You gotta help him."

"Where is he?"

"In jail."

"They didn't arrest you?"

"No. Told me to get out of the way. They cuffed him. Put him in the car. Then started going through the house. They kept me out-side. I walked up the street to my sister's house. She let me use her car, but I didn't want to stay there. She'd be too easy for them to find."

"What did they charge Tinker with?"

"I don't know."

"Have you talked to him?"

"No. I just know he needs somebody to help him."

Connolly was still holding the door open.

"I can't help him."

"Why not?"

"Because I already represent Dibber."

"What's that got to do with it?"

"Tinker's involved in Dibber's case. I can't do it. It would be a conflict."

"I don't know how they ever found him."

Connolly looked away.

"Yeah, well, they have their ways."

She glanced around the house.

"I need a place to stay tonight."

Connolly felt uneasy. Tiffany glanced in the living room. She turned to him with a timid smile.

"Think I could stay here? Just tonight. I ain't got no place to go."

Connolly sighed and closed the door. He didn't want her there. No telling what she'd steal. But he was too tired to argue, and she wasn't going to leave regardless of what he said.

"Yeah. Sure. You can sleep on the sofa."

She dropped her purse on the floor and lay on the sofa. Connolly moved up the hall.

"But stay out of the kitchen."

"What do you mean?"

"No cooking."

He heard her giggle as he walked toward the bedroom.

Fifty-five

When Connolly awoke the next morning, Tiffany was gone. He stood near the sofa and sniffed the air. The house smelled like cigarette smoke. He glanced around the room to make sure nothing was missing then went to the kitchen for a cup of instant coffee. He drank it leaning against the counter by the sink.

An hour later he was showered and dressed. He checked his watch as he started out the door. It was ten thirty. Somewhere past Houston Street his cell phone rang. The call was from Mrs. Gordon.

"Somebody said you have an office downtown."

The sarcastic tone in her voice made him smile.

"Good morning, Mrs. Gordon."

"More like good afternoon."

"I had a late breakfast."

"Yeah. Didn't we all." Her tone changed. "DA's office called two or three times this morning. Gayle Underwood."

"What did she want?"

"Wants you to call her."

"Okay."

"You coming in today?"

"Be there in a few minutes."

"I'll believe it when I see you."

She hung up.

Connolly pressed a key on the phone for his call list and found the DA's number. After two rings Juanita answered. It took her a few minutes to find Gayle. By the time she came on the line, Connolly had turned onto Royal Street.

"We arrested Tinker Johnson last night."

The sound of her voice made him remember the laughter in her eyes.

"So I heard." Connolly propped his elbow against the car door. "Tell you anything you didn't already know?"

"We searched the nursery this morning."

Connolly made the turn onto Dauphin Street.

"What's in the barn?"

"Meth lab."

"How big?"

"Big. Hazmat team's still in there. It's a mess. Toxic waste dump. You'll read about it in the papers. We found the rest of Stephen Ellis."

"Where was he?"

"In a burn pile behind the barn."

Nausea struck Connolly in the pit of his stomach. He'd seen that burn pile the morning he was out there talking to Nick. Stood just a few feet from it. He turned the car into a parking space across from Bienville Square. The phone was still against his ear. Gayle's voice called to him.

"You still there?"

Connolly swallowed.

"Yeah. Find anything you could recognize?"

"Of what?"

"Stephen Ellis."

"They found his bones." She paused. "They don't burn too well." Her voice sounded solemn. "At least that's what someone said. Ted Morgan says we found all of them except the one you brought him."

"You were out there?"

"Yeah."

"Henry?"

"He came out for a little while."

Connolly sighed.

"So, what does this mean for Dibber?"

"Dibber?"

"Landry."

Gayle's voice found its laughter again.

"They call him Dibber?"

"Short for Dilbert."

"That's the other reason I called you. If he'll plead to theft of property, we'll drop the murder charge."

"What kind of sentence?"

"Year and a day. If you ask for probation, we won't oppose it."

"I'll talk to him today."

Connolly turned off the engine and grasped the handle to open the car door.

"I showed Henry the results on the forensic report for the bullets."

He let go of the handle.

"Forensics?"

"I had the lab compare the bullets from this case to the ones from that old case you asked about. Earl Givens."

Connolly leaned back in the seat.

"What did Henry say about that?"

"Don't worry about it. That's my problem."

"Did they match?"

"The lab says both bullets came from the same gun. Thirty-eight caliber revolver."

"Interesting."

"Yeah. We still can't find the pistol. It was checked into the property room with all the other stuff on that Givens case, but it's not there now."

Connolly frowned.

"Is that going to cause us a problem?"

"Not for your client. He might be able to loot houses in a hurricane, but I don't think he could get something from the property room."

Connolly leaned forward and grasped the door handle once more.

"Okay. I'll talk to Dibber and get back to you this afternoon."

"All right. Listen, we tried to find Nick Marchand this morning. Any idea where he might be?"

"He wasn't at the nursery?"

"No. What about his mother, Inez? Any idea where we could find her?"

Connolly chuckled.

"Is Hodges still in jail?"

"Yes."

"Maybe you should go talk to him."

"I don't think he'd see me."

"Send Henry."

"Henry doesn't talk to prisoners at the jail anymore."

Connolly laughed.

"I think you'll have to solve the rest of this case on your own."

"I figured."

When they finished talking, Connolly switched off the phone and laid it on the seat. He put the key in the ignition and started the engine.

This case was over. He might have to cajole Dibber into pleading to a theft charge for the jet ski, but that wouldn't take long. Judge Cahill would give him probation. If they could get to court that afternoon, Dibber would be back at home in time for dinner. The case was over for Dibber. But not for Connolly.

Some called it insatiable curiosity. Others called it just plain nosey. Whatever the trait, he never had been able to walk away from a case while questions remained unanswered. It wasn't a sense of duty. It wasn't a sense of loyalty. It was personal. Connolly wanted to know. Not for Dibber. Not for the good of the community. Not for the sake of humanity. Just for Connolly. He had no idea where Nick might be, but he knew how to find Inez. And he was pretty sure where to find the missing pistol, too.

Fifty-six

our blocks past Bilotti's restaurant Connolly turned onto Crenshaw Street and brought the car to a stop in front of Clyde Ramsey's house. The street was quiet. The house looked dark. He opened the car door and started up the walkway.

On the porch he cupped his hands around his eyes and peered through a window in the front door. A newspaper lay on the floor beside a chair near the sofa. Beside the paper was an empty coffee cup. He leaned away from the window and jabbed the doorbell button with his finger. When no one answered, he rang it again, then pounded the door with his fist. When no one appeared, he pounded on the door with both fists and shouted.

"Hey! I know you're in there!"

A moment later Clyde Ramsey appeared in the hallway. He called to Connolly from inside.

"What do you want?"

"Where's Nick?"

Ramsey came across the room and stood near the door.

"What are you talking about?"

"Where's Nick?"

"I haven't seen him."

"They searched the nursery. Cops are looking for him and Inez."

Ramsey gestured with both hands.

"Leave me alone."

"I know all about you and Inez."

Ramsey glared at him.

"You don't know anything."

"Is she here?"

Ramsey stared at him. Connolly goaded him.

"She's here. I can tell. She's here, isn't she?"

Ramsey unlocked the door and stepped outside.

"Listen to me. All I have to do is pick up the phone and you'll be in jail. So get off my porch and leave me alone."

Connolly pushed past him and stepped inside.

"Game's over, Clyde."

"You don't believe me?"

"Hodges is in jail. Police are looking for Inez and Nick. This whole thing is falling apart." Connolly glanced around the room, then moved toward the kitchen. "Look, I realize you were covering for her. And most people would understand you wanted to spare Nick the pain of a trial when he was a boy." He glanced around the kitchen then turned to face Ramsey. "But now we're talking capital murder. Two people are dead. The DA's coming for Nick and Inez, and when they find them here, they're gonna haul you in too." Connolly saw the look in Ramsey's eyes. "They were already here, weren't they?"

Ramsey looked away.

"Why the sudden concern for me?"

"You're Toby's friend. You've had a long, successful life. And, in spite of everything, you're a likeable guy. I'd hate to see it end in prison."

There was a noise from the hall. Connolly glanced around. Nick appeared in the doorway. In his hand he held a revolver.

"Ain't nobody going to prison."

Connolly glanced at the pistol then over at Ramsey.

"This isn't happening."

Nick grinned.

"Oh, it's happening all right."

Connolly was still looking at Ramsey.

"That's the pistol?"

Ramsey smiled.

"Couldn't let them keep it. Not after you started asking questions."

"But how'd you get ..." Connolly stopped when he saw the look on Ramsey's face. "Hodges gave it to you."

Ramsey's face went cold.

"Why did you do that?"

"Do what?"

"Why did you humiliate him on the stand like that?"

Connolly's voice grew loud.

"They were out to get my client. What was I supposed to do? Let them have him just to hide your affair with Inez?"

Ramsey smiled.

"That's what you think this is about?"

Suddenly all the pieces of the puzzle tumbled together. Connolly's chin dropped.

"You spent a lifetime enforcing the law."

Ramsey shrugged.

"Didn't get paid a dime."

"This was about money?"

"My daddy was a deputy. Worked hard all his life. Shot three times. Stabbed twice. Died without a thing to show for it." He cast a sideways glance toward Nick. "It ain't like he's selling it to schoolkids."

Connolly glanced at Nick. Nick smiled back.

"Don't matter now." He gestured with the pistol. "Let's go. Out the back."

Connolly turned to Ramsey.

"You would send a man to prison? Maybe see him executed? For this?"

Ramsey gave him a cold look.

"Somebody has to die. Ain't gonna be me."

Inez appeared in the hallway behind Nick. Connolly glanced at her then back at Ramsey.

"Edwin knew it was you in that beach house."

Ramsey smiled. Connolly continued.

"He knew you were going down there to that beach house with his wife."

The smile on Ramsey's face spread to a grin.

"He's always known it was me."

"That's why he was mad about the fingerprints."

Ramsey shrugged.

"He's been mad a long time."

"So if everyone knew, why did Hodges lie about the prints?"

Ramsey gave him a knowing look. Connolly's eyes grew wide.

"You wanted them to think it was Edwin?"

Ramsey shrugged again. Connolly frowned.

"You're ... eighty years old."

Ramsey grinned.

"So?"

Nick took a step closer.

"He's old. He ain't dead." He gestured to Connolly with the pistol again. "Let's go."

Connolly looked Nick in the eye.

"I'm not going anywhere."

Nick smiled.

"You ain't that tough. Get moving."

Inez reached over Nick's shoulder.

"I've had enough of this. Give me that gun. I'll take care of him right now."

Ramsey shouted at her.

"No. The neighbors will hear it."

She grabbed at the pistol.

"I don't care. I've had enough."

Nick turned to avoid her. Ramsey started toward her.

"No!" He grabbed at her arm. "Don't!"

Inez clutched at the pistol. Her hand locked around Nick's wrist. Ramsey stepped in to separate them. Connolly shoved his way past them and started toward the front door. Behind him he heard Inez shouting.

"Give it to me!"

"No!"

Out of the corner of his eye Connolly saw Inez point the pistol in his direction. Ramsey and Nick wrestled with her. As Inez squeezed the trigger, Ramsey stumbled in front of her. A shot rang out. The bullet tore through Ramsey's chest and exploded out his back. Blood sprayed across the room. Bone fragments peppered the side of Connolly's face.

Nick wheeled around and ran down the hall toward the back door. Connolly snatched open the front door and darted outside. He ran down the steps and crossed the lawn to the far side of the Chrysler. From the street he heard Inez screaming inside.

"Clyde! No! Call an ambulance! Please! Somebody! Call an ambulance!"

Connolly crouched beside the Chrysler and took the cell phone from his pocket. As he flipped open the phone, he heard a car backing down the driveway beside the house. He raised himself high enough to see through the Chrysler's windows. A yellow Chevrolet Caprice came down the driveway with Nick at the wheel. Connolly ducked low and moved around the rear bumper of the Chrysler.

The Caprice bounced across the curb into the street then sped away. Moments later a patrol car screeched to a halt beside the Chrysler. An officer jumped out, pistol drawn. Connolly stood motionless, hands at his side, still holding the cell phone. The officer was all business.

"You make the call?"

"No, sir."

"Somebody heard a gunshot. Where's the shooter?"

"Inside."

"Who was that in the yellow Chevy?"

"Her son."

A second patrol car came to a stop behind the first. Two officers got out. Connolly recognized one. The officer acknowledged him with a nod.

"What we got?"

"Lady inside tried to shoot me. Man in there tried to get the gun away from her. I think she shot him."

The officer frowned.

"You think?"

"I didn't wait around to see."

"Are you armed?"

Connolly shook his head.

"No."

"Wait here."

The first officer started toward the front door. The other two hurried around the end of the house. The first officer crouched at the steps and moved into position beside the door. He shouted into the house.

"This is the police!"

Connolly heard Inez scream.

"Get an ambulance!"

"Put down your weapon and come out!"

"I can't!"

Still crouching, the officer peeked around the doorway then stood and went inside. In a few minutes one of the officers who had

gone around back came from the house to the front porch, talking
on a cell phone.

Connolly stepped from behind the Chrysler. He slipped off
his jacket and folded it over his arm as he moved beside the car.
Spatters of blood covered the lapel and shoulder. He ran his fingers over his cheek and felt the fragments of Clyde's bones
against his skin. When he reached the driver's door, he opened it
and laid his jacket on the far side of the front seat. He plopped down
sideways behind the steering wheel. With his feet propped
against the curb, he lay back on the seat and closed his eyes. It
was going to be a long afternoon.

Fifty-seven

Minutes later paramedics arrived at Ramsey's house. Behind them came three more patrol cars. Paramedics worked with Ramsey for half an hour, but there was nothing they could do. The shot from the pistol had torn a hole through his chest. An hour later Ted Morgan arrived. Photographs were taken. Video cameras recorded the scene. Three policemen carried Ramsey from the house in a body bag. Connolly watched from the front seat of the Chrysler.

When the body was gone, the first patrolman came outside. He walked over to the Chrysler and took out a notepad.

"I need to ask you a few questions."

Connolly stood. The patrolman gave him an odd look.

"What's that on your face?"

Connolly stroked his fingertip across his cheek.

"Blood."

The patrolman looked concerned.

"Yours?"

"No." Connolly glanced at the tacky red film on his fingers. "Ramsey's."

The patrolman stepped away. In a moment he returned with an evidence technician. The technician cleaned the side of Connolly's face and placed the soiled wipes in an evidence container. When he was gone, the patrolman turned to Connolly.

"You knew the decedent?"

"Yes."

"What's his name?"

"Clyde Ramsey."

"You know the woman's name?"

Connolly nodded.

"Inez Marchand."

Just then a pickup truck screeched to a halt in the street. The driver's door flew open. Edwin Marchand leaped from the truck, his eyes wide. He called out.

"Inez!"

No one answered. His eyes darted from side to side.

"Inez!"

He saw the patrolman and started toward him.

"Where is she?"

Before the patrolman could answer, Edwin spotted Connolly and elbowed the patrolman aside.

"What happened?"

Connolly took a step back and slid along the side of the Chrysler. The patrolman stepped in front of Edwin.

"Excuse me. You'll have to leave."

Edwin shoved the patrolman aside.

"Where is she? Where's Inez? Where's Nick?"

Three patrolmen appeared from nowhere and wrestled Edwin to the ground. Connolly watched from the fender by the rear bumper. As Edwin struggled to get free, he called out to Connolly.

"Where is she?"

The patrolman turned to Connolly.

"You know this man?"

Connolly nodded.

"Edwin Marchand. That's his wife inside."

The officers placed Edwin in handcuffs and lifted him to his feet. Edwin glared at Connolly.

"Where is she?"

Connolly pointed toward the house.

"She's inside."

"Is she all right?"

"I think so."

Edwin's face seemed to soften.

"What about Clyde?"

Connolly glanced away.

"I think he's dead."

"What happened?"

Connolly shook his head.

"You'll have to ask her."

"What do you mean?"

"I mean I can't help you. You'll have to talk to her."

A patrolman tugged at Edwin's arm.

"Let's go."

The patrolmen led Edwin toward a car. As he ducked his head to get inside, the front door of the house opened. Two patrolmen led Inez down the steps. Blood soaked the front of her dress. Her hair was matted on one side, sticking out on the other. Edwin stared at her, his eyes pleading for an explanation. Her eyes stared back in his direction, but she seemed not to notice him. In the commotion the patrolman who had been talking to Connolly disappeared.

As Connolly watched, Toby LeMoyne appeared at his side. Connolly gave him a nod.

"You taking over for Hodges?"

Toby shook his head.

"Just answering a call. I don't think Hodges will be available for a long time."

Connolly chuckled.

"I guess not."

Toby folded his arms across his chest and leaned against the fender of the car. He sighed and shook his head.

"Hard to believe Clyde was mixed up in something like this. She shot him?"

Connolly nodded.

"It was an accident."

"You don't think she wanted to kill him?"

Connolly shook his head.

"Nah."

"How do you know that?"

He glanced at Toby.

"She wanted to kill me."

Toby chuckled.

"They'll need a statement from you."

Connolly nodded. They watched as patrolmen guided Inez into a car. Toby glanced over at Connolly.

"You all right?"

"I think so."

"Why did she want to kill you?"

"Because I found out the truth."

"That's about all it takes these days."

Connolly sighed.

"It is if your whole life has been built on a lie."

"Which was?"

Connolly shrugged.

"I'm not sure now."

Toby frowned.

"What do you mean?"

"They were having an affair."

Toby shot him a look.

"Who?"

"Clyde and Inez."

"You mean they had an affair."

Connolly shook his head.

"I think it was still going on."

"He's got to be ..."

"Eighty."

"At least."

Connolly grinned. Toby had a pained look on his face. Connolly laughed.

"What's the matter, Toby? Age doesn't have anything to do with it."

Toby covered his eyes with his hand and shook his head.

"I don't need these visuals in my mind."

Connolly laughed. Toby dropped his hand and looked at Connolly.

"Are you just messing with me?"

Connolly quit laughing.

"No."

"So, what's this all about?"

"Well, an hour ago I would have said Inez shot her father, Earl Givens, and Clyde was covering for her ever since. But now, I'm not certain."

"I'm confused."

Connolly nodded.

"I have a hard time keeping it straight myself."

"What's all this got to do with Dibber?"

"Dibber just happened to be in the wrong place at the wrong time."

"He saw what happened?"

"No. That man in the beach house was dead long before Dibber came around."

"So, how'd he wind up getting charged with murder?"

"Hodges."

"Hodges?"

"Found Clyde's prints in the beach house."

Toby shook his head.

"He did all that for his father-in-law?"

"Loyalty's a powerful thing. That and whatever they were paying him."

"You heard about that meth lab?"

Connolly nodded.

"Gayle Underwood called me."

"It was huge."

"The super lab you were looking for."

"Yep." Toby sighed. "You think Hodges was in on it with them?"

Connolly moved to the driver's door of the Chrysler.

"Looks like it to me. But you'll have to figure that one out. I've done about all I can do with this. I've got to go get my client out of jail."

Connolly took a seat behind the steering wheel. Toby pushed the door closed and leaned through the window.

"They'll want a statement from you."

"Give me a call when they're ready."

Toby nodded. Connolly started the engine.

Fifty-eight

Connolly slouched against the car door as he drove down Crenshaw Street. Shadows from the trees that lined the street covered the pavement. The rearview mirror above the windshield caught the reflection of the blue lights from the patrol cars. The glare made Connolly's eyes blink. Up ahead was his mother's house. He stared at it as he rolled past.

The lawn was mowed. The bushes trimmed. Dead branches that had littered the walkway were gone. The house was dark, but it no longer looked threatening. A sense of freedom washed over him. She hadn't made him cut the lawn. He had done it on his own. He didn't do it because she demanded it. He did it because he had wanted to, because of who he was. Because of who he had become. He pressed the gas pedal. The Chrysler picked up speed.

Getting Dibber out of jail took longer than Connolly expected. Dibber was reluctant to admit he stole the jet ski. Convincing him was more difficult than Connolly imagined. Judge Cahill took his plea as the last case of the day. By the time he was released from jail, it was almost dark. Carl met them in the lobby and took Dibber home.

When they were finished, Connolly walked with them from the jail to the street then turned toward the Chrysler. The day had been long and stressful. His body wanted to collapse across the bed and sleep, but there was still one more thing he had to do.

It took five minutes to reach Barbara's house on Ann Street. He brought the car to a stop in front and hopped out. As he started up the walk, he snatched the For Sale sign from the ground. He lifted it in the air and rested the stick against his shoulder like a picket sign at a protest rally. When he reached the steps, he bounded up to the porch and rang the bell. After a moment, he rang it again, then knocked on the door with his fist, but no one answered. He walked to the end of the porch and leaned over the rail to check the driveway. The car was gone.

Disappointed, he took the cell phone from his pocket and dialed Barbara's number. Her voice mail answered. He left a message then closed the phone and carried the sign down the steps.

At the car he opened the driver's door and tossed the sign on the backseat. He slipped behind the wheel and turned the car around in the driveway.

It was almost dark when Connolly turned into the driveway at The Pleiades. As he moved past the main house, the headlights from the Chrysler fell on a 1963 Chevrolet pickup parked near the guesthouse. A grin broke across his face. The car came to a stop behind the truck. The truck door opened. Hollis stepped out. Connolly came from the car, still grinning.

"Everything all right?"

Hollis shoved both hands in his pockets, a sheepish smile on his face.

"Yeah." He nodded. "Everything's fine."

"Have any trouble?"

"Nope. No trouble at all."

"Victoria see enough of Disney World?"

Hollis's eyebrows lifted.

"Oh, we saw a lot of it."

"Where is she?"

"She's over at Mrs. Gordon's. Had some stuff over there she wanted to get."

Connolly glanced at his watch.

"Y'all just get back?"

"Yeah. I tried to tell her it could wait till tomorrow, but you know women."

Connolly nodded.

"Yeah. I know." Then he corrected himself. "Well, actually, I don't. But I fake it pretty well. Did they get the house ready?"

Hollis nodded.

"House is ready." He leaned against the truck. "I still got my shack down there." He looked away. "But the house is ready."

"Something you want to talk about?"

Hollis shook his head again.

"Nah."

"Being married isn't much like dating someone."

Hollis smiled.

"No, it isn't."

"Barbara and I fought nearly every day the first year we were married." He looked away. His voice dropped. "Toward the end we didn't fight at all."

Hollis took a deep breath and let it slowly escape.

"Language barrier is a little more than I expected."

"Yeah."

"And sometimes ... it's like she's this wild animal in a cage, trying to figure out if she should bust loose or stay put."

"You probably feel the same way."

Hollis chuckled.

"Yeah. I do."

"It'll all work out. If you keep working at it. It'll all even out. Want to come inside?"

"Nah. Better get back. She'll be ready to go."

Hollis opened the door of the truck. When he was seated, Connolly pushed the door closed and leaned against it. He spoke to Hollis through the window.

"I'm glad you're back."

"Got something you need me to do?"

"Yeah. But we can talk about it later."

"Have any good cases while I was gone?"

"One."

"Who's the defendant?"

"A guy named Dibber Landry."

Hollis looked surprised.

"Dibber Landry? I know Dibber."

"Yeah?"

"Yeah. Me and him used to go fishing all the time. Then he took a job in Virginia. He's back?"

"Yeah."

"What happened?"

"I think he got in a fight with the foreman."

Hollis frowned.

"He killed a guy on the job?"

"No. He got in a fight in Virginia and came home. He was living in his uncle's house on Dauphin Island. They said he killed a guy in a beach house down there during the storm."

Hollis had a skeptical look.

"During the hurricane?"

"Yeah. You know. Said he was looting a beach house. Surprised somebody inside. Killed him."

Hollis shook his head.

"Don't sound like Dibber. Looting a house during a storm, yeah. But not shooting somebody. Unless they was about to shoot him."

Connolly tipped his head to one side.

"We got it all straightened out."

"Good."

Hollis leaned around the steering wheel and turned the key. The engine started. He turned back to the window. A grin spread across his face.

"Hear anything from Raisa?"

"She left a message from the airport in Atlanta."

"Miss her?"

Connolly shrugged.

"I did at first."

The grin on Hollis's face grew wider.

"She had it bad for you. Think she'll be back?"

"Not for me."

Hollis nodded.

"Just as well." He put the truck in gear. "I'll see you later."

Connolly stepped away.

"Come by the office tomorrow."

"Okay."

Hollis backed the truck from the house. Connolly called after him.

"Glad you're back."

Hollis waved out the window as he started down the drive.

Connolly stood there watching as the truck made the corner and disappeared up the street. Night had fallen while they talked.

The garden behind the main house looked dark and mysterious. The sultry night air invited him into the shadows. He glanced up through the trees toward the sky. A cluster of stars was visible through the haze. Sweat trickled down his back.

As he turned to go inside, the cell phone rang. The call was from Barbara.

"Where's my sign?"

"You got any iced tea?"

"Yes. Where's my sign?"

"Pour me a glass. I'm coming over."

"It's too hot."

"Your air conditioner doesn't work?"

"It works fine. It's too hot to sit outside."

"I thought we could sit in the den."

Barbara fell silent. Connolly grinned.

"You there?"

"Yeah." Her voice broke. "I'm here."

"Pour the tea. I'm on my way."

He closed the phone and stepped toward the Chrysler.